REWILD YOUR DRAWING

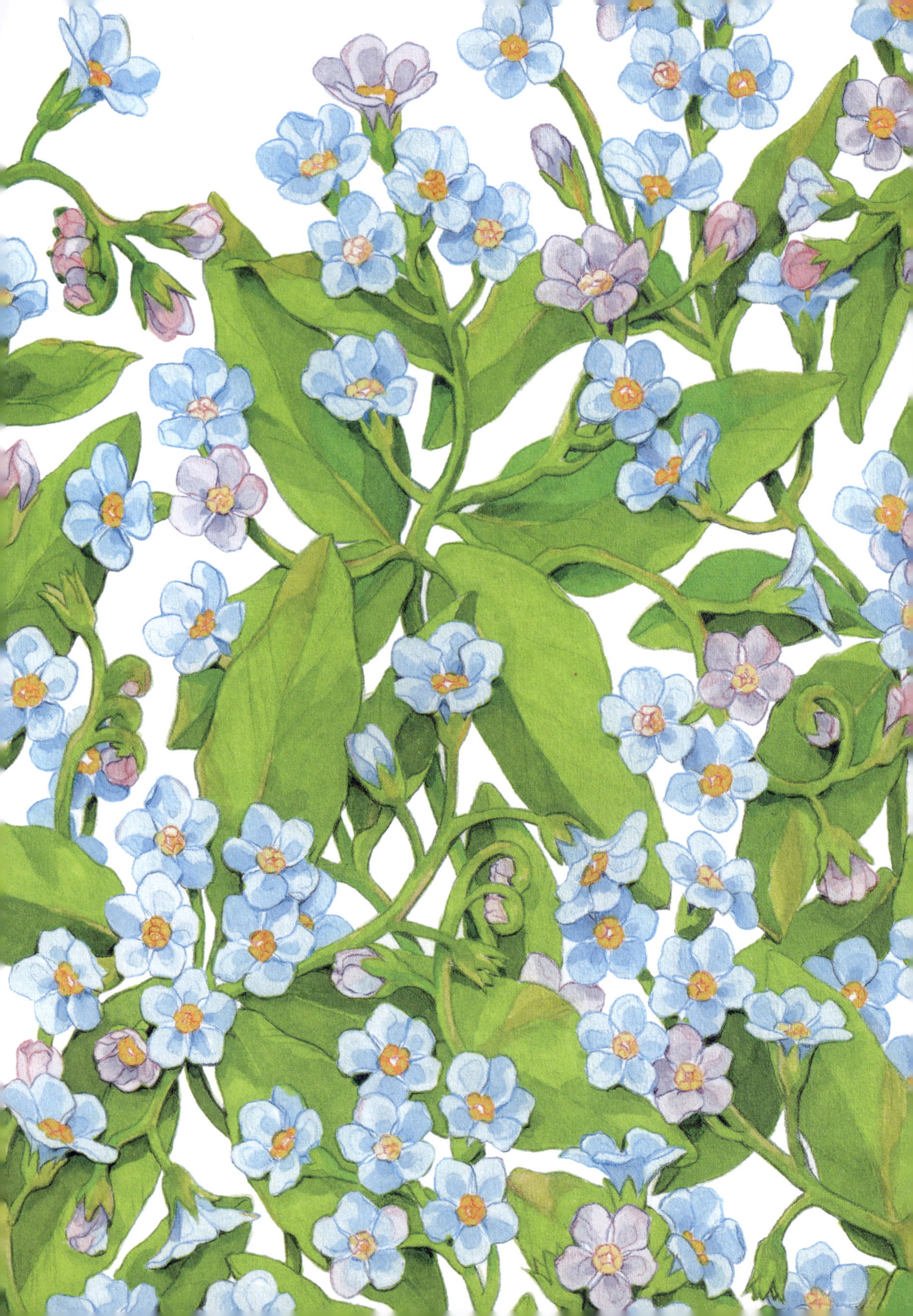

REWILD YOUR DRAWING

How to draw botanicals

MARTA
GŁOWACKA-SIĘBOR

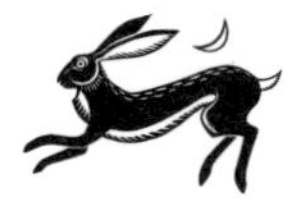

Leaping Hare Press

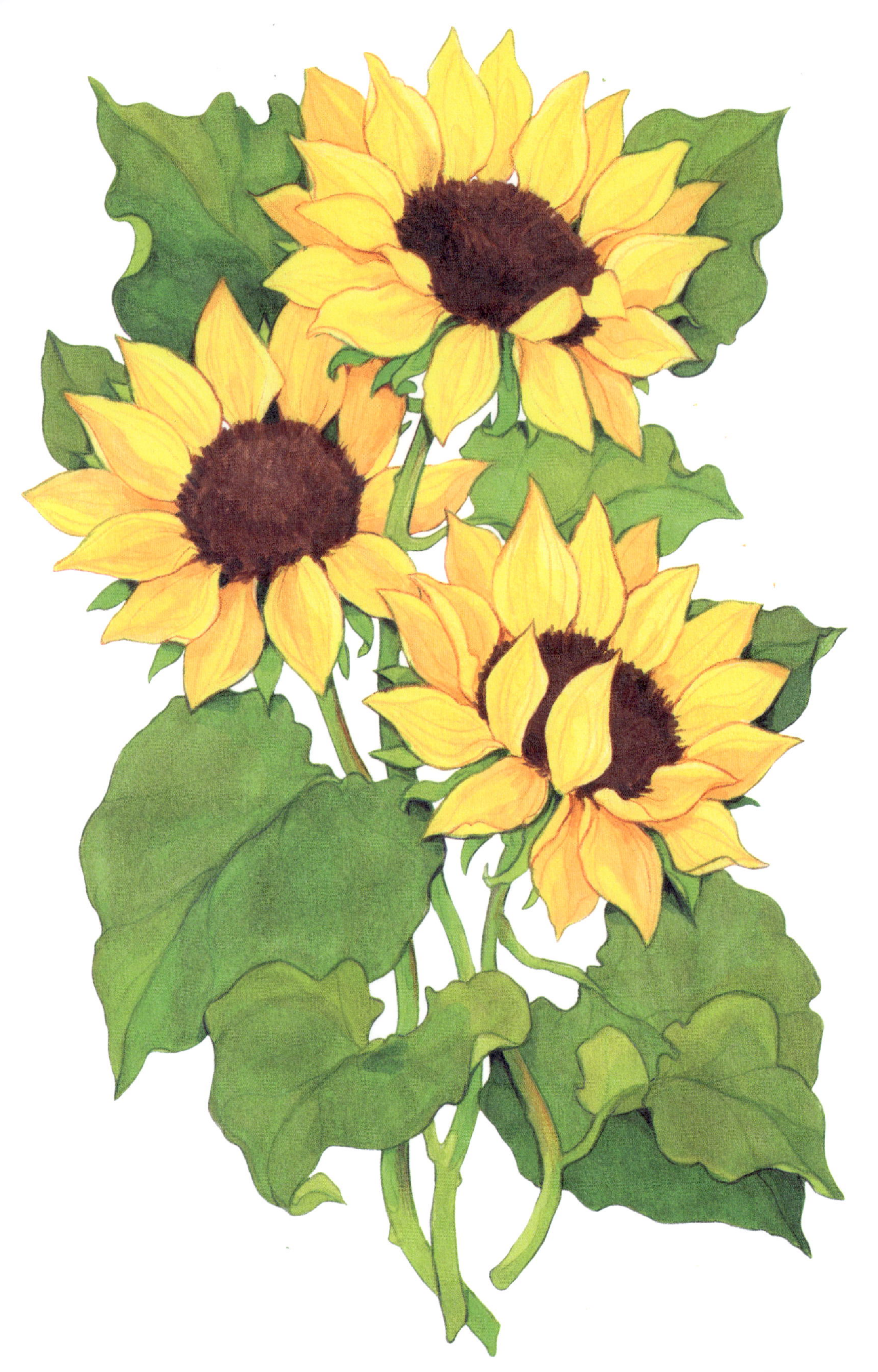

Contents

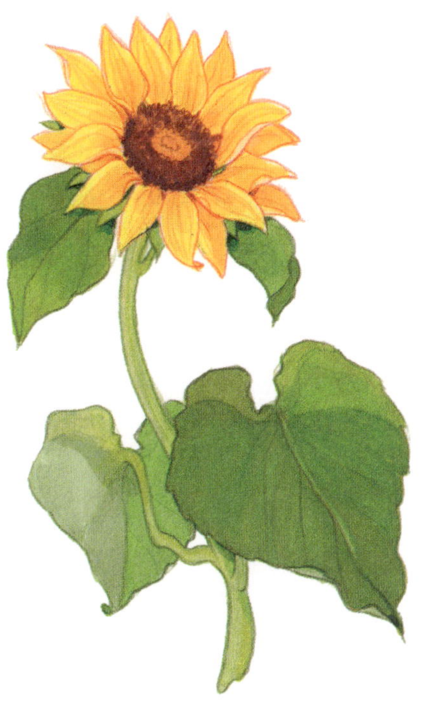

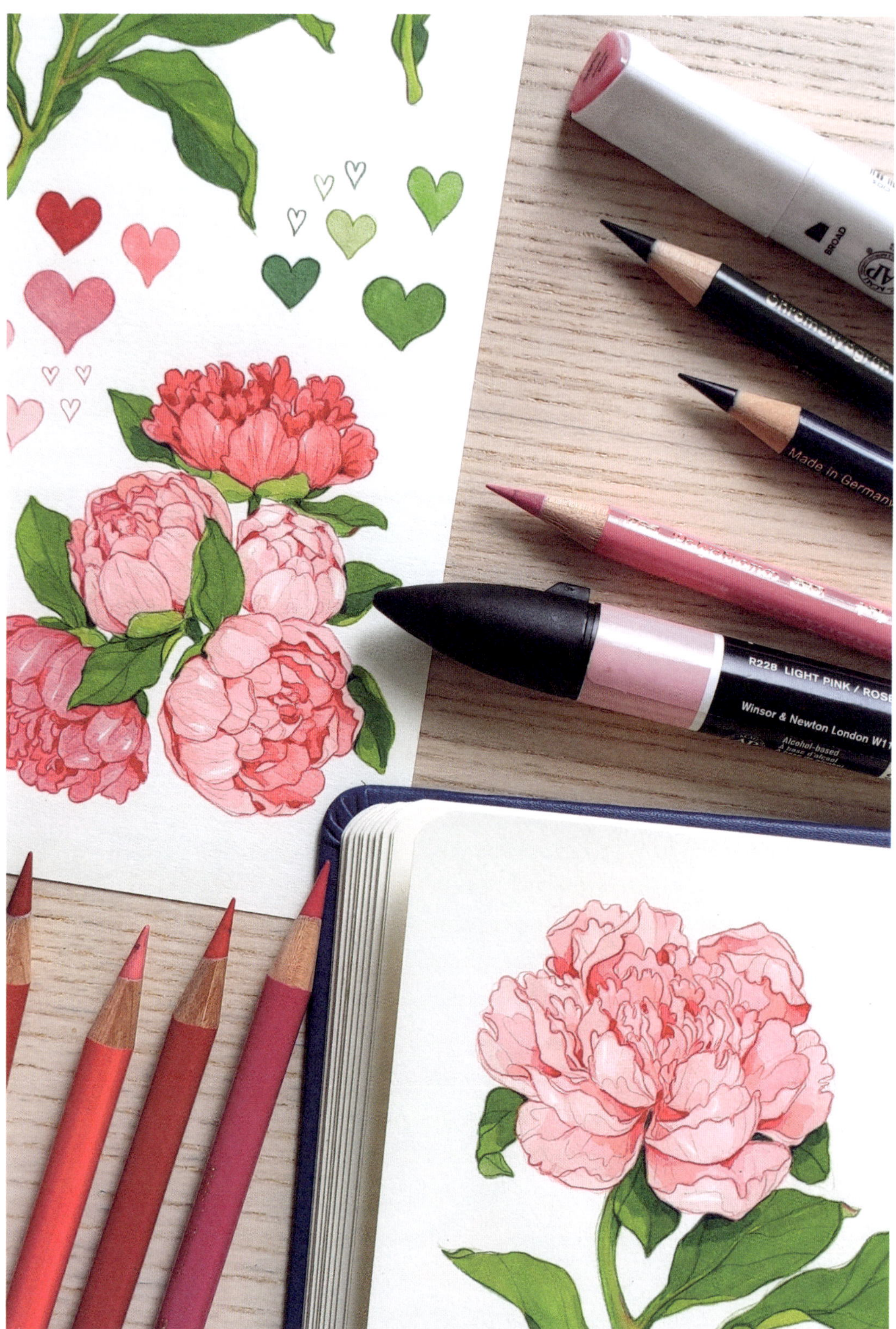

BROAD
Made in Germany
R228 LIGHT PINK / ROSE
Alcohol-based

Introduction

Why draw botanicals? Drawing botanicals can give you pleasure in so many ways. The act itself of choosing a flower or plant to draw is a peaceful, calming process, whether you are outside in a beautiful garden, leafing through a magazine or admiring the work of other artists. Then, once you have chosen your subject, you can start the process of building the flower from sketch to finished drawing, step by step.

You may have many reasons for wanting to draw botanicals. Perhaps you want to start a new hobby or expand an existing one. Or, if you're a gardener or outdoors enthusiast, drawing botanicals could be a new way to appreciate the plants that you already know and love. Maybe you want to find a way to connect with your surroundings or evoke fond memories, such as the awe of seeing an exotic-looking flower as a child, the joy of being gifted a flower from grandma's garden, or the beauty of a wedding bouquet.

Once you start to draw plants you will notice so much more about their structures and features - the way tendrils wrap around a stem or the multiple layers of petals in a big, showy bloom. If you are like me, you may also be drawn in deeper, becoming more curious about the plants themselves. Some of them have interesting origins, some are connected to fascinating myths, while others have been used in unexpected ways. At the back of the book, you will find some of the wonderful plant facts I have learned on my botanical journey.

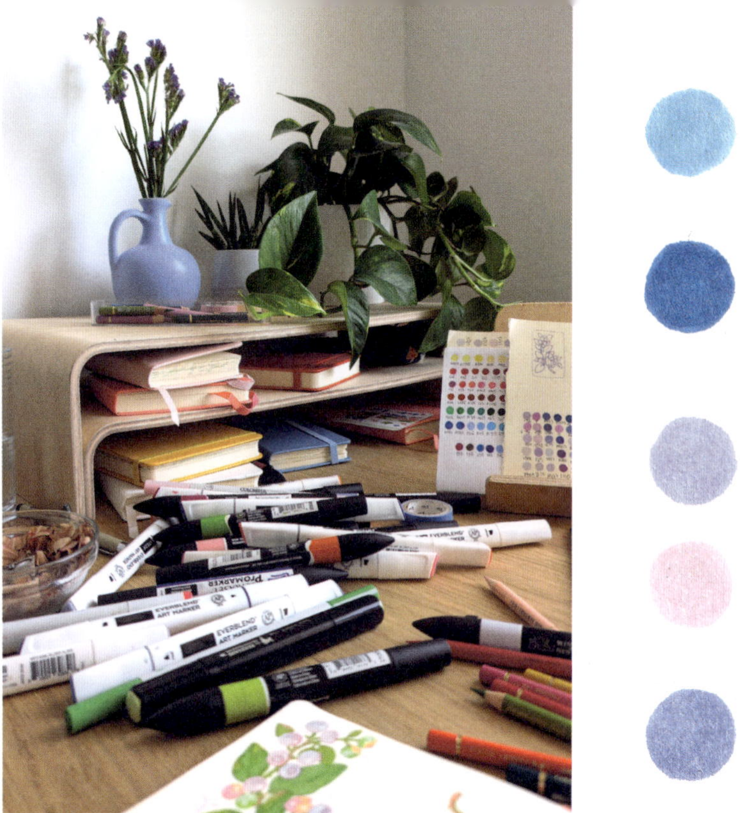

Why use marker pens?

Alcohol-based markers are a wonderful medium to explore at any skill level. Available in an astonishing range of colours, they were initially developed to allow artists and designers to get their ideas down on paper quickly. Fashion designers and architects were quick to adopt the medium, but it was not long before it became widely used in multiple industries. Today, they are also associated with manga artists and adult colouring books.

The reason for their success is that marker pens are so versatile that amazing results can be achieved with even a small colour range, regardless of whether you're a beginner or a seasoned artist. They also offer a portable medium that is quick and easy to use. There is no need to prep a large working space or to invest in a wide range of supporting materials as there is with many other painting mediums. There is no need to mix colours and there is rarely any need to allow for drying time when building layers. Best of all, there is barely any tidying up required after a drawing session.

About me

I'm a self-taught artist. As a child, I was obsessed with field guides. I grew up in a city but lived near a forest, where my parents, my sister and I used to go for Sunday walks. I'd always take a field guide with me, hoping to identify all the plants and animals I would see. I also spent a lot of time drawing.

In my late teens, I saw marker illustrations on the internet and instantly fell in love with the opaque vibrant colours. I bought a set of markers, even though I didn't know how to use them or even how to draw properly. At first I got into drawing people, but after a while I realized it wasn't my calling. At some point I switched to making digital art, so the journey to discover what and how I really wanted to draw wasn't straightforward. A couple of online art challenges led me to explore the world of plants, taking me back to my childhood days in the forest. I began to make plant studies and something clicked in my brain. From that moment on, all of my illustrations have revolved around plants and flowers. I started making double-page sketchbook illustrations and that soon became my 'thing'. Today, I make all of my illustrations in sketchbooks using markers and coloured pencils. Everything I have learned has been by trial and error.

Before I start a drawing, I read about the plant I have chosen, studying the shapes of its leaves and flowers in detail. This helps me to draw accurate botanical illustrations, but also to create them in my own particular style. I tend to draw a plant over and over again in a range of compositions and my all-time favourite things to draw are berries, especially blueberries. I drew these for the first time after a visit to my grandma's garden, and drawing them brings back sweet summer memories!

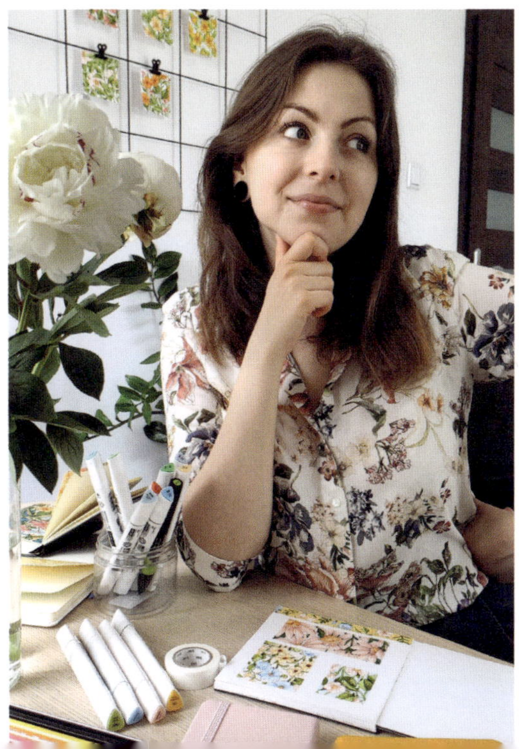

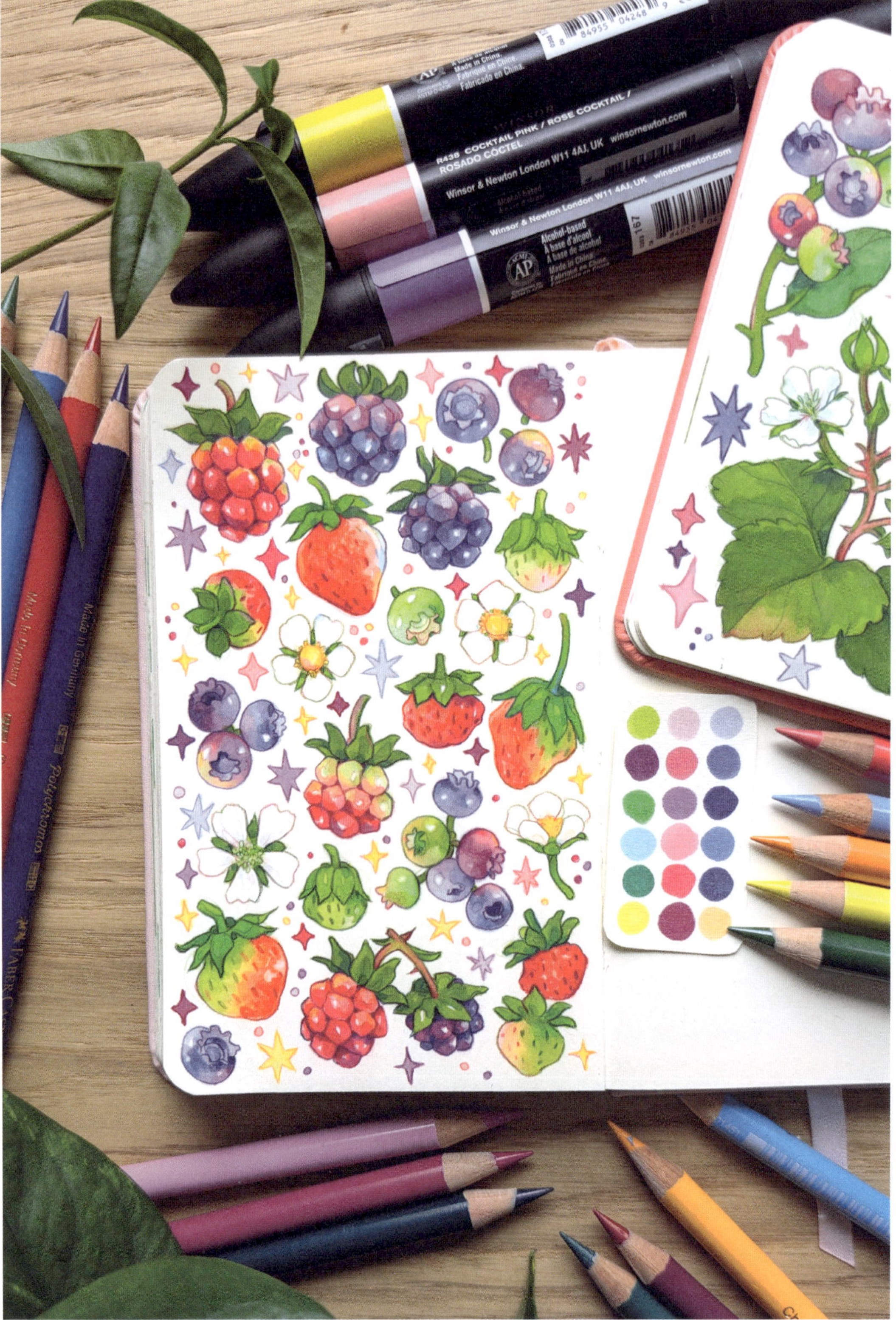
R438 COCKTAIL PINK / ROSE COCKTAIL /
ROSADO CÓCTEL
Winsor & Newton London W11 4AJ, UK winsornewton.com
Winsor & Newton London W11 4AJ, UK winsornewton.com
Alcohol-based
À base d'alcool
A base de alcohol
Made in China.
Fabricado en China.
Made in Germany
Polychromos

BASIC MATERIALS

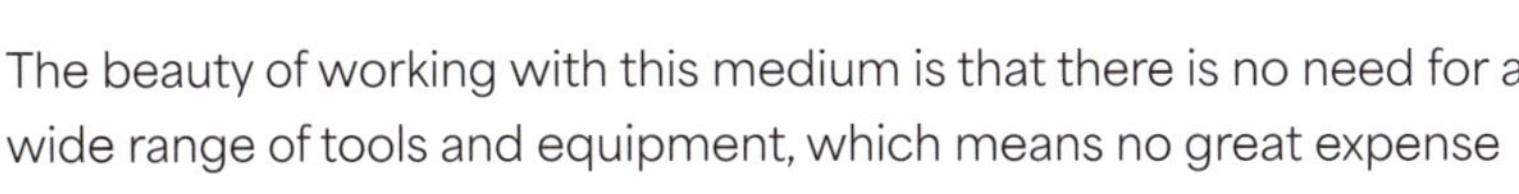

The beauty of working with this medium is that there is no need for a wide range of tools and equipment, which means no great expense when starting out.

Markers

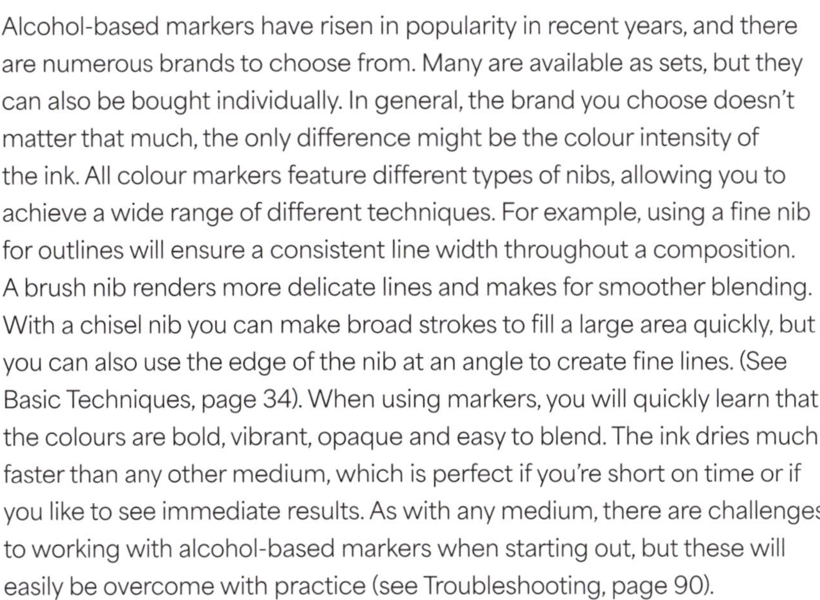

Alcohol-based markers have risen in popularity in recent years, and there are numerous brands to choose from. Many are available as sets, but they can also be bought individually. In general, the brand you choose doesn't matter that much, the only difference might be the colour intensity of the ink. All colour markers feature different types of nibs, allowing you to achieve a wide range of different techniques. For example, using a fine nib for outlines will ensure a consistent line width throughout a composition. A brush nib renders more delicate lines and makes for smoother blending. With a chisel nib you can make broad strokes to fill a large area quickly, but you can also use the edge of the nib at an angle to create fine lines. (See Basic Techniques, page 34). When using markers, you will quickly learn that the colours are bold, vibrant, opaque and easy to blend. The ink dries much faster than any other medium, which is perfect if you're short on time or if you like to see immediate results. As with any medium, there are challenges to working with alcohol-based markers when starting out, but these will easily be overcome with practice (see Troubleshooting, page 90).

Coloured pencils

Coloured pencils work really well as a secondary medium when drawing with alcohol-based markers, helping to achieve a more organic look in the finished artwork. You can use pencil to create subtle textures, to add small details and to give definition to your outlines. Pick pencils with soft or hard tips, depending on what you are trying to achieve. Wax-based pencils tend to be softer, which allows you to blend colours more smoothly. Oil-based pencils are harder and remain sharp for longer. These are ideal for creating really fine outlines and details. You can control the intensity of the colour by applying more or less pressure on the pencil.

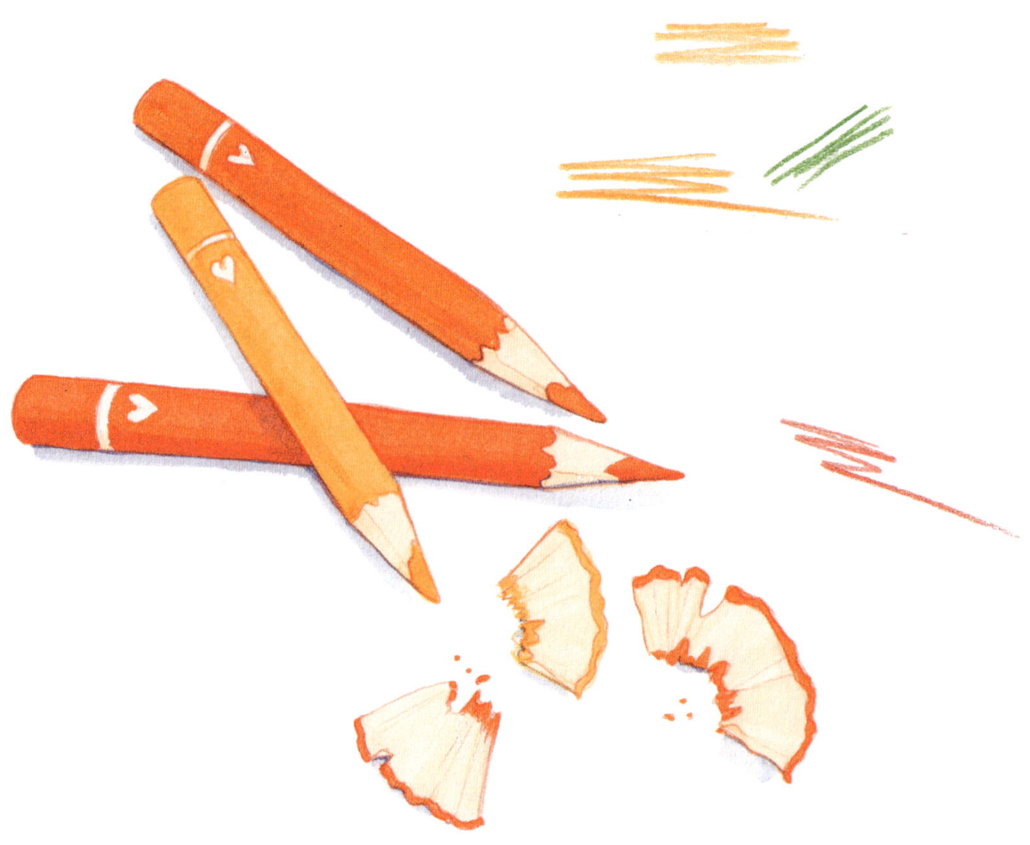

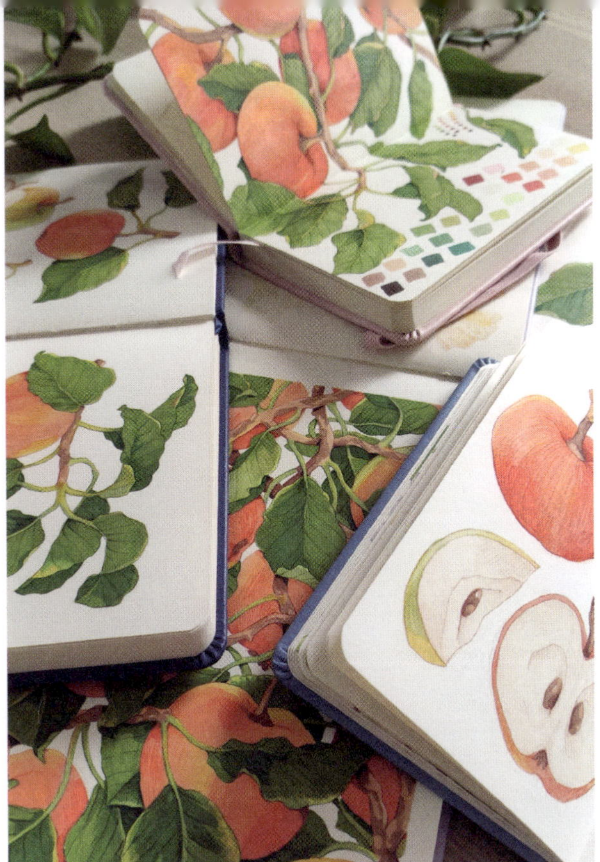

Paper

Lots of different types of paper are available and it may take a while for you to find your preference. The type of paper most typically used with alcohol-based markers tends to be very white, smooth and thin, almost semi-transparent. Usually it comes in some form of drawing pad. Some brands offer heavier paper, too. White paper is the industry standard because it doesn't affect the colour of markers. Ivory paper, on the other hand, makes some colours appear less vibrant or desaturated.

Most mixed media sketchbooks have slightly textured paper, which tends to absorb more ink, shortening the life of a marker - the more textured the paper, the more ink is used. Very heavily textured paper might even damage a marker's nib. One thing to be aware of when using smooth paper is that the ink smears more easily if you accidentally touch your illustration before it dries completely. The best way to avoid this is simply to be careful when colouring. Work on one section at a time, preferably colouring from left to right (or right to left, if you are left-handed).

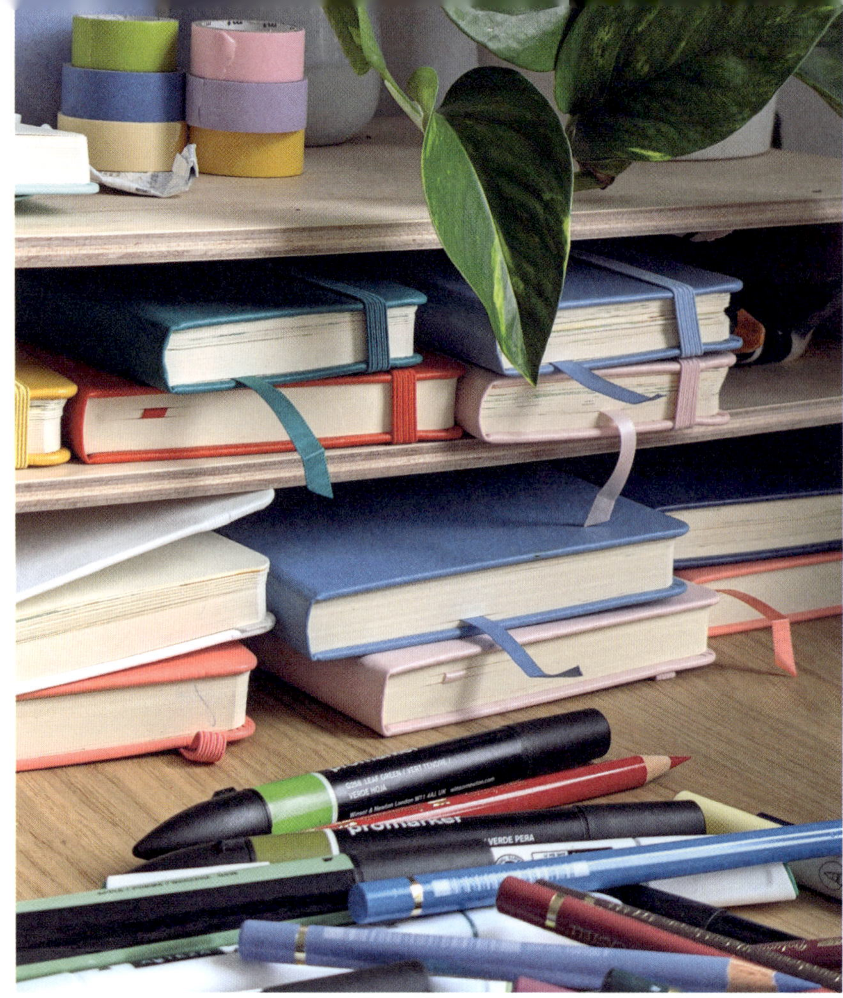

Using sketchbooks

It is a good idea to buy multiple sketchbooks in various sizes for greater creative freedom. Some formats might work better for different kinds of drawings. For example, I find A5 works best for full-page illustrations, square sketchbooks for simple designs and multiple small pieces, and pocket-sized sketchbooks for double-page designs. Some people might experience 'sketchbook anxiety' and fear they might 'ruin' a sketchbook. This is another good reason for having several to work in. You can dedicate one of them for colour and composition tests and creative explorations, and there's no pressure to keep it looking 'pretty'.

I suggest always having a dedicated sketchbook on the go for pencil sketches and studies. It does not have to be one with heavy paper - in fact, if the paper is not suitable for markers, you will not be tempted to turn your sketches into illustrations. These should simply serve the purpose of giving you practice at drawing shapes, exploring plant forms and trying out different compositions. The more practice you have at drawing something multiple times, the better your finished results will be.

Try out different sketchbooks and see what works best for you. Come up with your own sketchbook system if you need one. I used to draw only pinkish and purplish things in my sketchbook that had a pink cover, just because the illustrations matched the cover - it doesn't have to make sense to anyone but you.

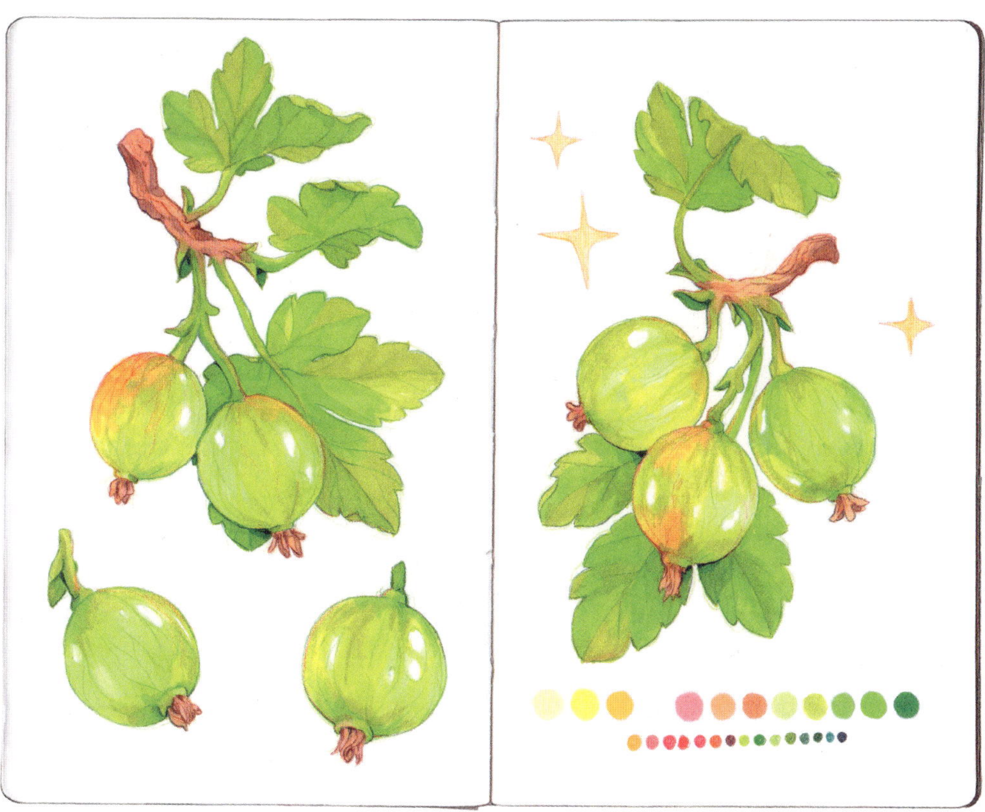

Other tools

Pencil sharpener

For extra crisp lines when using pencils, it is best to use a sharp pencil. Use a good-quality pencil sharpener for this and replace the blade every so often, or buy a new sharpener.

Eraser

An eraser is useful, but not essential, at the sketching phase, depending on how neat you want to make your art. Any pencil eraser is good, but a kneaded eraser is less likely to damage your paper or leave any residue. You can cut off a small corner from any eraser to allow you to reach small areas.

Washi tape

You can use washi tape to create a clean frame for an illustration, which can be removed once the art is finished, without damaging the paper. Washi tape can also be used to secure a sheet of paper when tracing or transferring a sketch.

Light pad

An A4 light pad, or box, is useful for tracing over sketches or transferring a design to a sketchbook. Most tablets can also be used as light pads, so perhaps see how often you need one before investing in a dedicated tool. You can also trace a sketch using a window, taping the sketch and your paper to the surface before starting.

White gouache paint

White gouache paint comes in handy when you are painting white objects, especially if you are not working on pure white paper. It acts as a clean layer beneath the markers (see page 57). You can use any brush, depending on the size of your illustration - a flat brush is good for filling big areas, a round brush for flowers, and a long slender brush for superfine details.

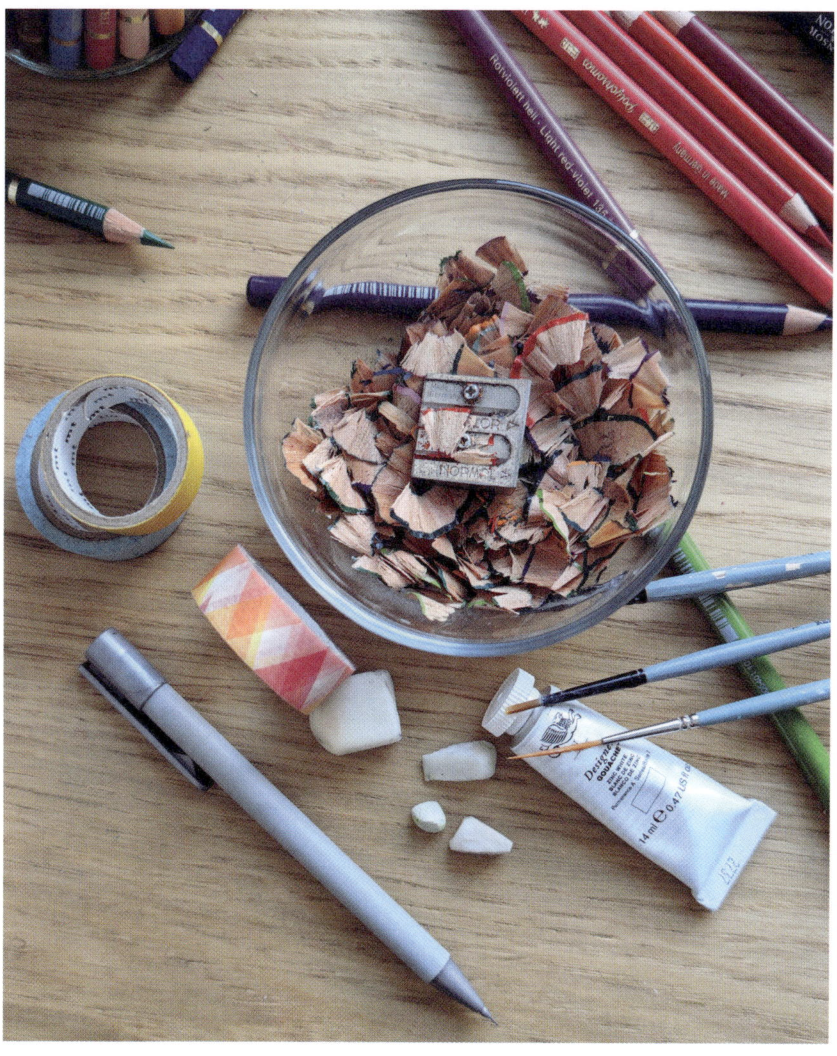

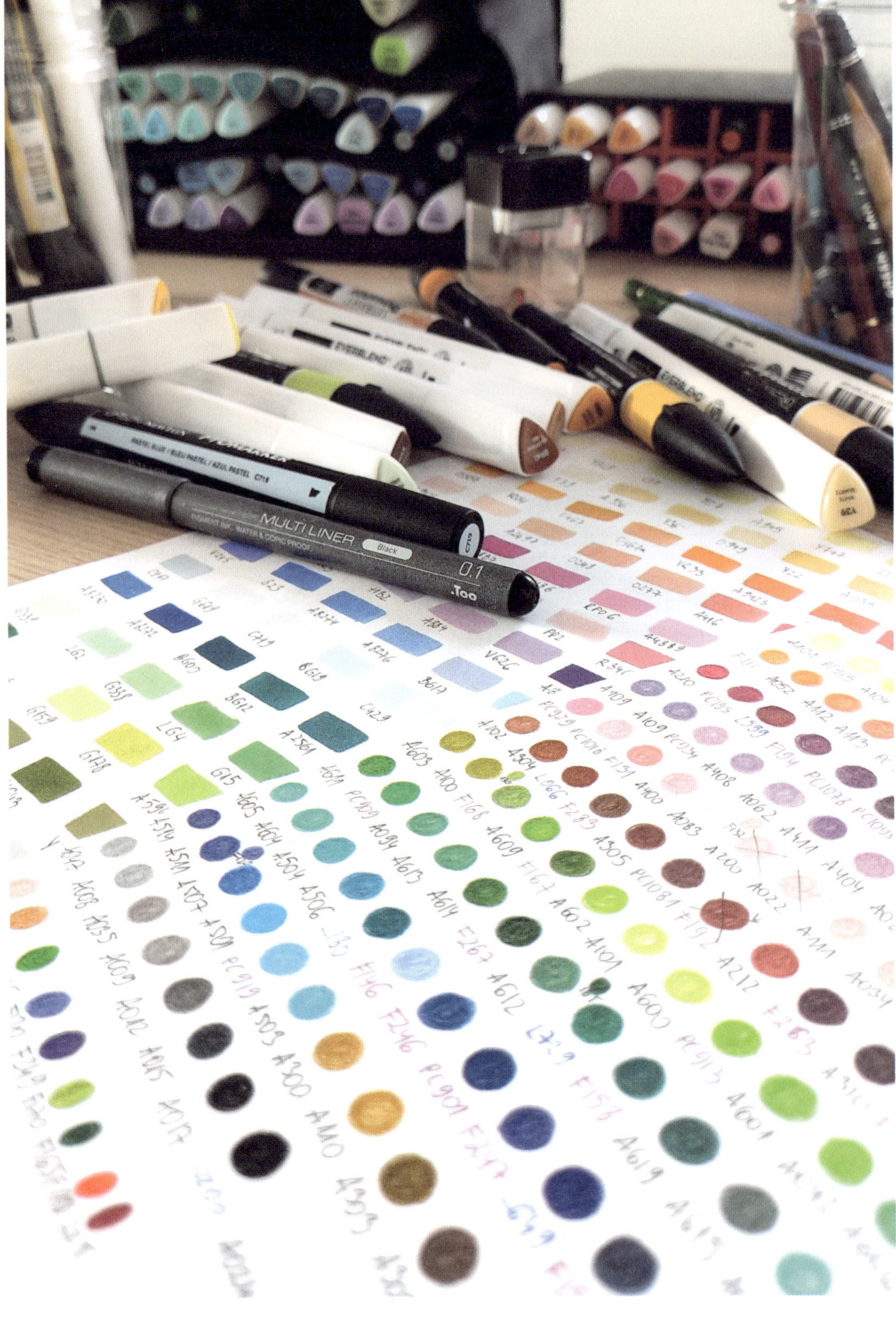
PASTEL BLUE / BLEU PASTEL / AZUL PASTEL C718
MULTI LINER
Black
0.1
.Too
PIGMENT INK, WATER & COPIC PROOF
EVERBLEND

BASIC COLOUR THEORY

All colour theory revolves around the colour wheel, a basic tool that allows artists to see the relationships between colours at a glance. For example, it shows which colours are harmonious with each other, and which are not, depending on where they sit on the wheel.

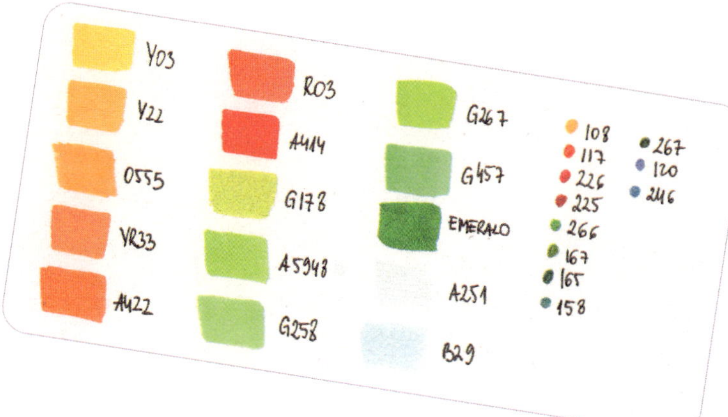

The colour wheel

A colour wheel can feature any number of colours in multiples of three. Twelve colours is a good number to settle on for basic colour theory as this establishes primary, secondary and tertiary colours.

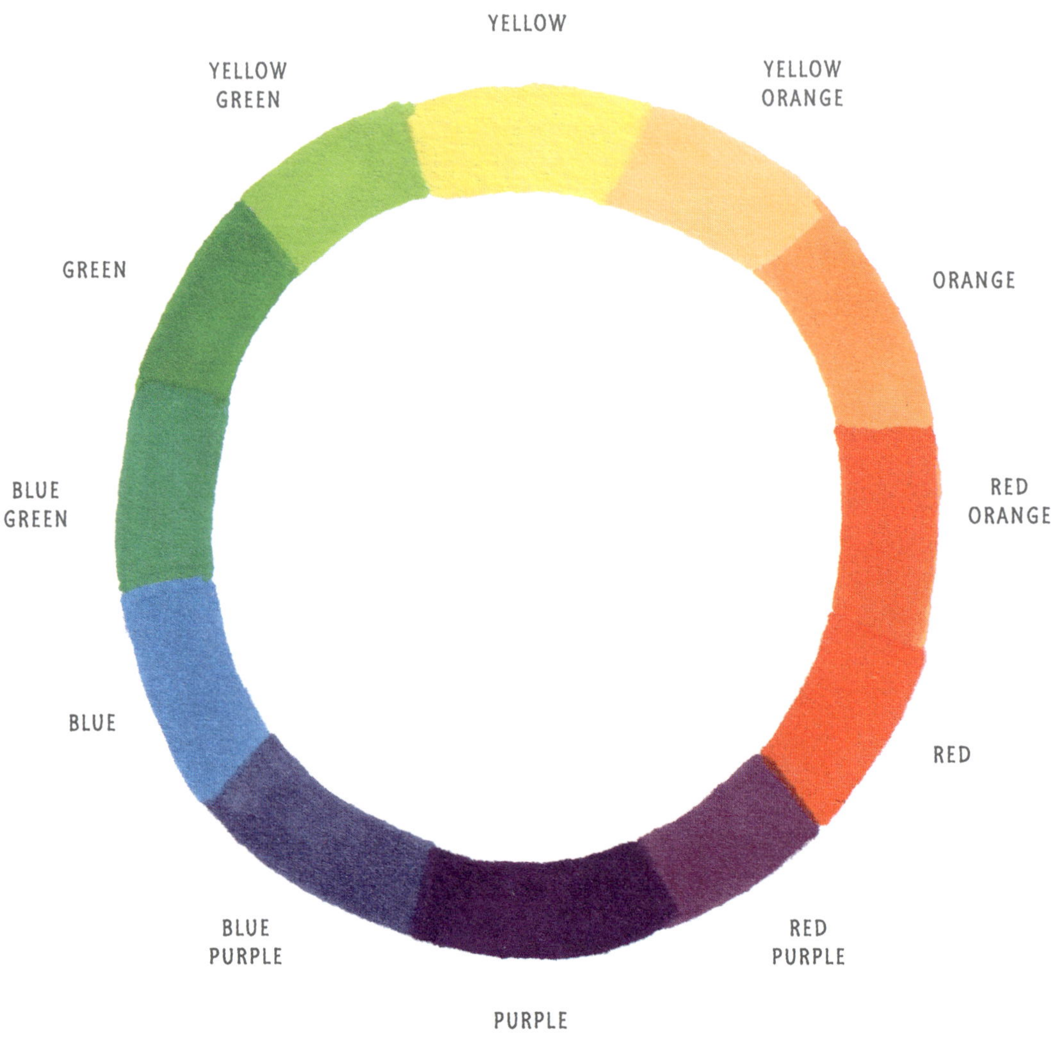

PRIMARY COLOURS - yellow, red, blue - sit at equal distances from one another on the wheel.

SECONDARY COLOURS - orange, green, purple - sit exactly halfway between the two primaries used to make them. So, orange sits between red and yellow; green sits between yellow and blue; and purple sits between blue and red.

TERTIARY COLOURS are mixes of adjacent primary and secondary colours and sit between them. So, red-orange sits between red and orange; yellow-orange sits between orange and yellow, and so on, all the way round the wheel.

Armed with this knowledge of where primary, secondary and tertiary colours sit on the colour wheel, artists can make informed decisions when choosing colours for a drawing, depending on whether they are looking for complementary, analogous or triadic combinations.

Complementary colours

Complementary colours sit directly opposite each other on the colour wheel and each makes the other really stand out when used together. Classic combinations here are the primary colours and their opposites:

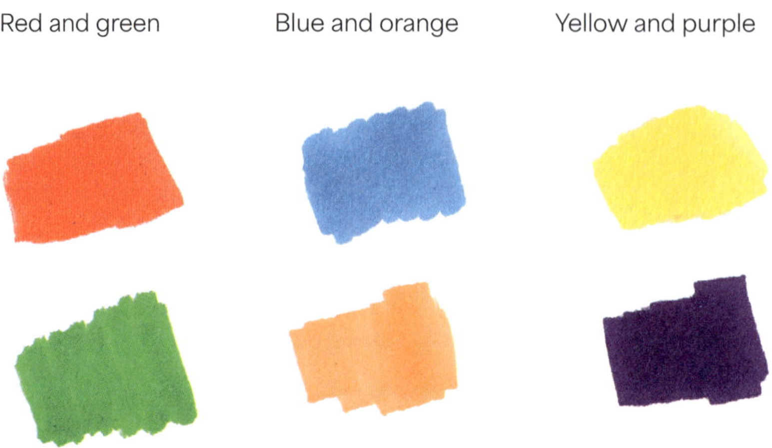

A complementary colour scheme can be taken a step further by using the tertiary colours adjacent to the primary or secondary colour. Such a combination provides contrast and energy yet are softer than a straightforward complementary scheme. So, for example, you might use red alongside blue-green and yellow-green. Or purple alongside yellow-green and yellow-orange.

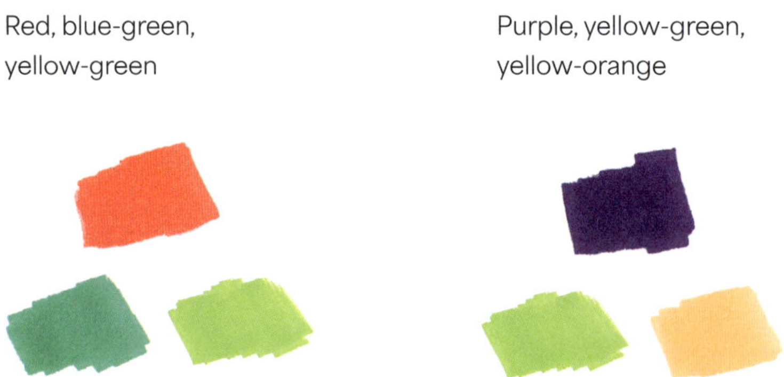

Analogous colours

Analogous colours are those that sit in the same area of the colour wheel, creating a more harmonious look when used together. Classic combinations here would be:

Blue and green | Red and purple | Yellow and orange

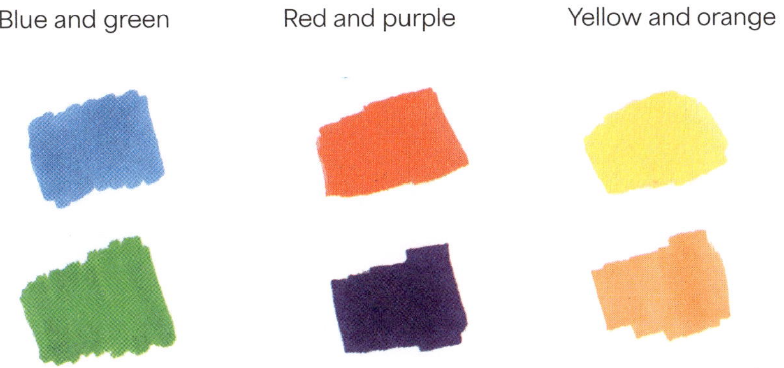

Triadic colours

Triadic colour combinations involve three colours that are evenly spaced around the colour wheel – they form a triangle when looking at the wheel. Triadic colour schemes are the most vibrant. Classic combinations here would be:

Red, yellow, blue | Orange, green, purple | Blue green, red purple, yellow orange

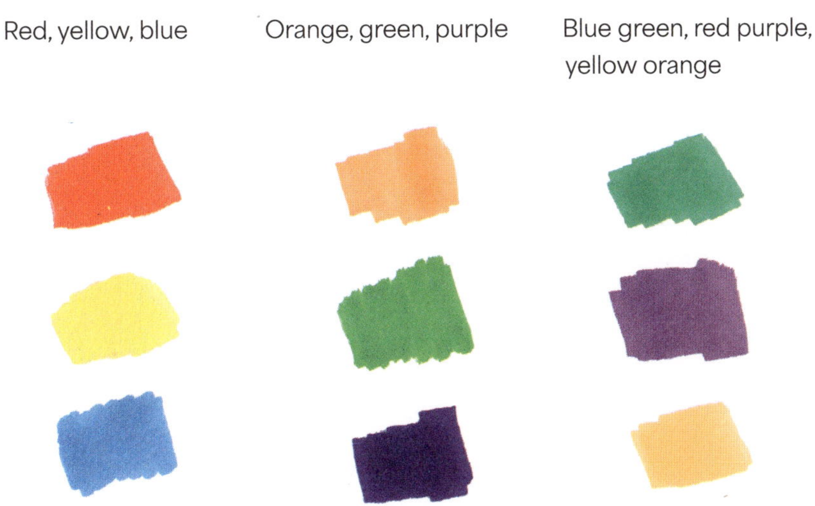

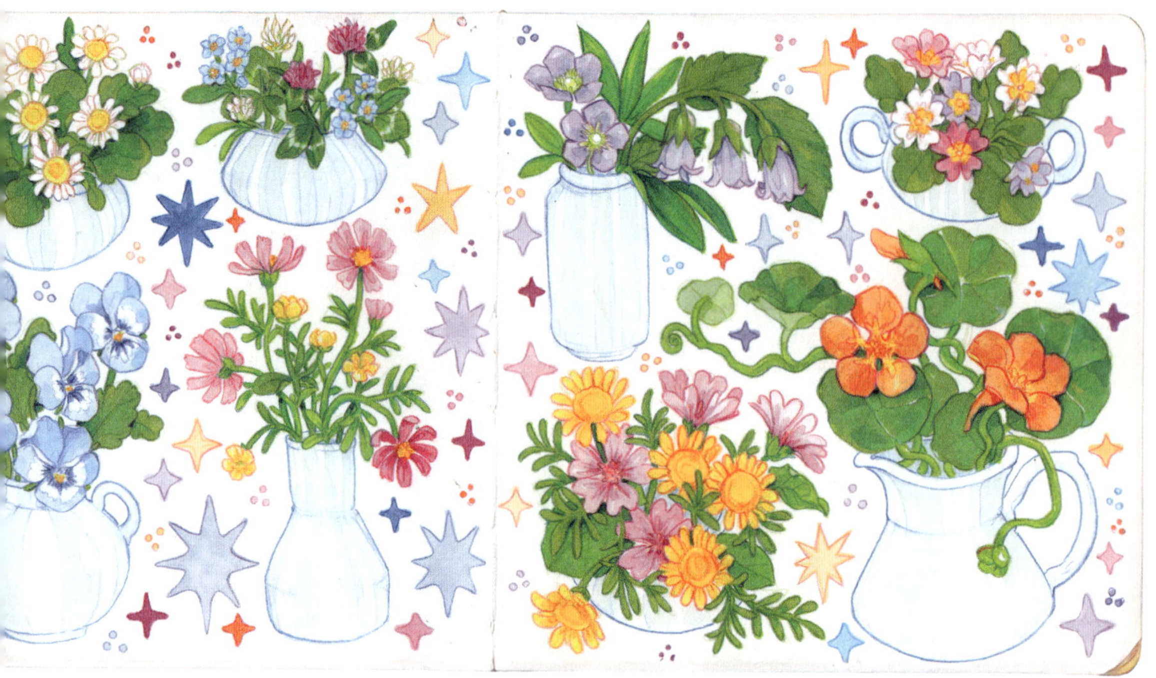

BASIC TERMINOLOGY

HUE: The property of a colour that allows the viewer to distinguish it as red, blue, green, and so on. The term is often used interchangeably with 'colour'.

SHADE: A variation of a given hue or colour.

SATURATION: Colour intensity, vividness of a colour. Pure colours are most saturated, whilst colours that appear closer to white, black or gray are more muted and softer.

VALUE: The lightness or darkness of a colour. The higher the value, the lighter a colour is.

Drawing tips

When creating a colour scheme it's good to use three shades of each colour - light, medium and dark. It is also important not to confuse the terms 'saturation' and 'value'. In the examples for saturation pictured below, both colours are similar but one appears more grey whilst the other is vivid. In the examples for value, both colours have the same intensity, but those on the right are slightly darker - their value is lower.

Use saturated colours to create bold, energizing illustrations and muted colours for calming drawings. Of course, you can also create a nice balance by using both saturated and muted colours - for example, vibrant flowers with muted leaves and vice versa.

To add dimension to an illustration, use colours with different values, so both light and dark colours. To see if the values are right in an illustration, take a photo of it and use a black-and-white filter. You are looking for a nice contrast where different shades of gray really stand out. Alternatively, squint your eyes; this will make your eyesight slightly blurry, helping to see if the contrast is strong enough.

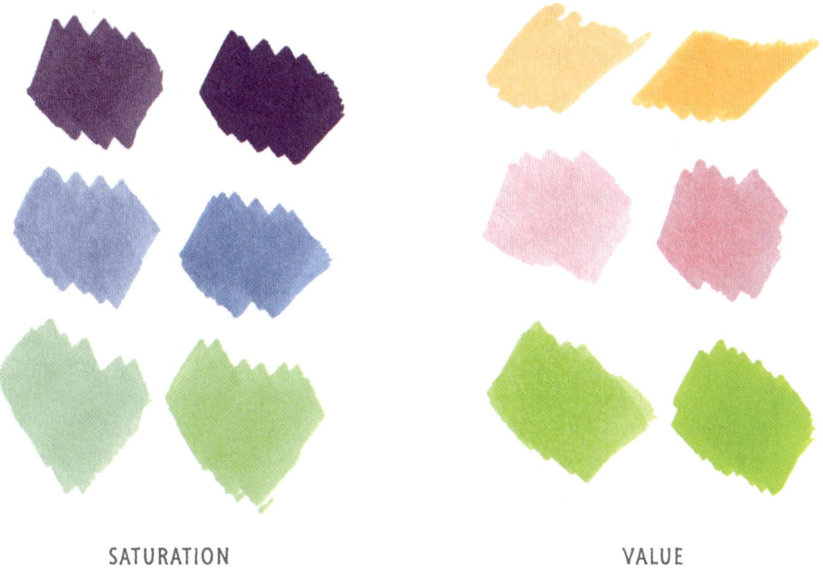

SATURATION

VALUE

Cool vs warm colours

Colours can have either cool or warm undertones. This is quite relative and depends on the viewer's eye and on how the colour makes them feel. In general, warm colours resemble warm things, such as fire and sunlight - they typically evoke joyful, cosy feelings. Cool colours resemble nature's calm elements, such as sky, water and foliage and can create a soothing effect.

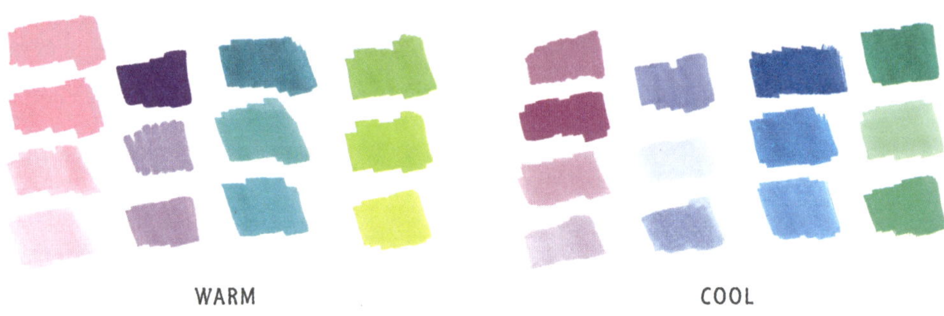

Very often, what one person sees as a warm blue, another might consider to be a cool green. If you have trouble identifying whether a colour is warm or cool, just look at the colour wheel. For example, a pink that is closer to purple would be considered cool, whereas a pink closer to orange would be warm.

Knowing about warm and cool colours allows you to use them more effectively in your art. For example, you could restrict an illustration to using only cool or only warm colours, depending on the vibe you're going for. Another approach could be to use warm colours in those parts of an illustration that are supposed to be 'hit by the sun' and cool colours for elements that are further away from the viewer. Or, you could use a cool background colour for a warm-coloured illustration. A mix of warm and cool tones makes a nice contrast in an illustration - it's the approach I take in most projects in this book.

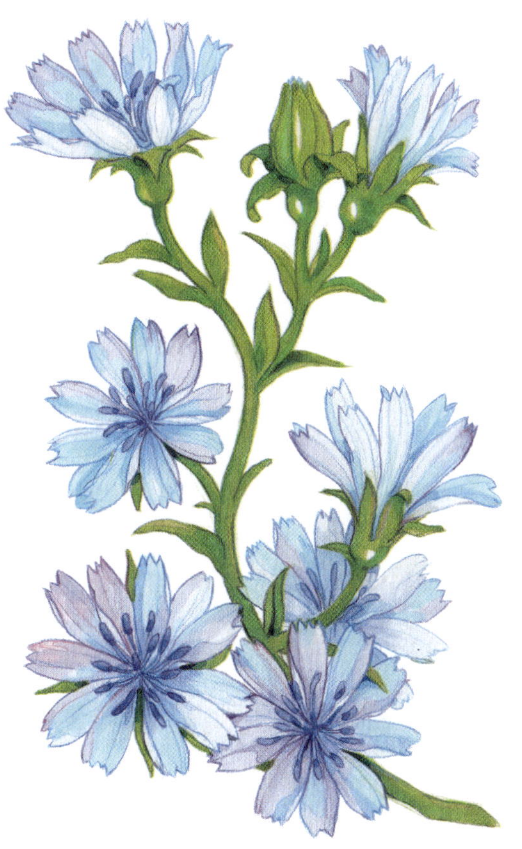

Applying a pencil outline offers another way to play with warm and cool colours - using a warm outline for mostly cool-coloured illustrations or vice versa. Traditionally shadows are cool toned, so use a cool blue or bluish-purple outline for the shadows but add warmer colours elsewhere. For illustrations of spring flowers, reddish-pink outlines work well on stems and young leaves.

In this illustration, the flowers are a cool-toned blue, and the lighter green parts have warmer tones. Then the darker, shaded green parts have cooler tones.

In this illustration, only warm colours have been used.

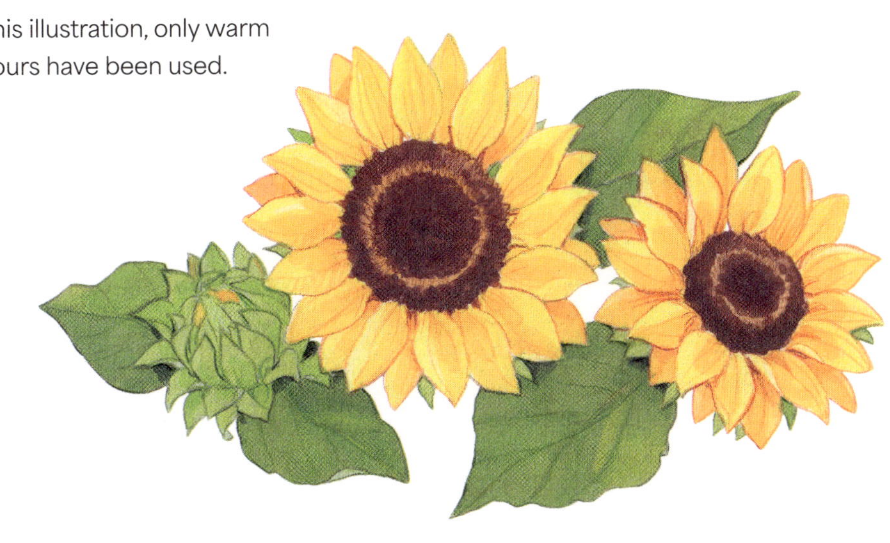

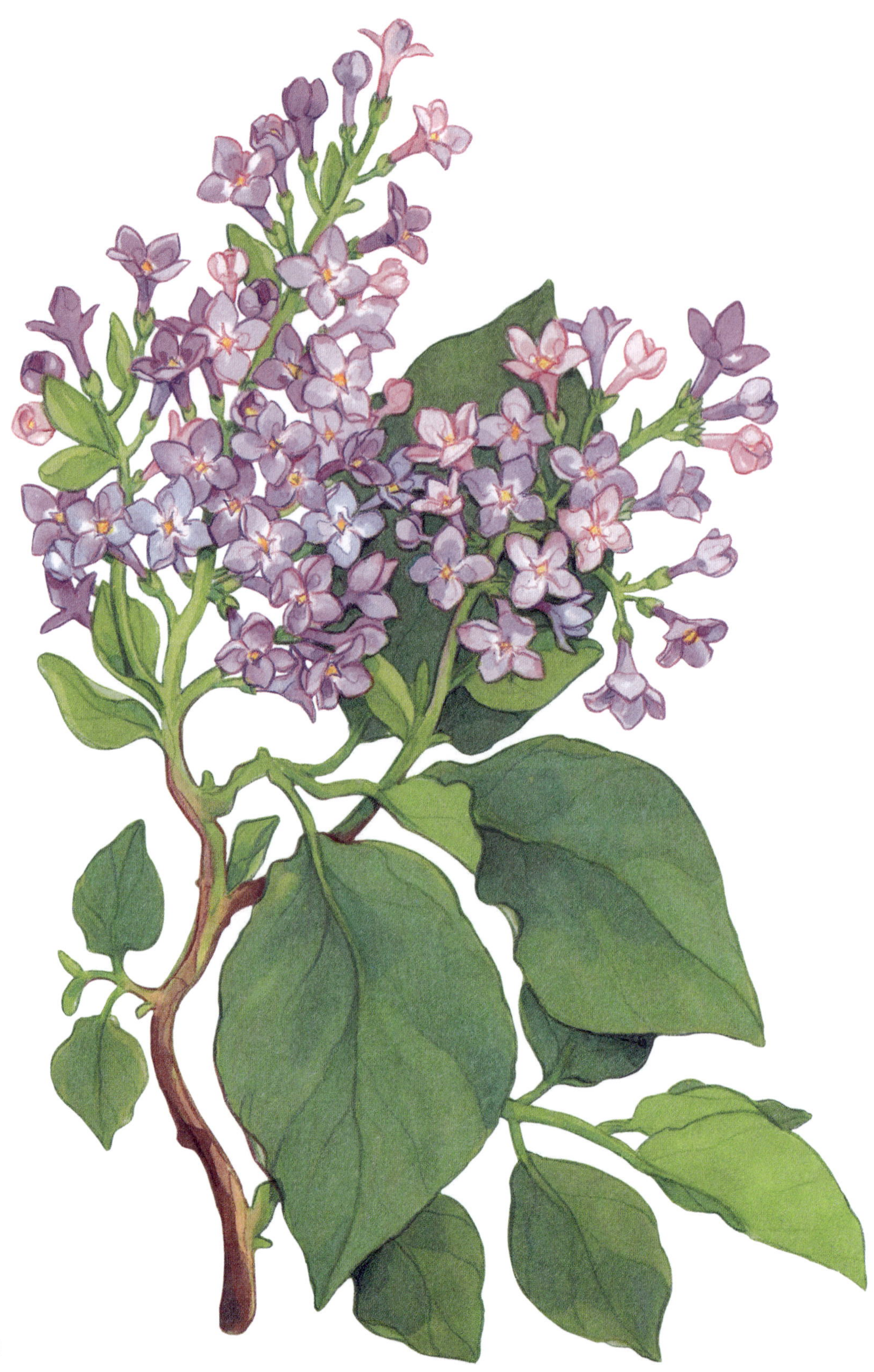

COMPOSITION BASICS

Composition

Composition can be static or dynamic. Botanical illustrations, unless they're heavily stylized, are usually dynamic. This is because plants are living matter and are rarely stiff. Dynamic compositions rely on smooth, flowing, curved lines rather than rigid or straight ones. When starting on a composition for a botanical illustration, you need to decide on what shape the subject should take on the paper.

Here are several basic options to choose from:

- An S-curve composition
- A C-curve composition
- An X-shape composition
- A triangle-shape composition

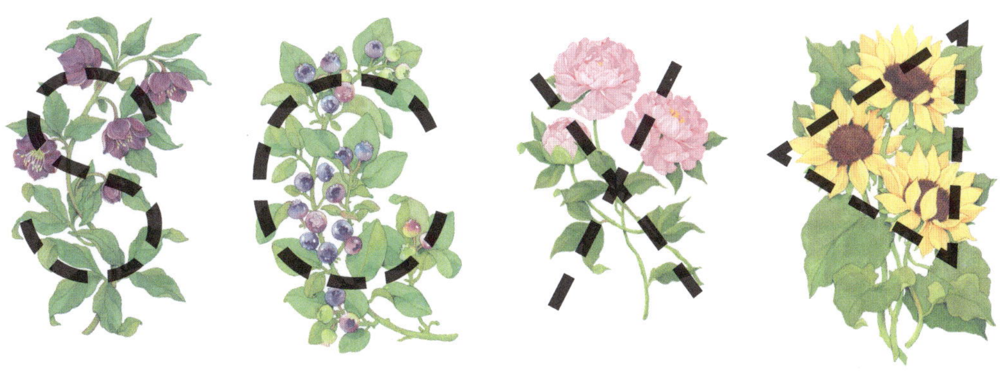

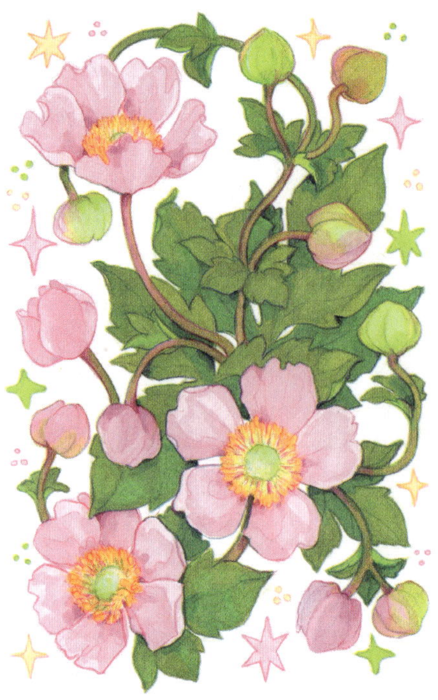

Tips for dynamic composition

A composition will look more natural and fluid if you avoid things looking too symmetrical. Make sure some flower heads are taller than others, that they face in different directions, that their stems are not rigid, but twist and turn on the page, and that some leaves curl and fold.

Within the same composition, draw flowers at different stages of growth: buds, emerging petals, fully open blooms. Whilst different objects can overlap, the two edges shouldn't meet.

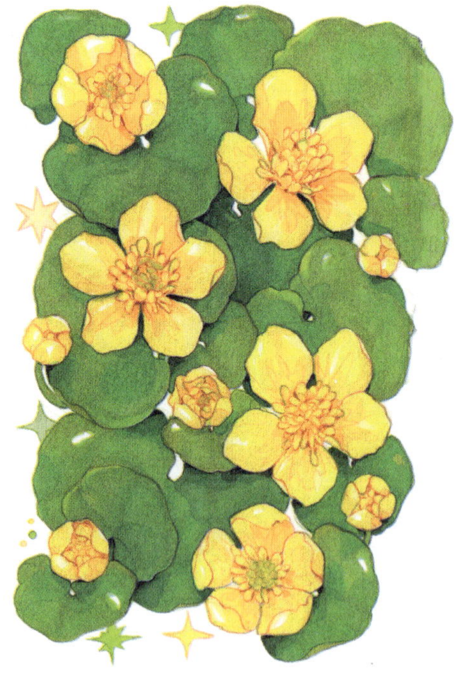

Draw objects in odd numbers (thee, five, seven etc) to make the composition look more organic. The fewer flowers, the bigger difference it makes. It is less noticeable in an illustration with lots of flowers but there is a huuuge difference between an illustration with two flowers versus one with three.

A triangle-shape composition is one used for many floral arrangements, usually using an odd number of blooms. The basic idea is to make the flower in the middle the tallest, with the other two at a similar height either side. The same principle can be used working from left to right (or vice versa), as with these tangerines.

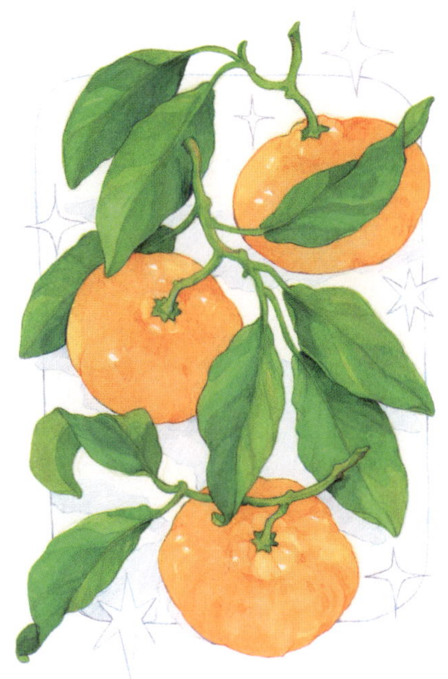

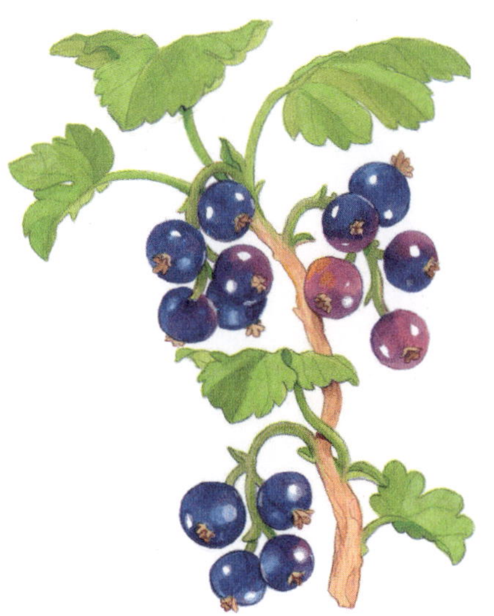

Adding bumps on woody stems and branches prevents your lines being too straight or rigid.

Consider allowing an illustration to 'run over' the edges of the page, so that some leaves and flowers at the edges are incomplete.

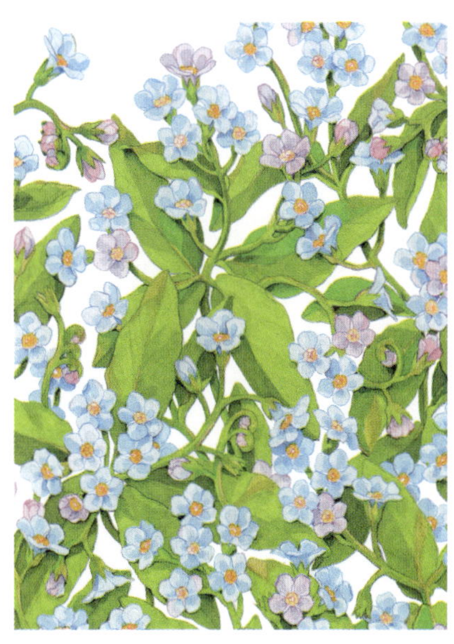

Adding a frame

Creating a composition within a frame can achieve pleasant results. You can use a rectangular shape (rounded edges add playfulness to the design) or an oval (especially suited to vintage illustrations). Furthermore, the frame can be smaller than the illustration, with some elements of the drawing overlapping - but not exactly touching - the edges. This is a good option for small illustrations.

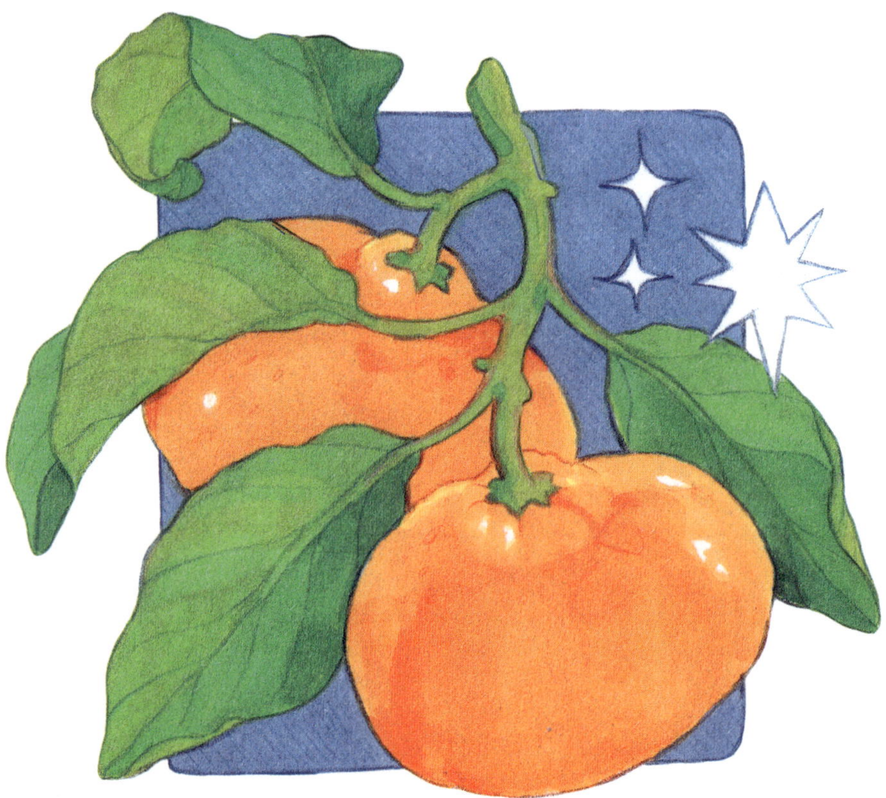

If you want crisp edges to an illustration, you can use washi tape or masking tape to create a frame within which to contain your illustration. This is particularly useful if you want to colour in the background (see Nighttime bloom, page 119), or if you wish to create more complex compositions contained within a finite space.

Creating thumbnails

Before starting on an illustration, it can be useful to try out your composition as a thumbnail sketch - or even as a series of thumbnails to decide on which composition works best. Simply draw a small rectangle with a similar ratio to the illustration you want to make and make a sketch of your proposed illustration. This will help you to work on the perspective, proportion and scale of all the elements, making sure they all work well together before committing to the 'live' work.

Thumbnail sketches can be as neat or as rough as you like. Compare the thumbnail sketches I made for the Peony illustrations on page 104 with those I made for the Blueberries project on page 112 (see below). The former are just quick pencil sketches to use as references. The latter are more polished and could be tiny pieces of art in their own right. Sometimes, it can be fun to create a thumbnail sketch on the same page as the finished art, to see how the project developed from start to finish.

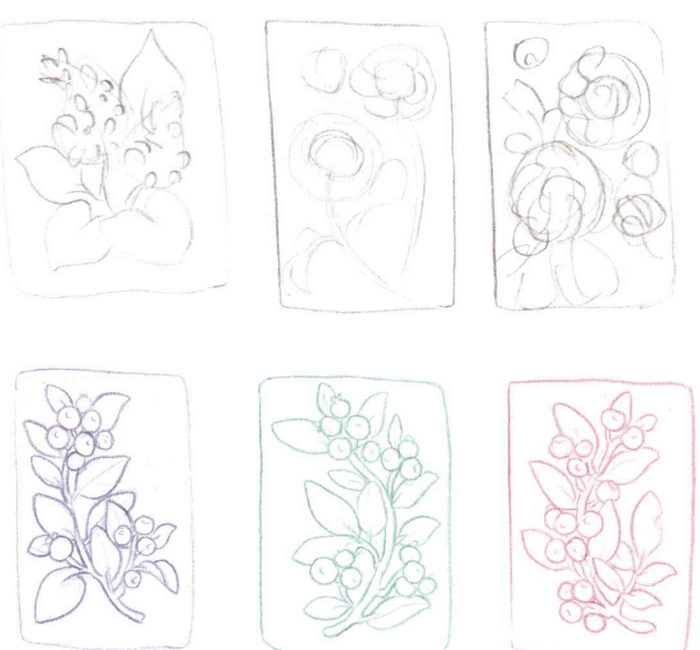

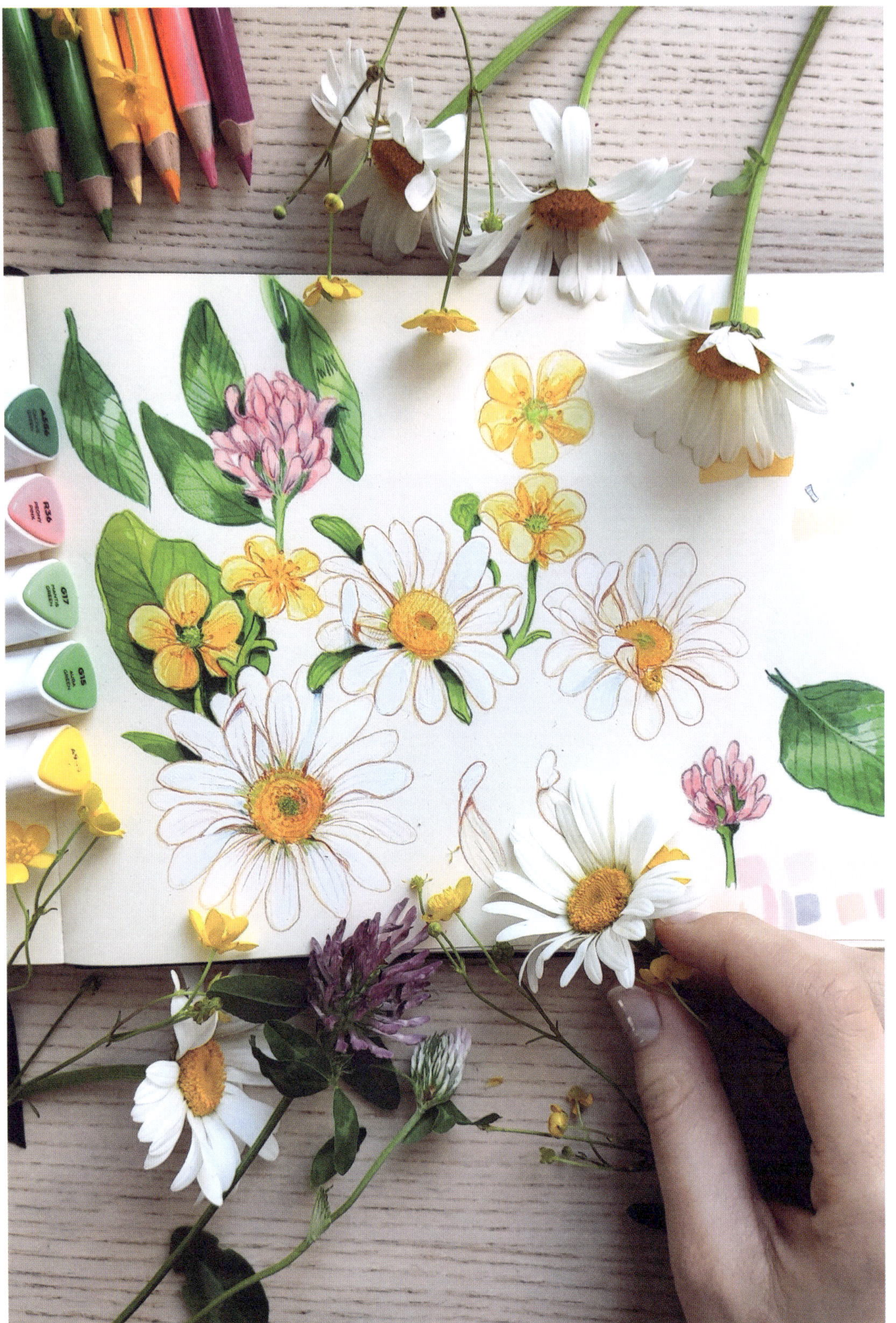

BASIC TECHNIQUES

Sketching

It is always a good idea to make an initial sketch for your drawing, even it is very loose. It will help you to plan the composition properly and to get a general idea of how the finished artwork will look. It will also serve as a guide whilst you are working - you can always refine the lines as you progress from one step to the next.

Always work lightly using pencil when creating an initial guideline or sketch. Good colours to use are light pink, baby blue or beige - colours that are barely visible. If you keep the pressure light as you draw, these initial lines will be covered by the layers of colour you add at each stage. This avoids the need to erase the initial sketch at the end of the process. Once you are happy with the sketch, you can refine the lines using darker colours and then move on to colouring using markers.

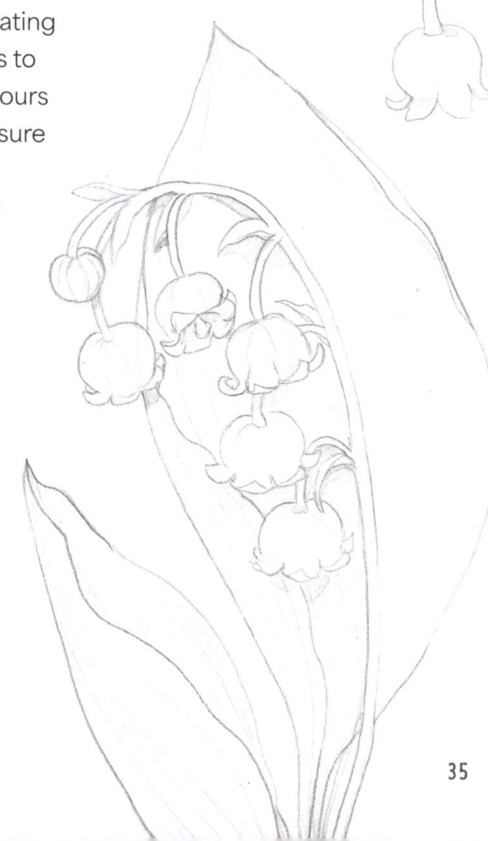

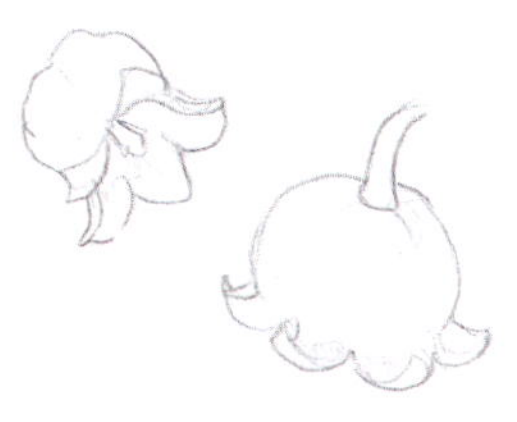

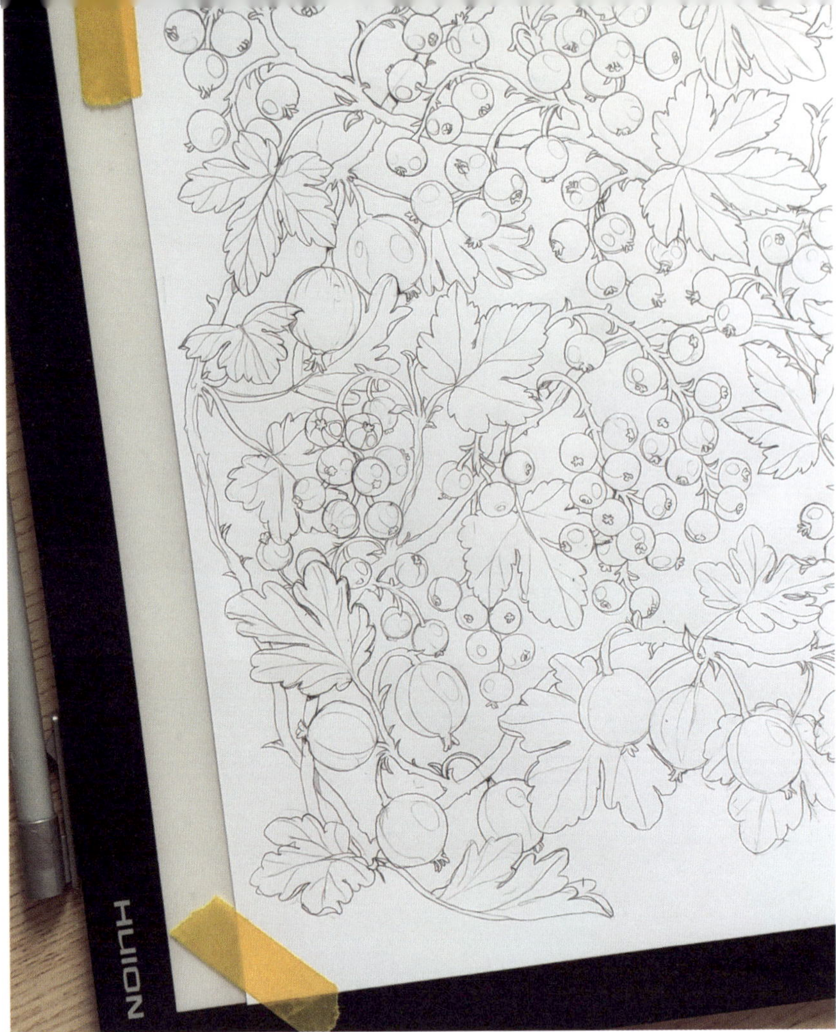

Transferring a sketch

Sometimes - say when you are out and about - you might want to make a sketch using a regular pencil on a loose sheet of paper and then trace that sketch into your sketchbook or another sheet of paper at home. The easiest way to trace a sketch is to attach it to light a pad or window using washi tape then place your sketchbook page or a second sheet of paper over your sketch and draw over the lines that show through. It can be quite time-consuming, but will lead to the cleanest results. This technique is particularly useful when drawing something you're not that familiar with, such as when making a first proper fully coloured study of a plant, or when creating more complex composition where objects overlap a lot.

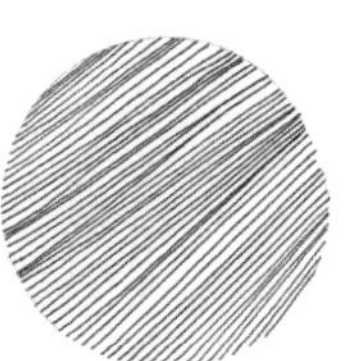
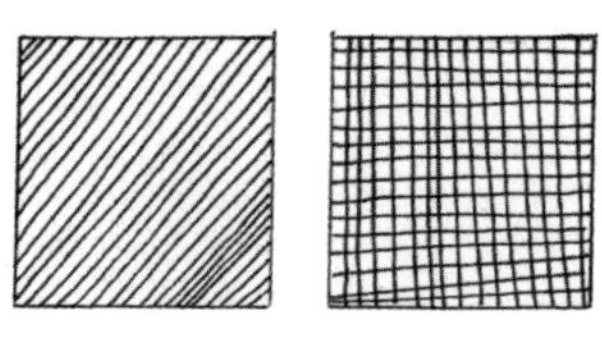
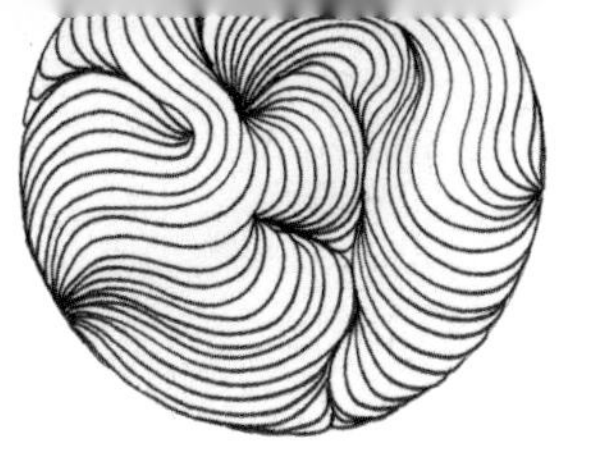
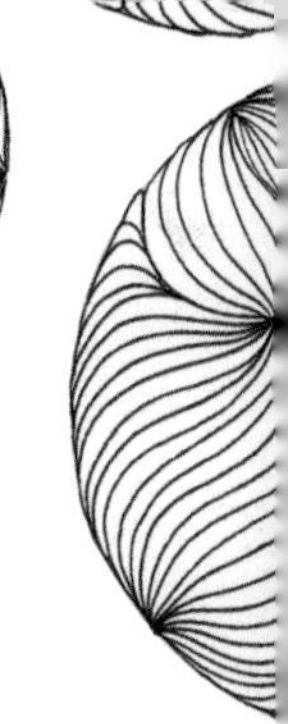

Warm-up doodles

Before making a start on any 'serious' illustration, it can be beneficial to doodle, simply to warm or loosen up your hand. Choose something abstract or draw items that are in your comfort zone so that you can adopt a relaxed approach as you practise drawing steady straight or flowing lines. That way, you can focus better on hand stability, line control and building confidence.

DOODLE WARM-UP

This is a great exercise for practising flowing, curvy lines – a skill that helps to make future illustrations look more organic and less 'stiff'.

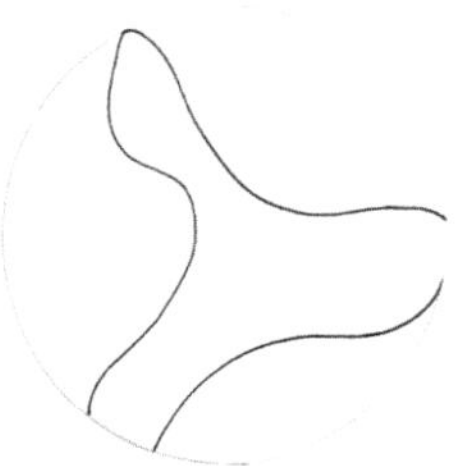

- Draw a circle by tracing around the top of a glass, saucer or similar. Now draw two or three flowing lines within the circle, making sure that none of them cross.

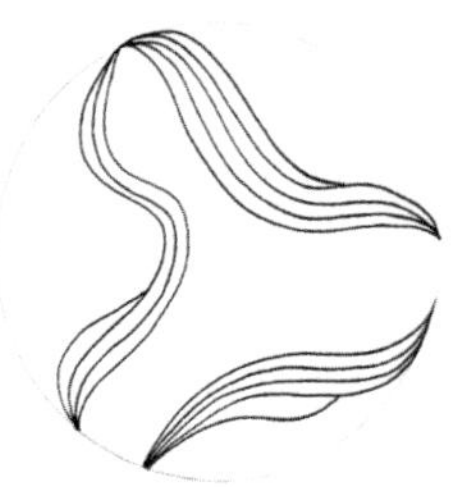

- Add in two or three lines running parallel to the lines you drew in the previous step, following the same curves and roughly the same distance apart.

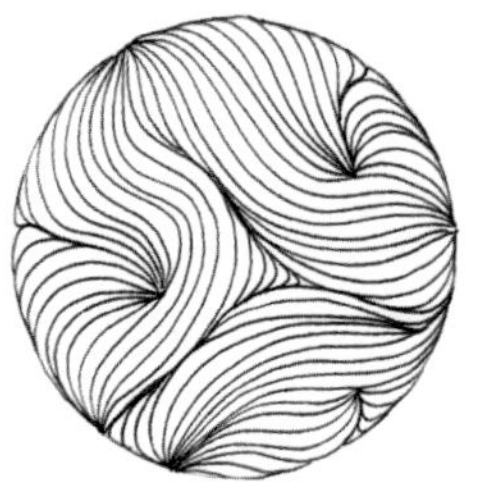

- Fill the remaining space with shorter lines, running either parallel or perpendicular to the first lines you drew.

Making studies

Building a 'visual library' of various different plant forms can be hugely beneficial to your practice. Though it may take some time, with each plant that you study you will become more skilled in knowing what to look for, in recognizing basic leaf and petal shapes, and in drawing plant forms confidently from scratch. With enough practice, you will reach a stage where you don't have to think about the 'anatomy' of a plant when painting and will be able to draw without looking at reference images, so focusing more on the finer details.

Get to see as many real plants as possible, whether as cut flowers, out and about in nature, or online. In the case of the last option, search for images on dedicated botanical sites and watch gardening videos on YouTube, which will allow you to see a plant from a range of different angles. Similarly, when you are out walking, look for interesting plants and take several photos to use for reference when you get home.

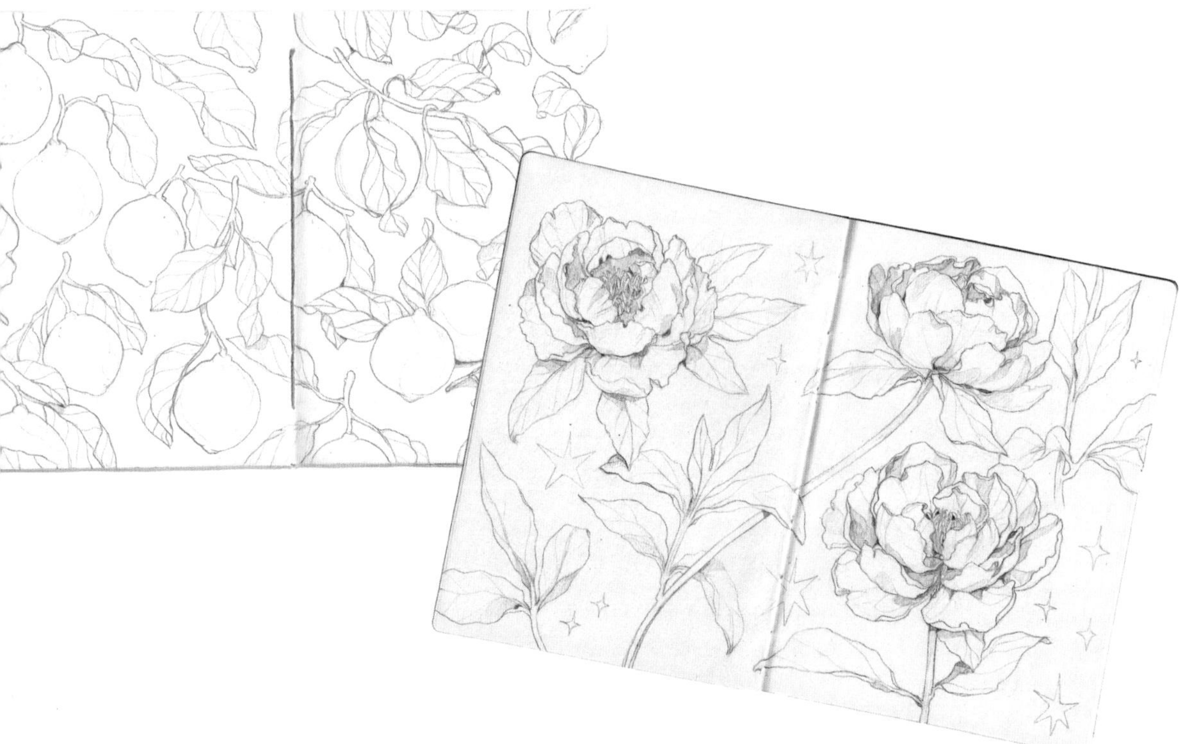

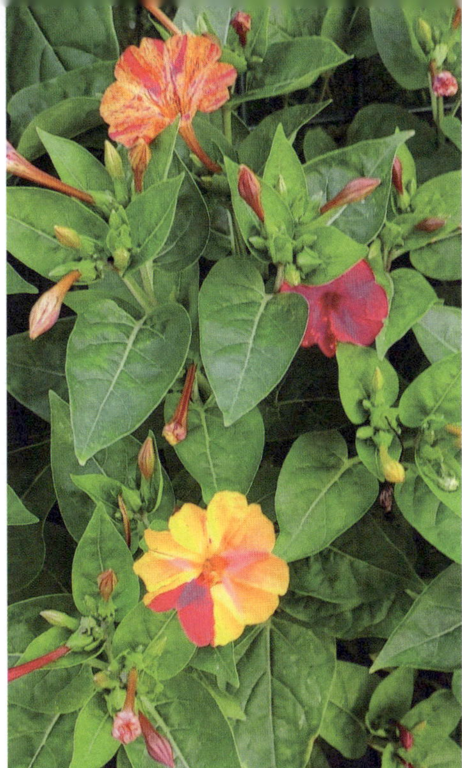

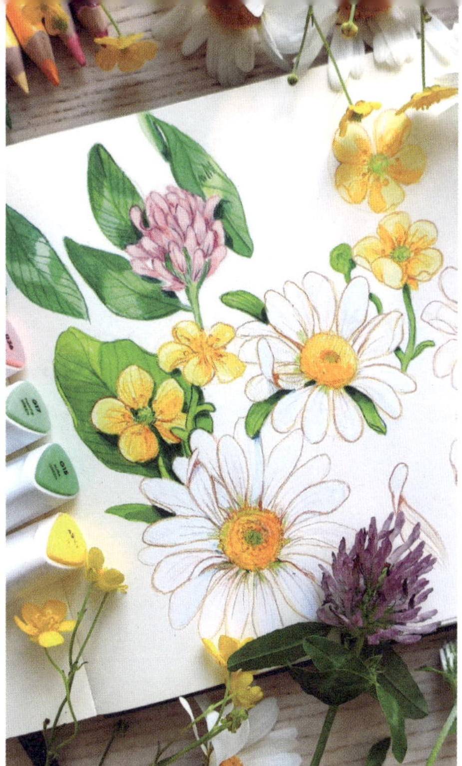

Initially, focus just on the basic shapes and general 'silhouette' of the plant. Examine each plant to familiarize yourself with its main features:

What kind of stem does it have?
What shape are the leaves and how do they join at the stem?
How many petals do the flowers have and what shape are they?

To help you make a first pencil sketch, combine your findings with the Tutorials on pages 58-76, where you will find examples of all the most common leaf and flower types and shapes.

As you build confidence, progress from graphite to coloured pencils and marker pens. Choose single flowers to work up as a collection of studies, as in the postage stamp tutorial on pages 80-85. Then progress to more complex compositions, trying several alternatives that show the plant from different perspectives. The more you practise, the better your drawing and painting skills will become.

Using marker pens

All of the techniques demonstrated in the following pages feature in the seasonal projects that follow. There is endless scope for variation and experimentation. As you develop your own style, you might like to practise them on scrap paper before committing to an illustration. Better still, use a dedicated sketchbook for your experiments so that you can keep a visual record of the things you have tried.

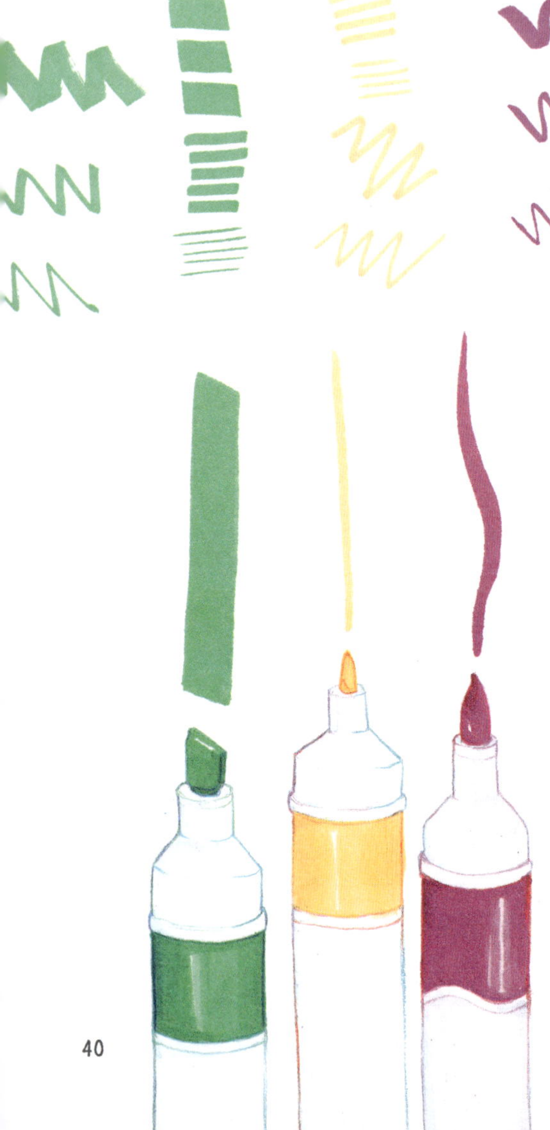

Basic pen marks

As described in the materials section, marker pens come with three different nib types: fine, brush and chisel. You can use them in various ways and it can be good to experiment. In general, use the finest nibs for crisp, even outlines, use the chisel for filling large areas of colour with broad strokes and use the brush nib for blending colours more smoothly.

COLOURING TIPS

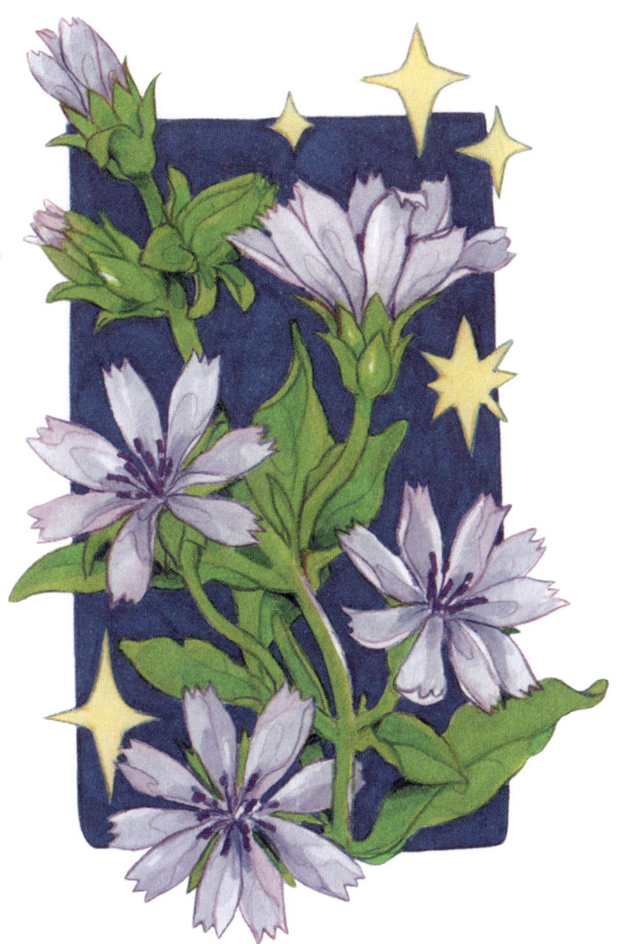

- When colouring large areas, work in sections so that the ink doesn't dry out before moving to the next section. This prevents harsh lines forming where sections meet.

- Work from left to right (or right to left, if you are left-handed) and from top to bottom to avoid potentially smudging your work.

- Avoid giving elements of a drawing a marker outline before filling in the rest. This will dry before you have finished colouring, leaving the outlines visible once you are done. It is better to colour in sections - say, between veins on a leaf.

- For a smoother finish, maintain contact between the pen nib and the paper for the whole time that you are colouring in a section.

- If you intend to include a colour background, think carefully about what colour it should be. A dark background can make other colours pop. You could also consider using a cool-coloured background for a warm-coloured illustration (and vice versa). Backgrounds that offer a degree of contrast work best.

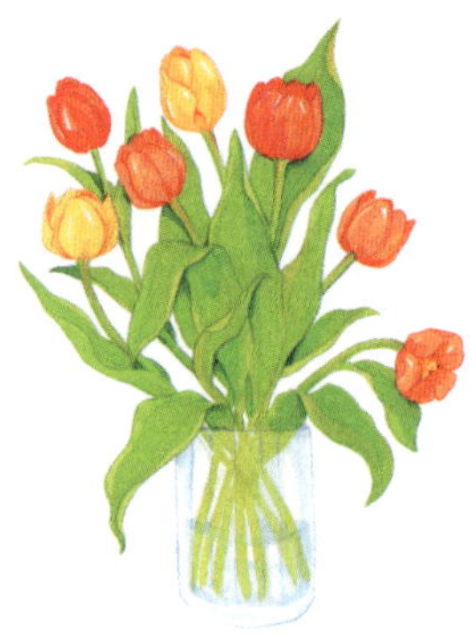

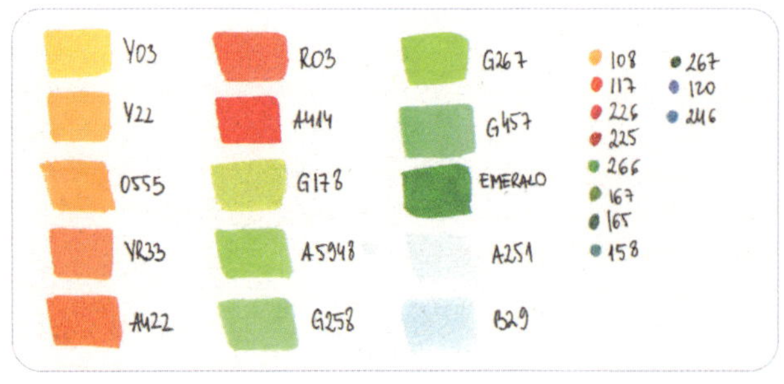

Creating colour swatches

Alcohol-based markers are notorious for having pen caps that do not accurately represent the colour of the ink on paper. Sometimes not even the name of the colour matches the true colour of the ink. For this reason, it's crucial to create colour swatches before working on any illustration. Also, inks dry differently, depending on paper type. In most mixed-media sketchbooks, paper isn't pure white; it's more ivory, and since alcohol-based ink is transparent, the slightly yellowish undertone of the paper will affect the final colour. Cool colours might look a bit desaturated (because yellow is a warm colour). Colours will look truest to those of the pen caps when you use smooth white paper. It is a good idea to make colour swatches on the paper you're actually going to use for illustrations.

Due to the nature of alcohol-based ink, in particular its readiness to fade (see page 92) always keep your swatches away from direct sunlight and create new versions every few months, or once you notice colours changing.

You can also create colour swatches for specific illustrations, as above. Or you might even consider making swatches part of the artwork, as here. Swatches can be both practical and fun.

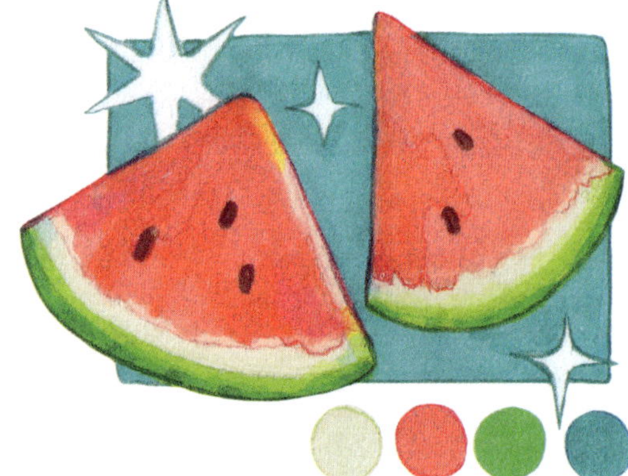

Building colour in layers

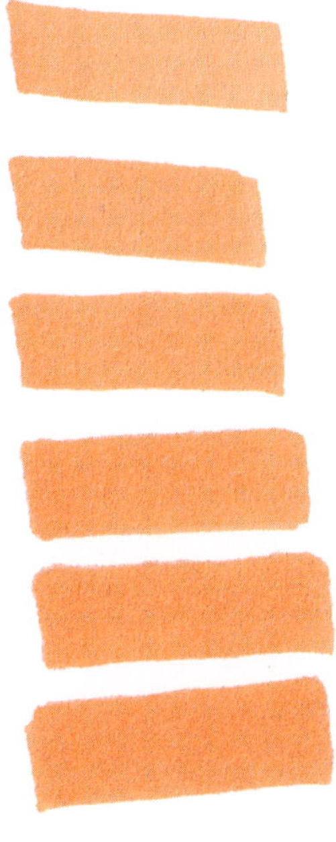

Alcohol-based ink is translucent, which allows you to build depth in an illustration and to create smooth gradients. The examples here show swatches of colour where a new layer is added as the swatches progress from top to bottom. See how the colour darkens with each layer until the paper cannot absorb any more ink (around layers three to five, depending on the colour). At this point, the colour will not get any darker and might cause soaking or bleeding through to the page below.

Whenever working in layers with colour markers - or any medium, in fact - the general rule is to work from light to dark. When shading a flower or leaf, for example, you might choose three to four tones and build up from the lightest.

Here are some examples of colour combinations working from light through mid to dark. For many images, the darkest tones are used sparingly for shadows in corners or where leaves, stems and other elements meet.

Blending colours

For smooth blending, you can use a wet-on-wet technique. It basically means applying the next layer of ink whilst the previous layer is still wet. To do this, you need to work quickly as alcohol-based ink evaporates fast. This technique takes some practice. If you apply the next layer too quickly or add too much colour, you might end up with feathery or fuzzy edges. Should this happen, you can fix it easily by adding a pencil outline later in the process. So, although you need to work quickly, give the first layer of ink at least a few seconds before applying the next. This technique is recommended for colouring berries, buds and other elements with round edges.

Should you allow ink to dry for longer - hours, days or even months - you can still blend smoothly. Simply reactivate the ink by adding another layer of the base colour. Note that this will darken the colour.

When blending, use colours with a similar level of saturation but a different value level (see pages 24-25). It's just easier to blend colours that are quite similar.

BLENDING FROM LIGHT TO DARK

As an example, take the Blueberries project on page 112. Always start with the lightest colour in your range as your base colour and, from that, add increasingly darker shades to build depth. Apply the mid-tone(s) where there are shadows, slightly overlapping the edge of the lighter tones where the colours meet. Draw circles or ellipses to spread the ink evenly and to create soft transitions. Finally, apply the darkest tone and repeat the previous step to blend the edges of the mid-tones.

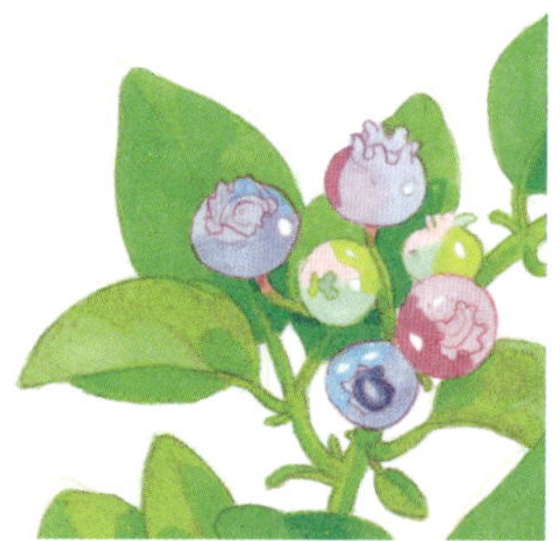

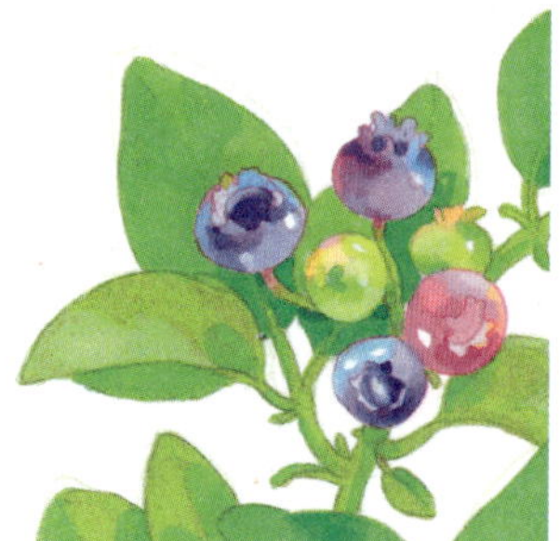

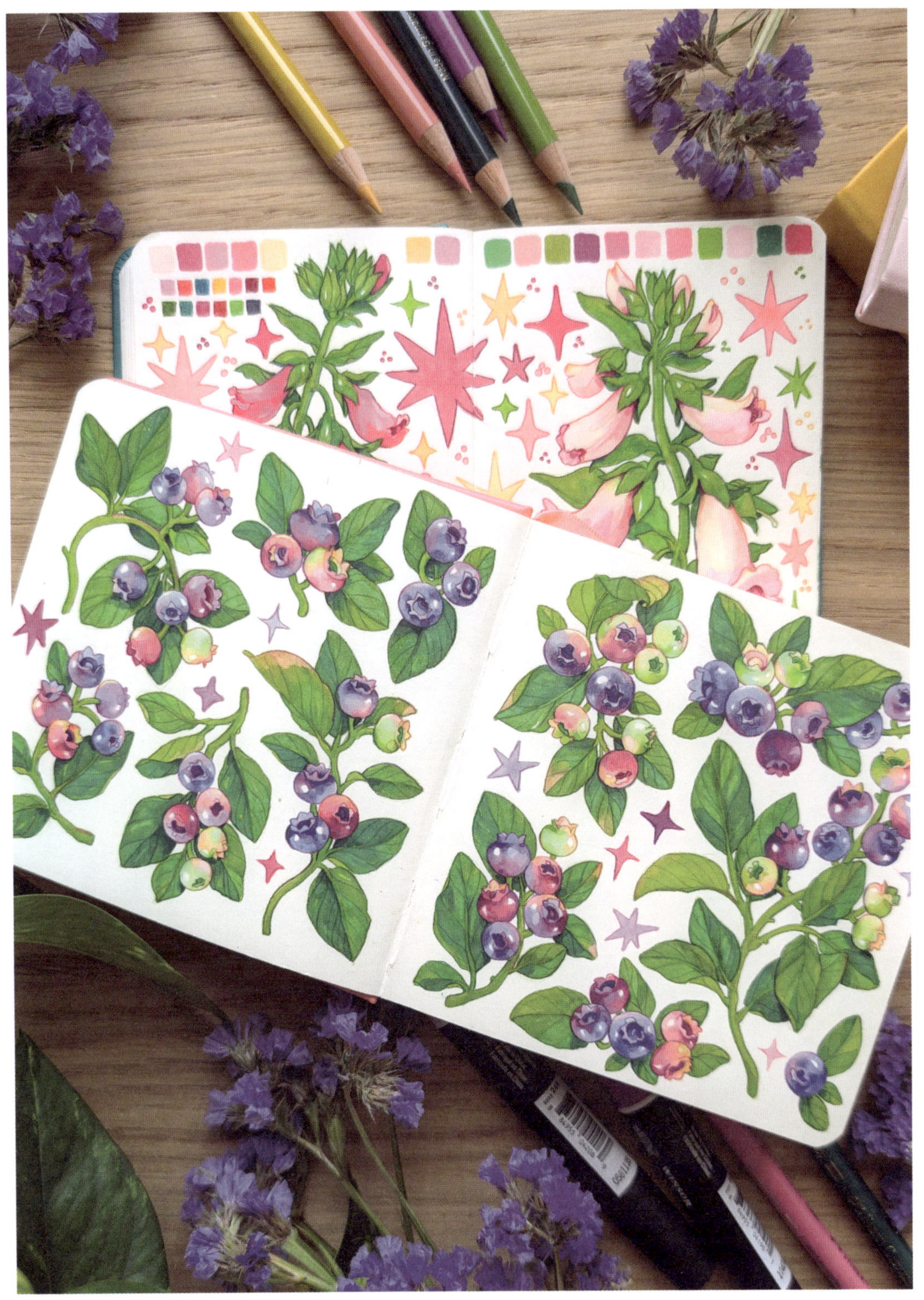

SOFTENING SHADES

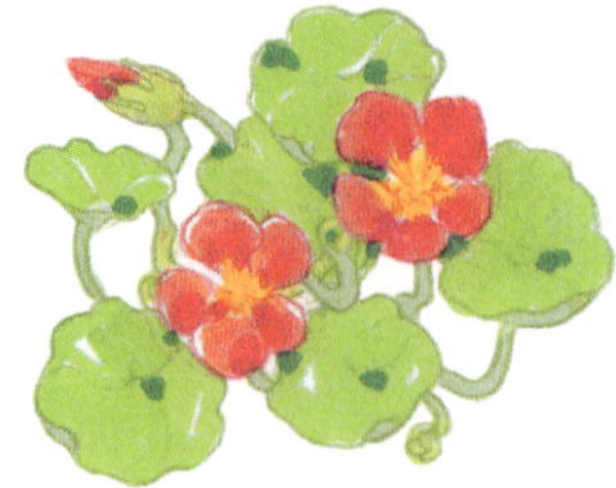

Even though the general rule is to go from light to dark, it is possible to work the other way around. This technique is used to soften the darkest shades, mostly used sparingly in small areas of deep shadow. You can see how this works in the Postage Stamp tutorial on page 80. The blending process starts with the lighter base colour. Then, instead of progressing to a mid-tone, you apply the dark tone and then blend where the edges overlap using a mid-tone. This makes the shadow appear brighter.

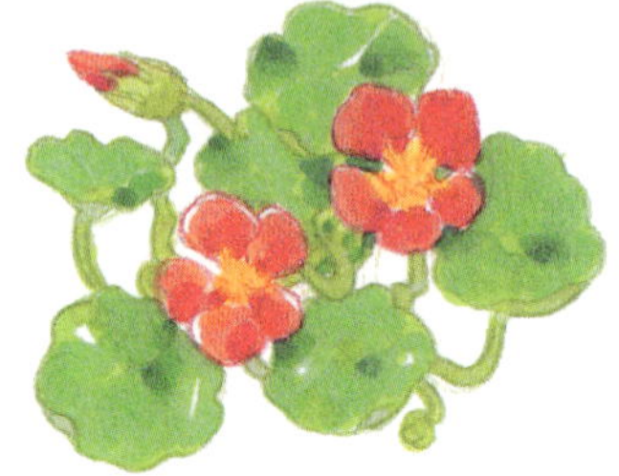

CREATING GRADIENTS

To create a gradient, you can apply the same technique as for blending from light to dark, except here there is no base colour. The tones simply shift from light to mid to dark. Do this by placing the colours beside each other, and blend the edges, using the light tone to blend the light to mid edges and the mid-tone to blend the mid to dark edges. In the examples here, the first shows a gradient created using colours that graduate from warm to cool, and the second using only warm colours.

Creating new colours

The ability to mix marker ink colours is limited, but not impossible. You cannot physically mix the ink to create new colours, as you might when using watercolour paints or gouache. Instead, new colours are created directly on the paper in a series of layers and not on a palette. This is a particularly useful technique for creating the more organic, natural colours of plants, since most markers in basic sets have rather saturated tones, especially when it comes to the greens. There are two main techniques: Using undertones and glazing.

USING UNDERTONES

An undertone is the base colour in an illustration and influences how other colours appear when laid over the top. Undertones can be used to add warmth or coolness to an illustration. For example a yellow-green undertone will make leaves appear more saturated and warmer. It works well for spring illustrations. Olive green makes other colours appear warmer and also slightly more muted. It is a great option for autumn illustrations and for illustrations in which the flowers or other elements are very saturated, as it helps to create a nice balance. Cool, blue-green colours can be used as undertones for winter illustrations, since they make other colours appear cooler.

As a general rule, an undertone needs to be lighter in colour and less saturated than the colours being applied on top of it. You can use different undertones in one illustration. For example, in the Meadow project on page 104, different plants have different undertones.

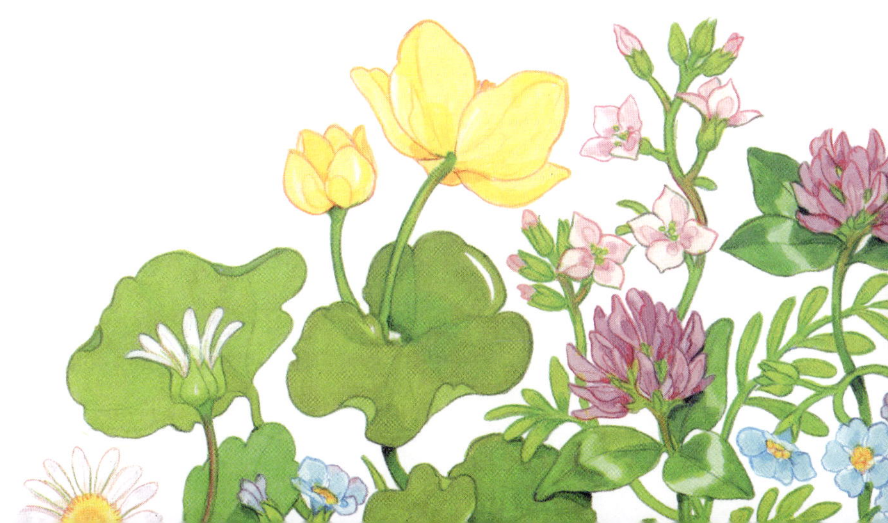

BUILDING COLOUR

As a visual example, see how the same olive green undertone affects other greens when looking for leaf colours. The first two colours look rich and natural. They are warm toned, so they blend beautifully. The third colour is slightly too bright and looks less natural. The fourth option doesn't work at all. If you use a significantly lighter colour over a darker one the two won't blend well. Since the ink is translucent, the dark colour will show through and will appear washed out.

The most reliable method for building leaf colours, therefore, is to use a warm colour on top of a yellow-green undertone (as in the first two examples). Subsequent layers can then be either warm or cool greens. This is how the leaves were coloured in the majority of projects that follow, including the Hellebore project on page 140.

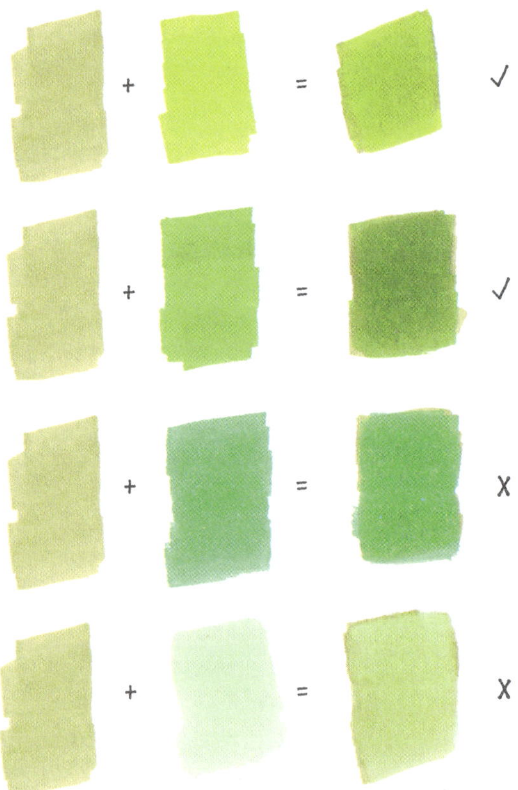

GLAZING

Glazing is a term used for applying a final layer of colour over the top of a finished illustration once it is complete. It allows you to build more depth. For example, you can glaze with yellow to make colours appear even warmer and more saturated - see the Colourful pumpkins project on page 132. Glazing with yellow works best when the colours in the illustration are analogous to yellow (see page 23). So, any red, pink or orange. If you try to warm colours that are traditionally considered cool (purple and blue, for example) with yellow, it'll make the colours appear muddy.

The same is true for making colours appear cooler. Glaze over the parts you want to change using blue. A cool-toned vibrant blue usually works best. Again, this works best when the colours in the illustration are analogous to blue. It is great for 'cooling' green tones and adding shades.

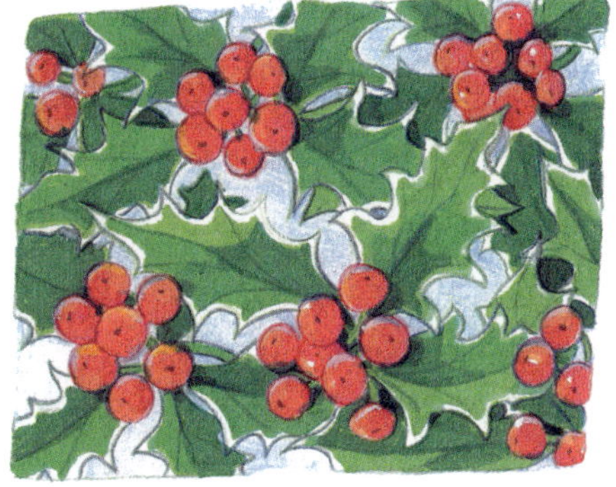

Glazing is also something that can fix poor blending. If you end up with harsh lines in a finished drawing, go over the area again using a mid-tone. The ink will reactivate and harsh lines will be smoothed. It's also a great technique for colouring round objects and creating a more cohesive look, a technique used in the Holly project on page 146.

Creating highlights

Highlights are the brightest parts of an illustration, seen on shiny leaves or petals and on round objects such as berries). They can be used to make elements look more three-dimensional.

The easiest way to create highlights is to leave some areas of the illustration free of colour, so allowing the white of the paper to show through. It is best to use light colours around a highlight in order to avoid harsh transitions. Alternatively, you can use a very light colour that coordinates with the colour of the object - light blue for a green leaf and pale yellow for red berries, for example. This will soften the highlight. See the Colourful pumpkins project on page 132 and the Peonies project on page 98 for examples of this.

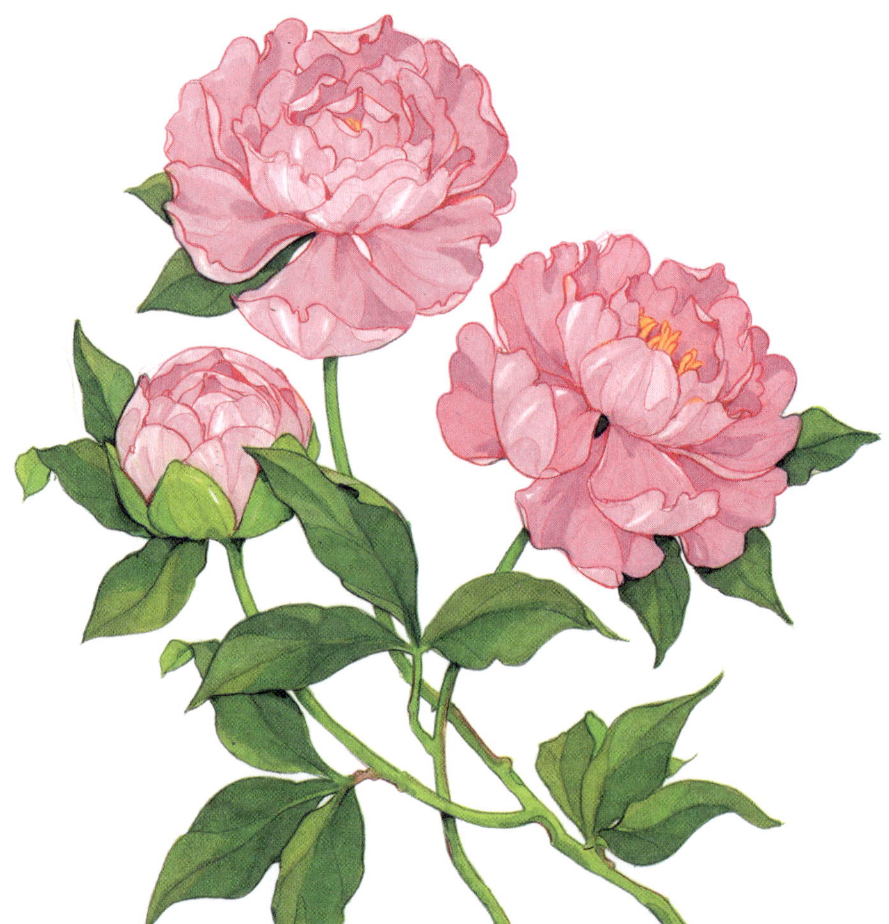

Another method is to use a white pencil, but this only works on dark objects - as on the berries in the Holly project on page 146. Use the pencil on the edge of a round object to create round highlights. Keep it as it is or use another light-coloured pencil on top of it, like sky blue or lemon yellow for more visual interest.

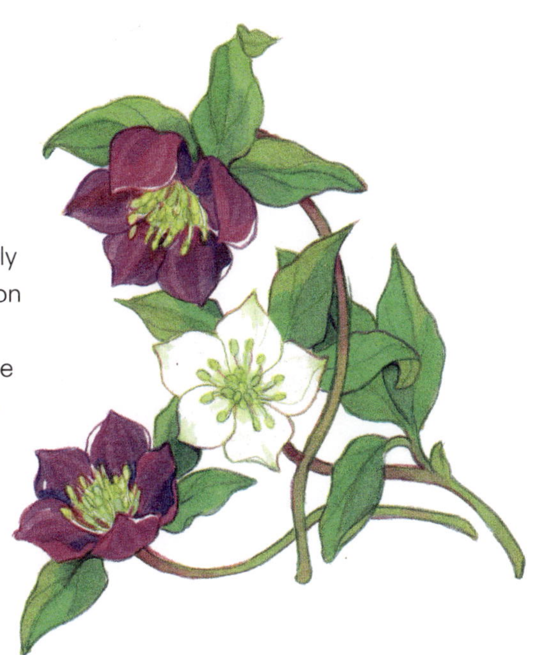

You can also use a colourless blender marker to create highlights. It washes out any colour beneath it. Any light colour similar to that of the illustration can work like this as well. Simply use a blender or a light marker in places where you want to create a highlight, a technique used in the Hellebore project on page 140. Results won't appear immediately, so wait a few minutes before you decide to reapply the blender.

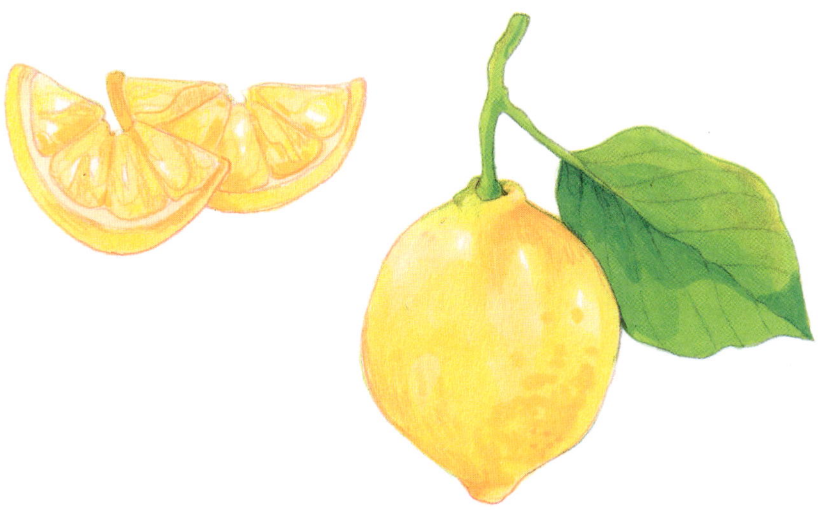

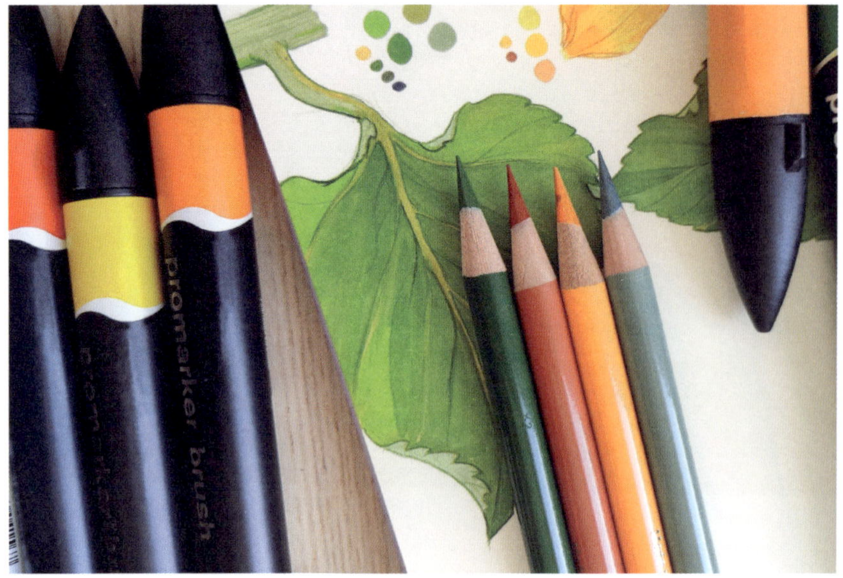

Mixing mediums

When working with more than one medium - in the case of the projects in this book, coloured pencils and alcohol-based markers - it is possible to create different effects depending on the order in which you use them. Coloured pencils, for example, are useful for creating an initial sketch that will effectively disappear once markers are worked over the top, or for giving super-sharp outlines to a finished drawing. But they can also be used in other ways to enhance your work.

Coloured backgrounds: pencil first

Once the main subject in a drawing is complete, you can add a coloured background. Use the tip of a coloured pencil, making sure it is blunt - this will allow you to cover the area more quickly and softly. Fill the entire background without applying too much pressure or trying to be too neat. Once the pencil layer is laid down, you can colour over it using a marker in a similar colour. This will 'smooth out' the pencil layer, filling any specks of white that might have been missed with the pencil as in the Holly project on page 146.

Coloured backgrounds: marker first

Once the main subject in a drawing is complete, fill in the entire background using a marker in a single colour, then use a pencil of a similar colour over the top of it to create a texture. Use this technique to create an interesting visual effect as in the example here. You can use the same technique to 'hide' the strokes of the markers, as in the Nighttime bloom project on page 118.

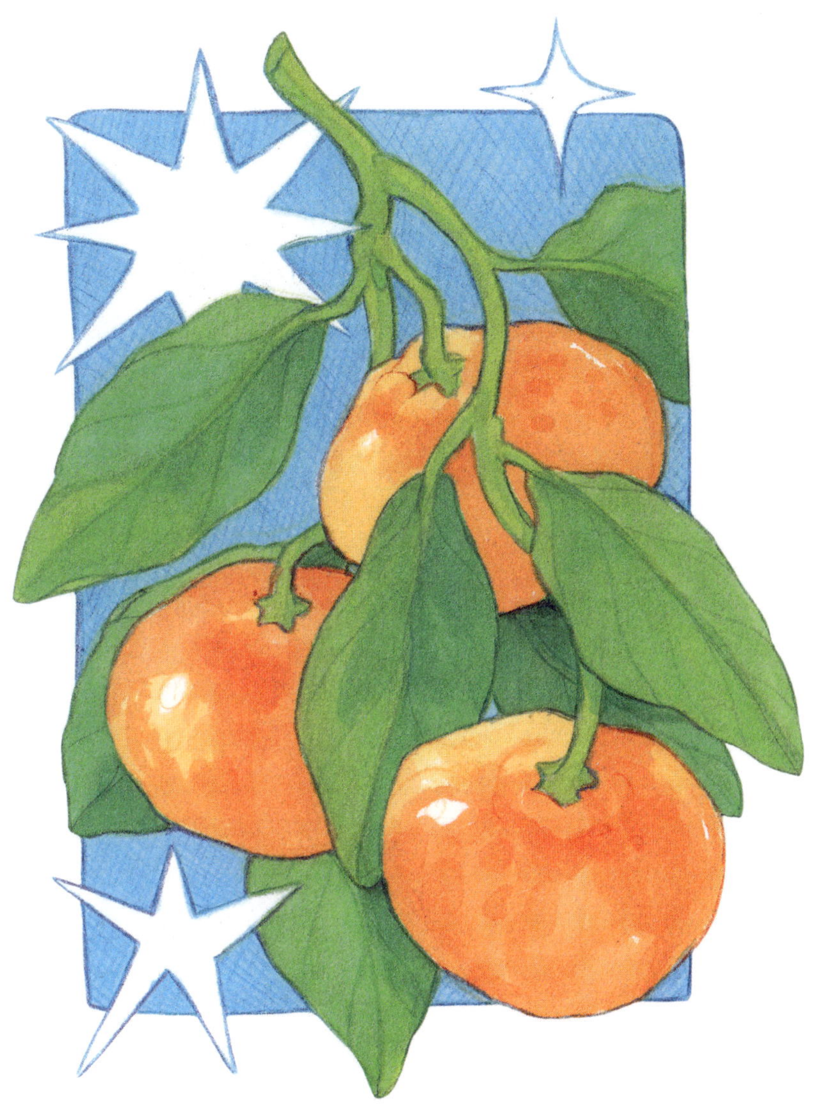

DIFFERENT EFFECTS

When a colour marker layer is applied over the top of a coloured pencil layer, the effect is smooth and soft.

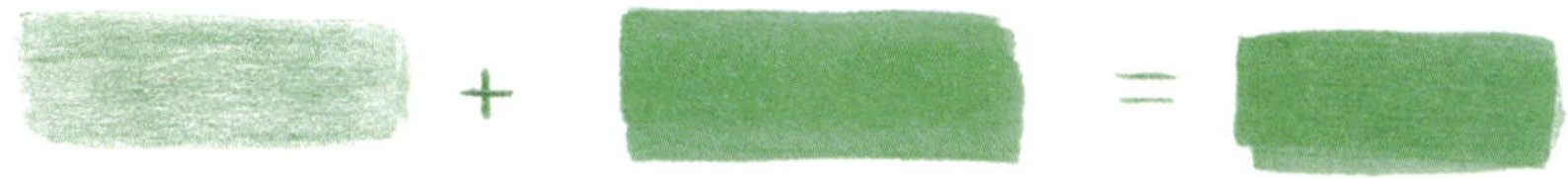

When a coloured pencil layer is applied over the top of a marker layer, the effect is rougher and more textured.

When a light marker colour is used on top of a darker pencil colour, the effect is more hazy.

Hatching

Hatching is a drawing technique achieved by using parallel lines to create shading, texture and depth. Below are some examples of the different kinds of hatching you can use. In all cases, the more layers of pencil you use and the denser the lines are, the stronger the effect will be.

BASIC HATCHING: Draw parallel lines in one direction.

CROSSHATCHING: Draw parallel lines in opposite directions so that they cross each other at an angle.

PATCH HATCHING: Create small areas of crosshatching over the surface.

SCRIBBLE HATCHING: Draw a series of overlapping circles or squiggles.

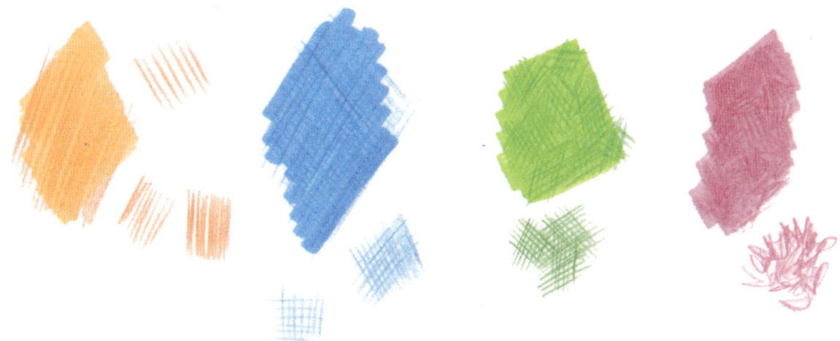

Hatching techniques can be used to create texture and visual interest in a drawing. They can also be used to add shading, especially when you are working with a limited range of colours. If you work the hatching in a different colour to the base colour, you can darken the background colour slightly or change it altogether.

HATCHING WITH TERTIARY COLOURS: This example shows how the pencil colour can change how the overall colour is perceived. A blue pencil over the background colour renders a cooler effect, whilst a purple pencil makes it warmer. You can use the same technique to create gradients (see page 46 for more on gradients).

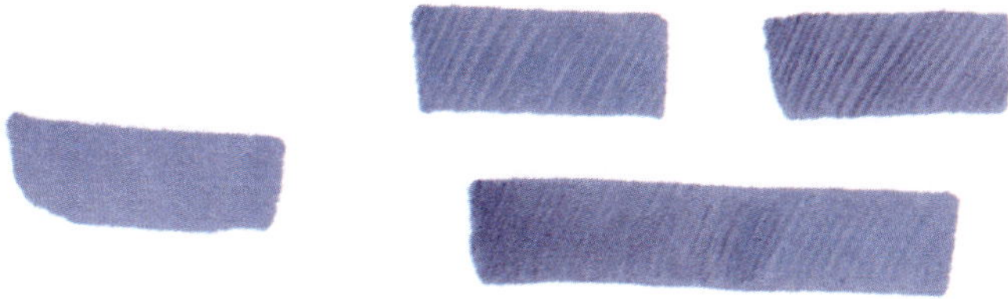

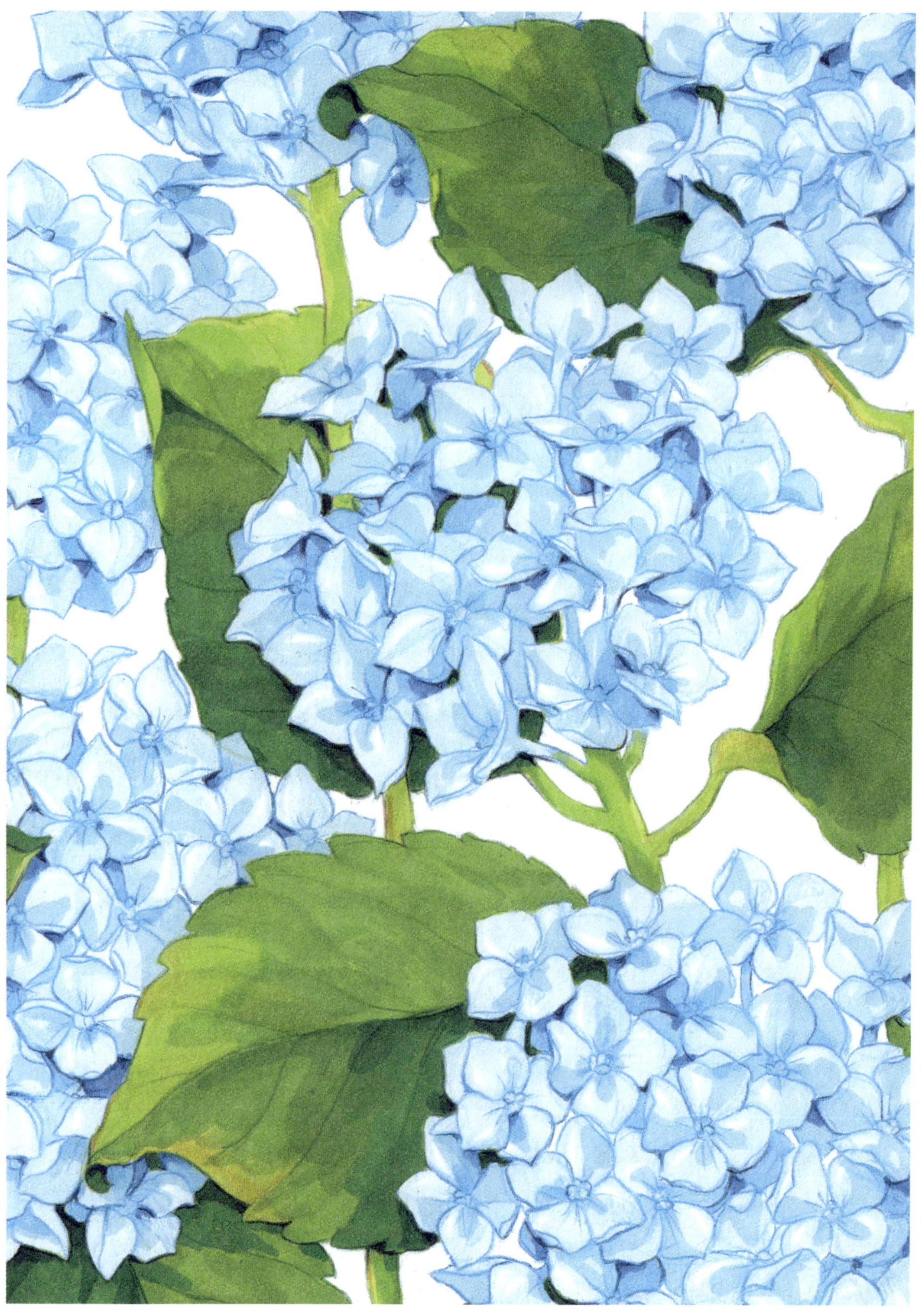

Working with gouache

White gouache paint can be useful when colouring white flowers, especially if the paper you are using is not pure white. There are several ways in which you can use it.

Apply it as a base colour across the whole illustration area and then, once the paint is completely dry, use coloured markers on top. The effect is to make the colours look much lighter and cleaner. The paint does not absorb a lot of ink, so use markers moderately, applying a maximum of two layers.

Use it as a base for white flowers, as in the Meadow project on page 104. This helps the flowers to stand out more and to achieve a purer white. Pencils can also be used on top of the paint; apply light pressure.

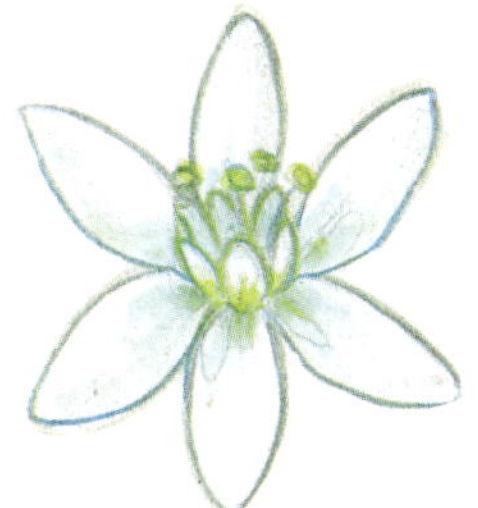

You can also create intricate details using white gouache. For example, paint leaf veins using a slender brush and, once dry, colour the leaf as usual using markers. The white gouache will make the veins appear lighter.

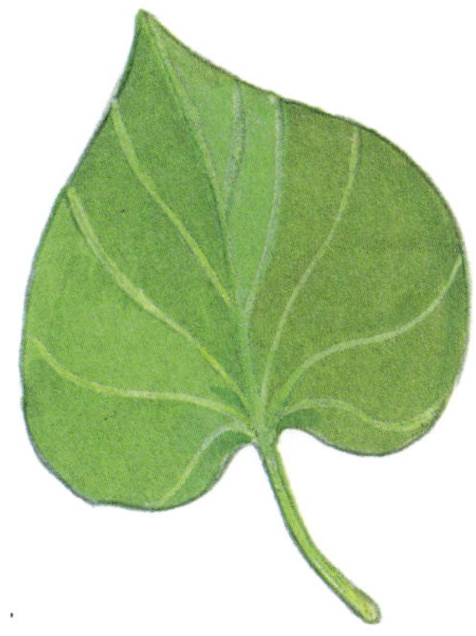

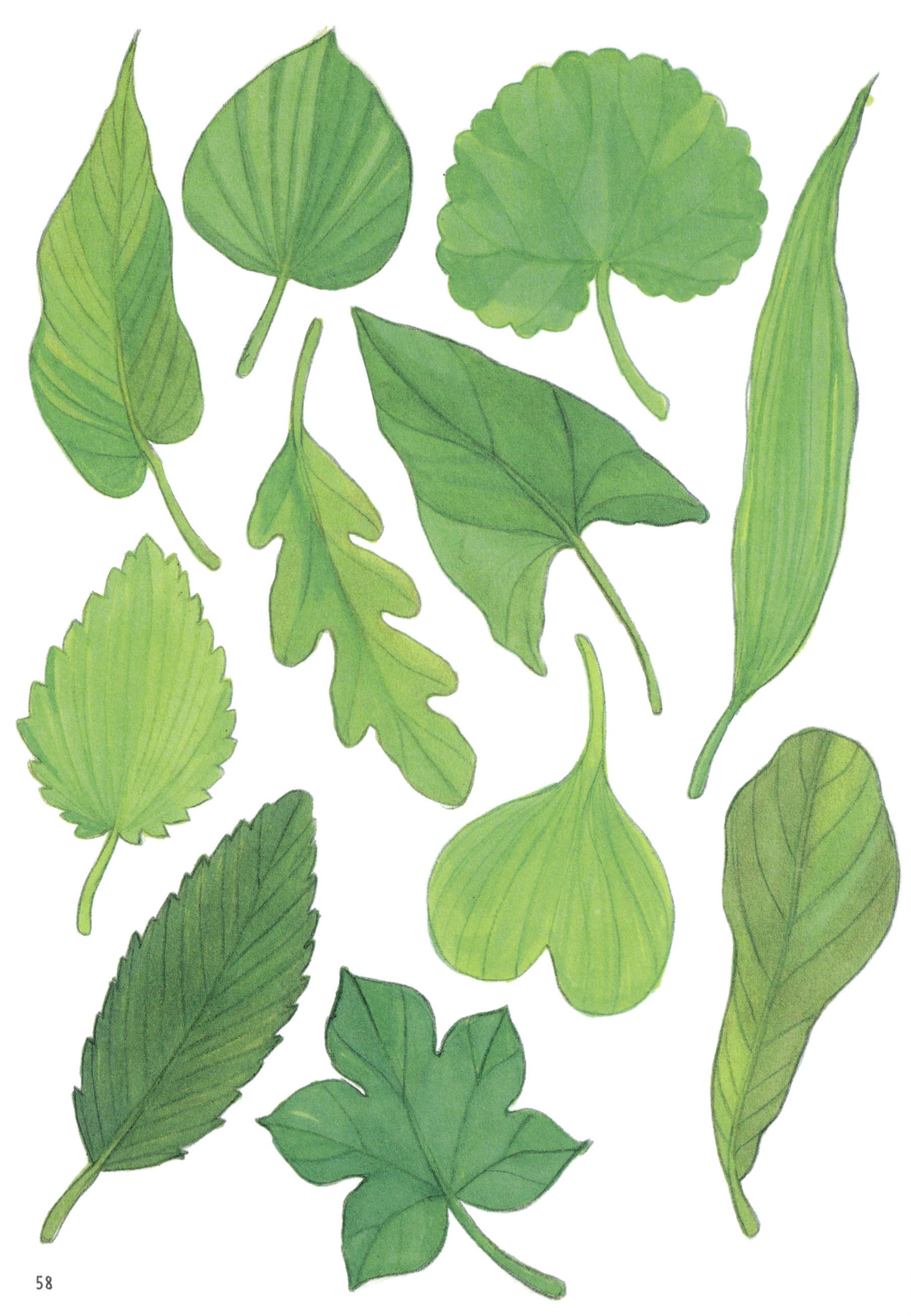

TUTORIALS

Leaf anatomy

When learning to draw plants it is good practice to have some knowledge of leaf anatomy - the different parts of a leaf and the terminology used for describing various leaf shapes. Besides these, things to consider when studying plants are venation and a leaf's arrangement on the stem.

1. **BLADE**: Green part of the leaf
2. **APEX**: Tip of the leaf
3. **MARGIN**: Edge of the leaf
4. **VEINS**: Vascular tubes that branch out across the blade
5. **MIDRIB**: Primary vein that runs through a leaf, from the base to the apex
6. **BASE**: Where the blade and petiole connect
7. **PETIOLE**: Stalk that connects the blade to the stem
8. **NODE**: Where the leaf connects to the stem
9. **STIPULE**: Small leaf-like structure, found at the node
10. **STEM**: Main axis of the plant

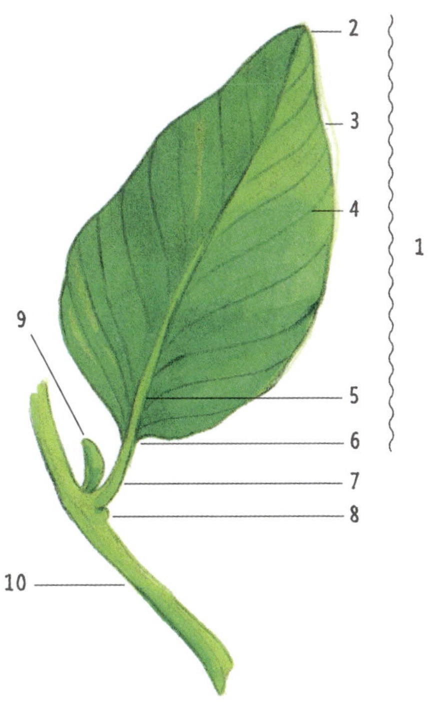

The apex

On a leaf, the apex is the tip of the leaf blade. The shape varies depending on the plant species.

1. **OBTUSE**: Apex is rounded.
2. **ACUTE**: Leaf gradually tapers to a short sharp point.
3. **MUCRONATE**: Ends in a short, sharp point.
4. **ACUMINATE**: Leaf tapers to a drawn-out, but sharp point.
5. **EMARGINATE**: Apex has a notch.
6. **TRUNCATE**: Apex is straight.

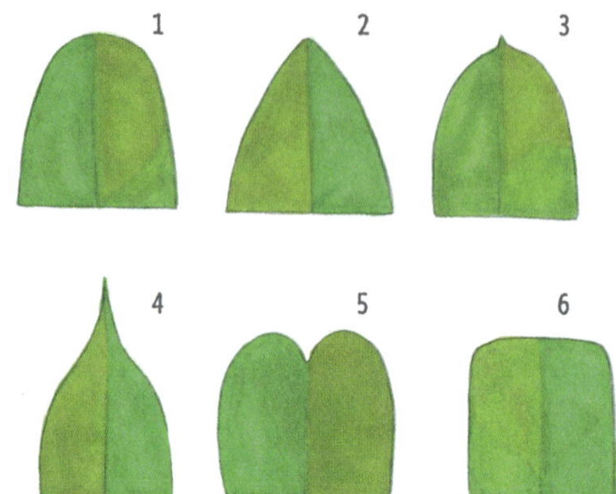

The base

On a leaf, the base is where the leaf meets the stalk or petiole.

1. **ACUTE**: Tapers gradually towards the stem.
2. **CUNEATE**: Tapers sharply towards the stem.
3. **CORDATE**: Forms a lobe either side of the stem.
4. **OBLIQUE**: One side of the leaf joins the stem lower down.
5. **ROUNDED**: A circular base.
6. **TRUNCATE**: A roughly square base.

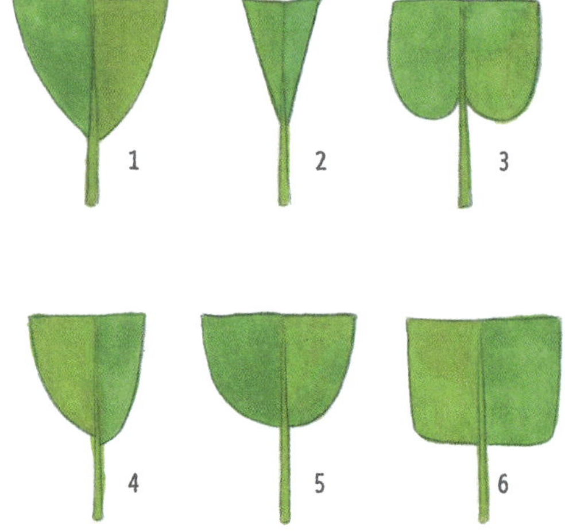

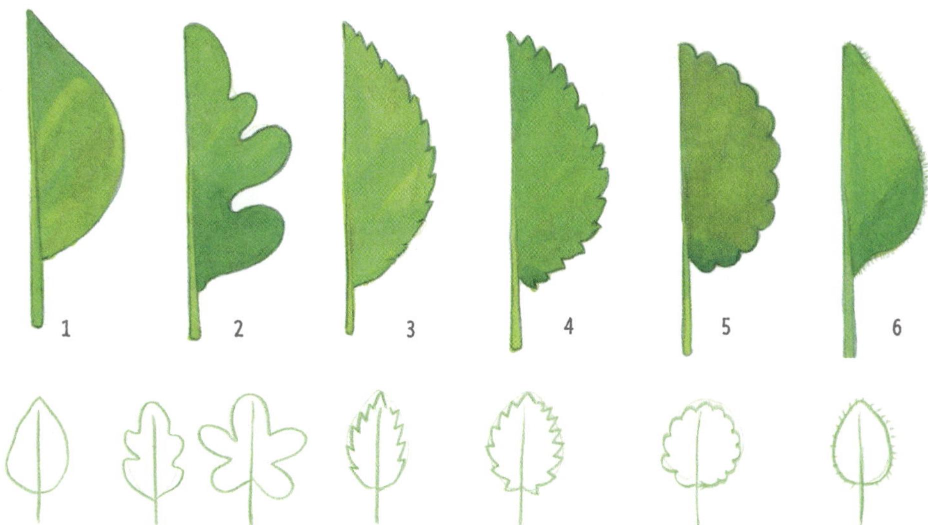

Margins

The margins of a leaf are its edges, or 'outline'. When drawing any leaf with indentations start with a leaf with smooth margins and draw the lobes or 'teeth' later on. This will help to keep the right shape.

1. **ENTIRE**: Smooth and even; no teeth, no notches, no indentations.
   Example: beech
2. **LOBED**: Deep indentations, usually symmetrical. They can have different shapes and depth. Palmate lobes radiate out from the base of the leaf, resembling fingers of the palm.
   Examples: oak, sycamore
3. **SERRATE**: Toothed leaf, where teeth point towards the apex.
   Examples: sweet chestnut, birch
4. **DENTATE**: Toothed leaf, where teeth point outwards.
   Examples: hazel, elm
5. **CRENATE**: Similar to dentate but rounder and wavy rather than sharp.
   Examples: golden ragwort, sweet violet
6. **CILIATE**: With short, thin hairs around the margin.
   Example: ivy-leaved speedwell

Venation

A network of vascular tubes, veins create visible lines and patterns on a leaf, branching out across the blade. The types described here are the most common ones.

1. **PINNATE**: Branch out from the midrib in pairs and extend towards the margins.
   Examples: avocado, cherry
2. **PALMATE**: Radiate from a single point at the base of the leaf.
   Examples: eastern redbud, papaya
3. **PARALLEL**: Run up the leaf in the same direction, without intersecting.
   Examples: grasses, lily of the valley

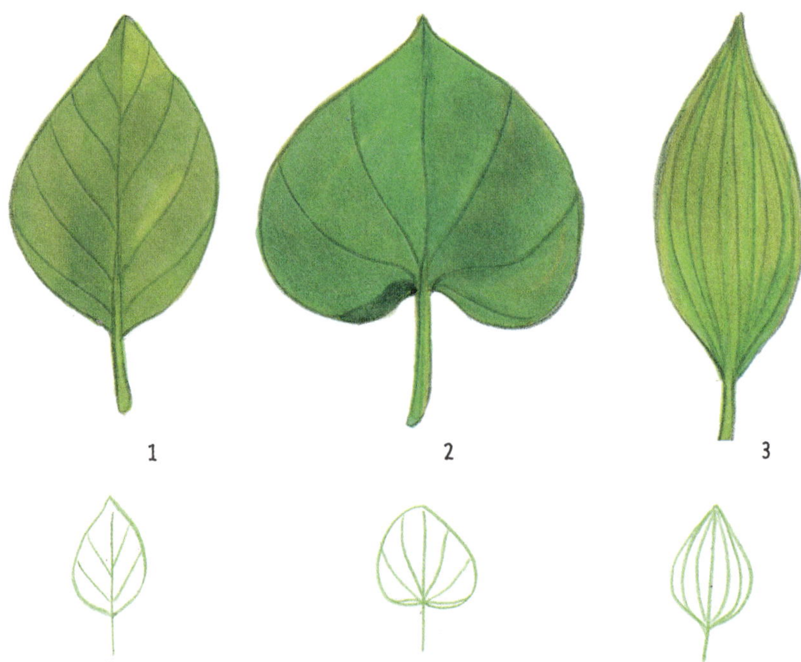

Leaf arrangements

There are three ways in which leaves can be arranged on, or attached to, the stem. Some plants can have more than one leaf arrangement, but usually just one is dominant.

1. **ALTERNATE:** One leaf per node on the stem.
   Examples: holly, sunflower
2. **OPPOSITE:** Two leaves per node, on opposite sides of the stem.
   Examples: maple, flowering dogwood
3. **WHORLED:** Two or more per node, growing around the stem.
   Examples: macadamia, catchweed

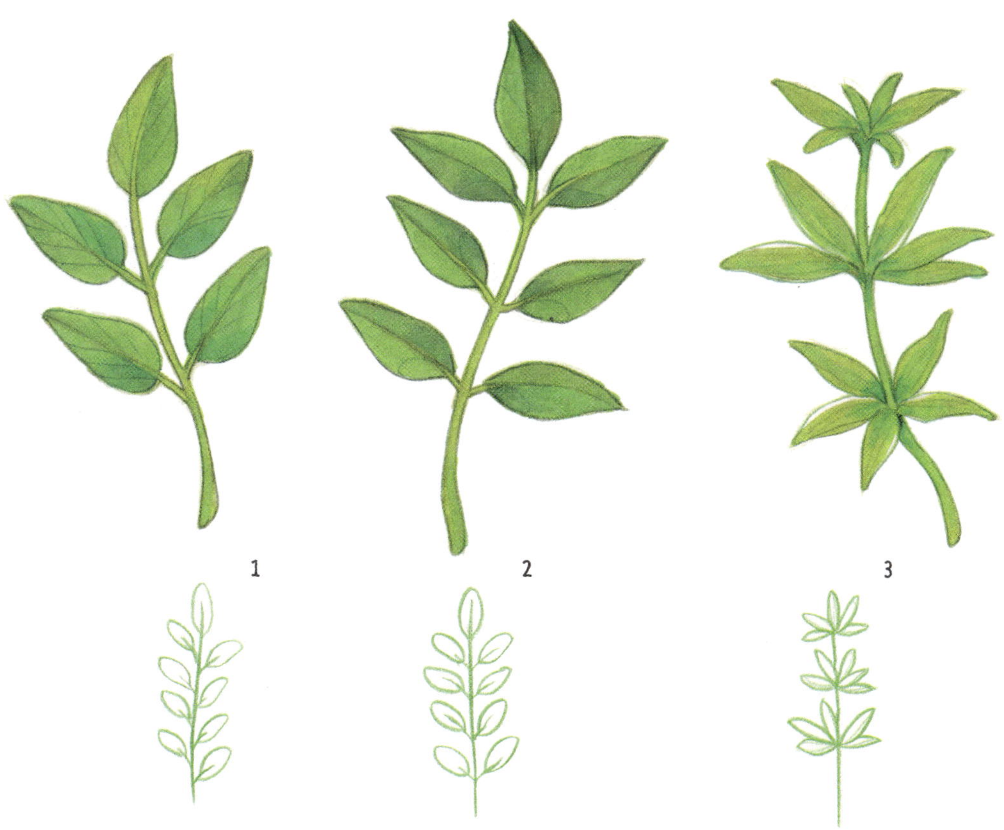

Leaf shapes

Here are some of the more common leaf shapes from the plant world. The illustrations show simplified versions of the shapes; it is normal for a leaf to be somewhere in between these - they can even vary from one leaf to another on the same plant. Besides a leaf's shape, it is important to note its proportions - that is, the ratio between length and width. On the guides below, the dotted lines show the leaf's widest point.

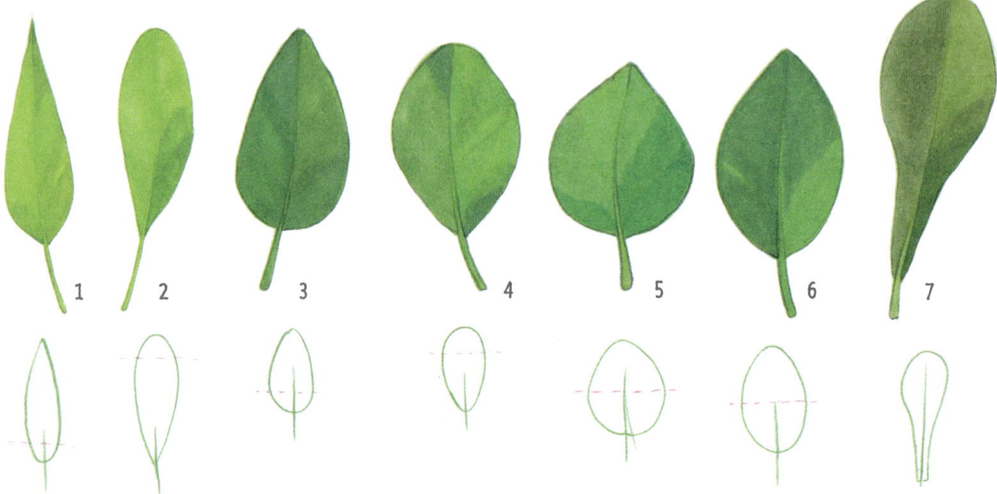

Common shapes

The most common leaves are generally a little longer than they are wide.

1. **LANCEOLATE:** Widest towards the base.
   Examples: bamboo, willow
2. **OBLANCEOLATE:** Widest towards the middle or apex.
   Example: rhododendrons
3. **OVATE:** Egg shaped; widest towards the base.
   Example: serviceberry
4. **OBOVATE:** Egg shaped; widest above the middle.
   Examples: smoke tree, honeysuckles
5. **OVAL:** Resembles an elongated circle; widest at the middle.
   Example: basil
6. **ELLIPTIC:** Similar to an oval leaf, but longer.
   Examples: mint, cherry
7. **PATULATE:** Spoon-shaped; broader and more rounded at the apex.
   Example: water oak

Long and narrow

The leaves in this group are significantly longer than they are wide.

1. **ACICULAR**: Needle-shaped; narrow, pointed and stiff.
   Example: pine
2. **LINEAR**: Long and narrow; edges almost parallel.
   Examples: grasses, cornflower, rosemary
3. **OBLONG**: Elongated, roughly rectangular.
   Example: rubber plant
4. **FALCATE**: Curved and tapers to a point.
   Examples: *Acacia stricta*, some *Eucalyptus*
5. **RUNCINATE**: Long and deeply lobed leaf, with many toothed lobes that point downwards.
   Example: dandelion
6. **LYRATE**: Long and lobed with a very broad rounded apex.
   Examples: fiddle-leaf fig, kale, white oak

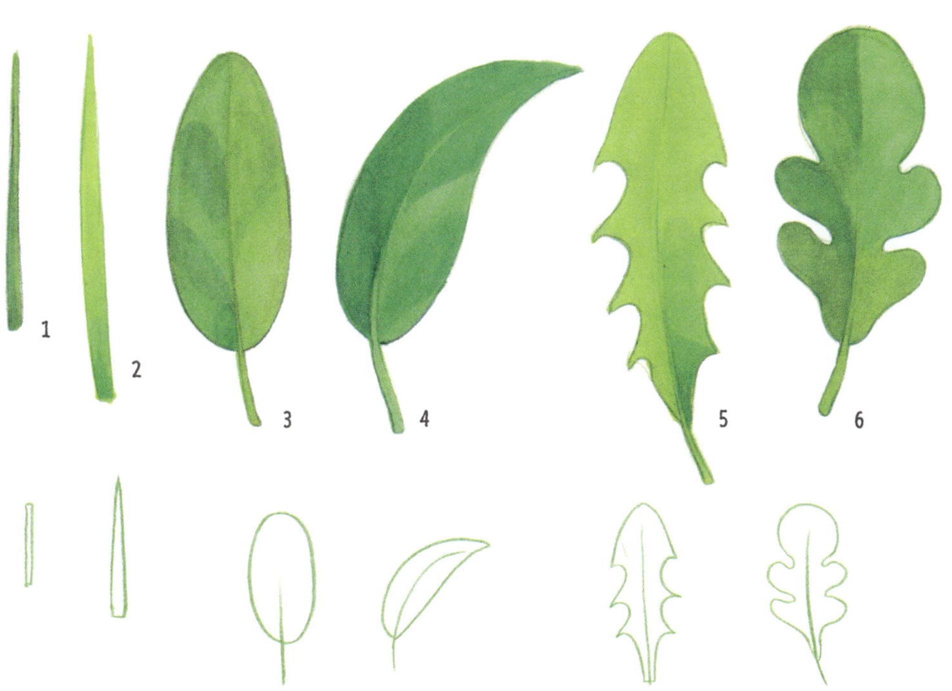

Circular

Leaves in this group are usually wider than they are long, with a rounded or blunt apex.

1. **ORBICULAR**: Near-perfect circle, the petiole (stalk) is attached to the centre of the leaf, not to the base. Examples: nasturtium, money plant
2. **RENIFORM**: Kidney-shaped. Examples: mud plantain, ground ivy
3. **FLABELLATE**: Fan- or wedge-shaped. Examples: ginkgo, fan-leaved columbine

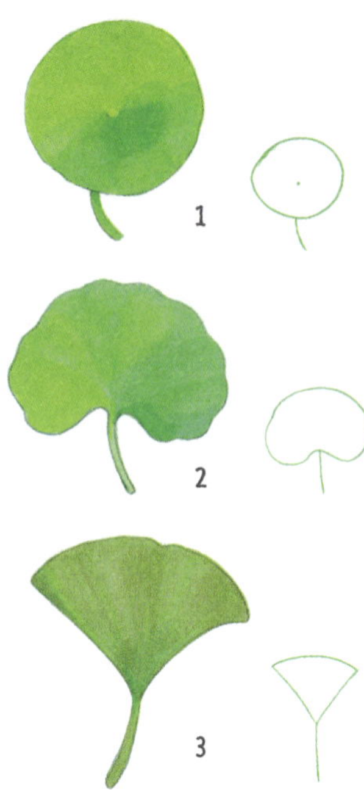

Triangular

Leaves in this group tend to be more angular.

1. **DELTOID**: Triangle-shaped with a broad base. Example: eastern cottonwood
2. **CORDATE**: Heart-shaped leaf; widest part at the base. Example: sweet violet
3. **OBCORDATE**: Heart-shaped leaf; widest part at the apex. Example: *Hoya kerrii*
4. **RHOMBOID**: Diamond-shaped leaf. Example: rhomboid mercury
5. **SAGITTATE**: Resembles an arrowhead. Examples: duck potato, arrowhead vine
6. **HASTATE**: Resembles a spearhead. Example: spearleaf violet

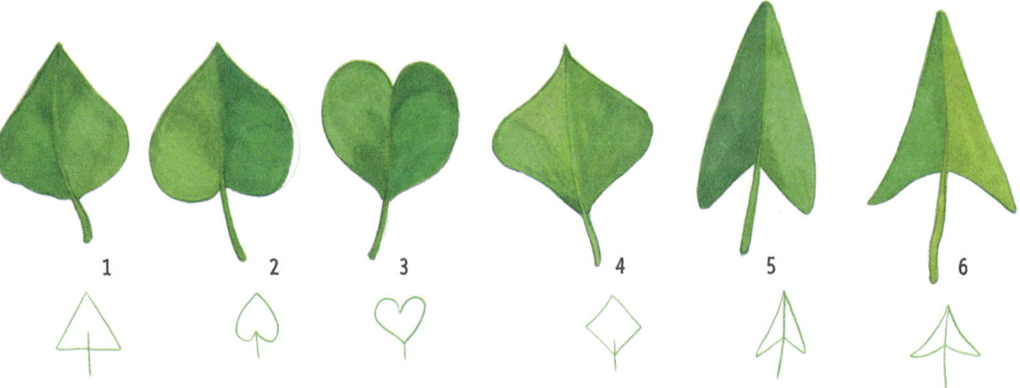

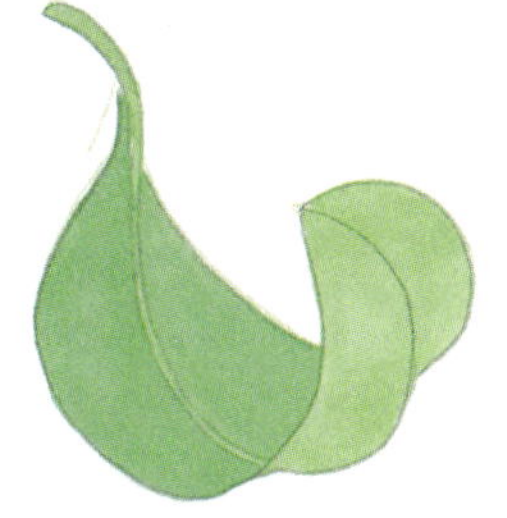

Basic leaves

There's nothing wrong with drawing simple, two-dimensional leaves. To make your illustrations more interesting, however, you can easily make them three-dimensional by adding some twirls and folds. All it takes is three, simple curved lines - do your best to draw each one with a single, flowing stroke. You've got this!

Following this method, you'll be able to draw any leaf in future projects. Since this is a tutorial, the steps below are shown using different colours to make it easy to see the construction of the leaves. When leaves feature in your projects, however, you should use just one colour for your outlines.

Materials:

- Acid-free paper (a sketchbook, drawing pad or a loose sheet of paper)
- 3 coloured pencils; I chose green, orange and blue.

1. Start with the green pencil, and draw a simple curved line using a single, fluid stroke. This is the central vein of your leaf.

2. Now use the orange pencil to draw a second curved line that connects each end of the green line, again using a single fluid stroke. Make sure the orange line crosses over the green line at some point.

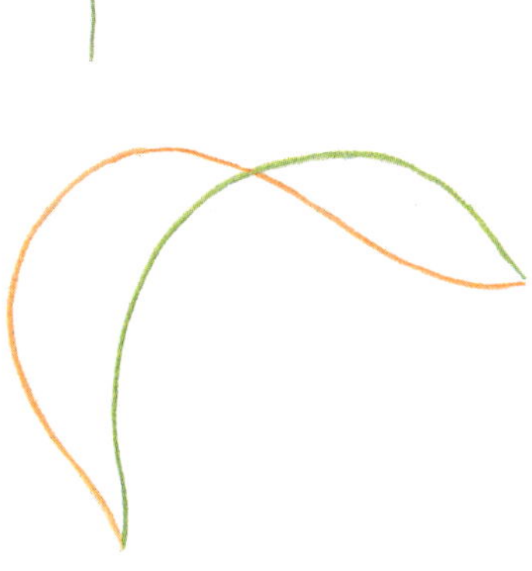

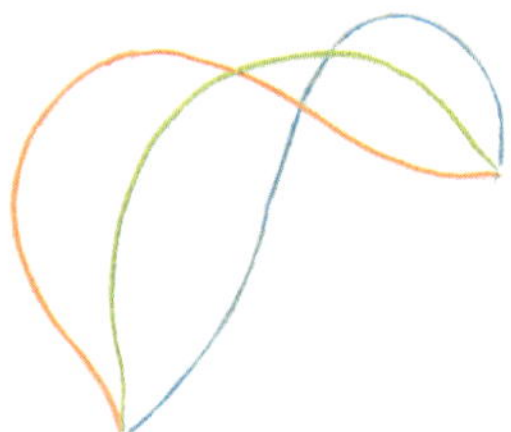

3. Draw a third curved line using the blue pencil. It should start and end at the exact same points as the orange line, and it should also cross the green line. This time, however, make sure it doesn't cross at exactly the same point.

4. Decide which of the lines you drew in Steps 2 and 3 is the edge of the leaf that's closest to the viewer and trace over it using the green pencil. Notice how this edge of the leaf is fully visible, whilst the back edge is not. In the examples here, the orange line is closer to the viewer in the top leaf and the blue line is closer in the bottom leaf.

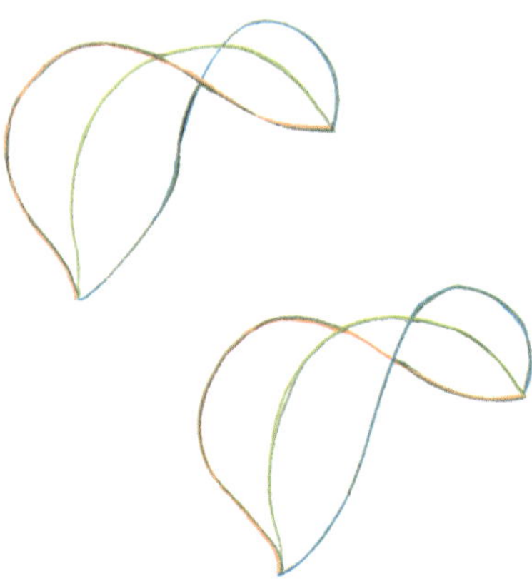

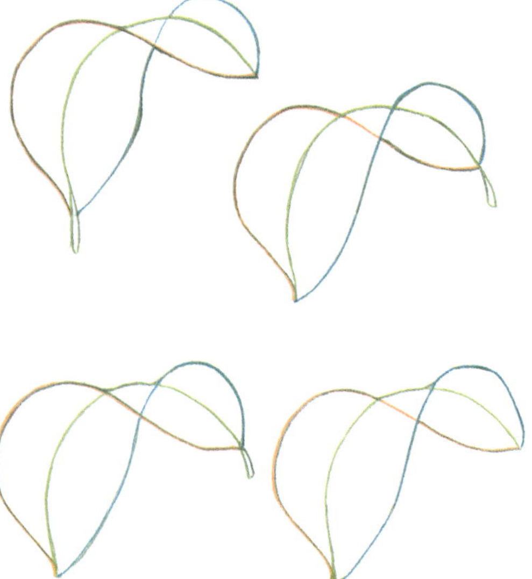

5. Draw the petiole - the stalk joining the leaf to the stem. The placement of the petiole determines whether the leaf folds towards the viewer or away from them. Here, the top two leaves fold towards the viewer and the bottom two leaves fold away.

With these few simple lines, you can create many different results using the same construction.

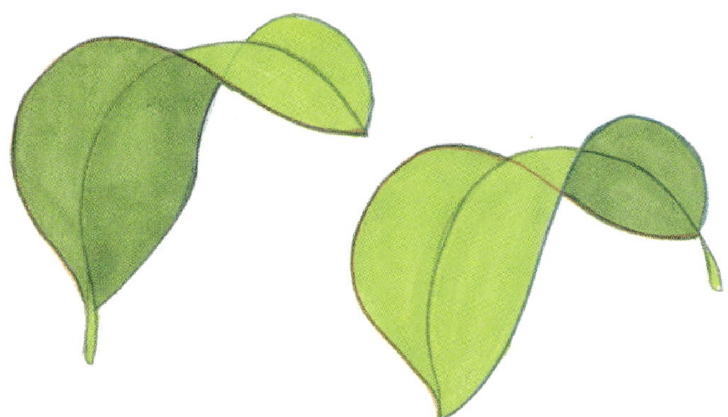

6. Colour the leaf, using two different tones of green. I like to pick a darker colour for the underside.

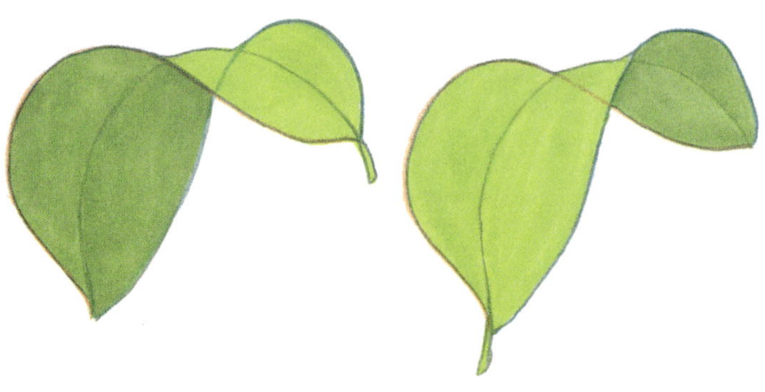

I chose three different pencils so that it's easier to see which line is which in this exercise, but once you've mastered the technique, there's no need to use different pencils anymore.

Flower anatomy

When learning to draw plants it is good practice to have some knowledge of flower anatomy. The following pages show simplified versions of flowers with basic terms that can be applied to most typical blooms. I use the terminology broadly and consistantly across plants, rather than using exact, scientific names. Not every flower will have all of the parts shown. Also, some flowers, such as daisies and sunflowers, are built differently.

1. **PETAL**: The most noticeable part of the flower; collectively, petals form corolla of the plant.
2. **PISTIL**: Female reproductive organ.
3. **STAMEN**: Male reproductive organ, typically composed of a stalk-like filament and anther that produces pollen.
4. **SEPAL**: The outermost parts of the bloom, sepals shield a developing flowerbud, fruit or seeds. Typically green and leaf-like, collectively, the sepals form the calyx.
5. **STALK**: Primary stem that supports a flower or an inflorescence.

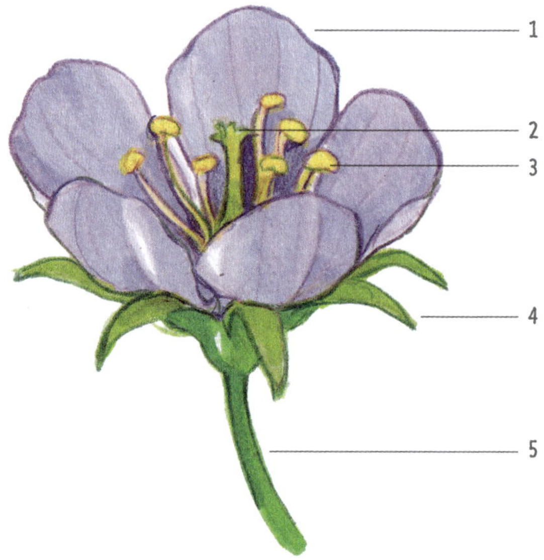

Symmetry

When looking at a flower the first thing you see is its symmetry and most flowers fall into one of two types in this respect.

1. **RADIAL SYMMETRY**: The flowers radiate around a central feature, with petals of the same shape and size; there are multiple planes of symmetry. Examples: buttercup, daisy, rose, lily
2. **BILATERAL SYMMETRY**: Petals have different shapes and sizes and there is only one plane of symmetry. Examples: violet, nasturtium, germander speedwell

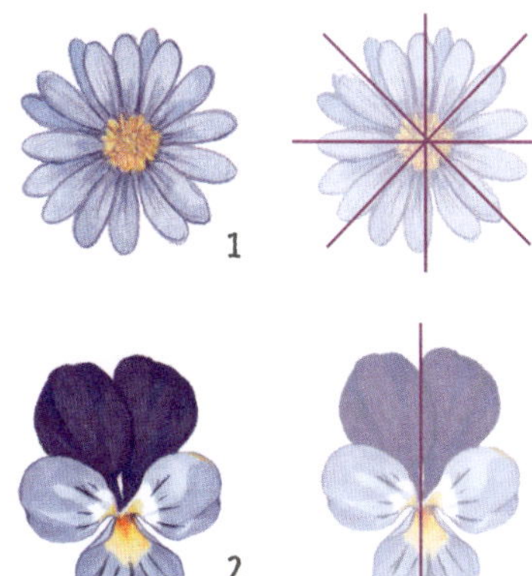

Corolla shapes

There are many corolla shapes. Some are obvious and easy to identify, and sometimes even the common name of the flower matches the shape of the corolla.

1. **CUP-SHAPED**: Petals curve upwards, forming a bowllike shape; the flower is circular and well balanced. Examples: winter aconite, buttercup
2. **SAUCER-SHAPED**: Petals point outwards, but can be slightly upturned, creating a flat saucerlike rim. Examples: wild geranium, California poppy

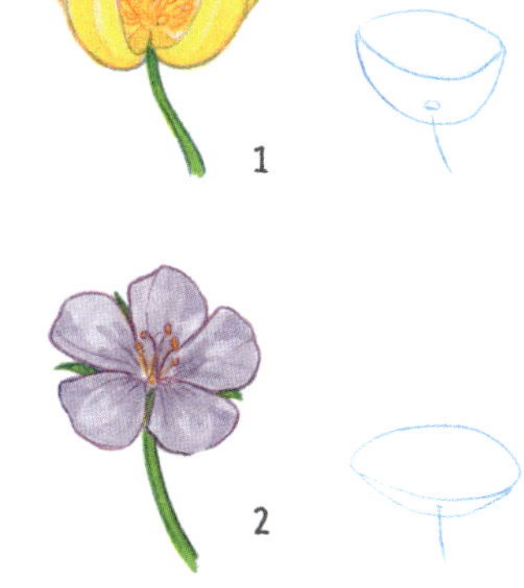

3. **TRUMPET-SHAPED**: A long narrow tubular base, flared out at the end.
   Examples: four o'clock flower, morning glory
4. **SALVERFORM**: A slender tubular base, flares outwards sharply, creating a disc-like opening; there is no curving of the petals.
   Examples: cape leadwort, primrose
5. **CRUCIFORM**: Four petals arranged in the shape of a cross; has radial symmetry.
   Example: cuckoo flower
6. **STAR-SHAPED**: Petals radiate outwards from the centre, resembling a star.
   Example: grass star lily
7. **BELL-SHAPED**: Bell-like structure, often with five petals and a rounded base.
   Example: harebell
8. **URN-SHAPED**: Bell or vase-shaped flower with a narrow opening.
   Examples: blueberry, heather

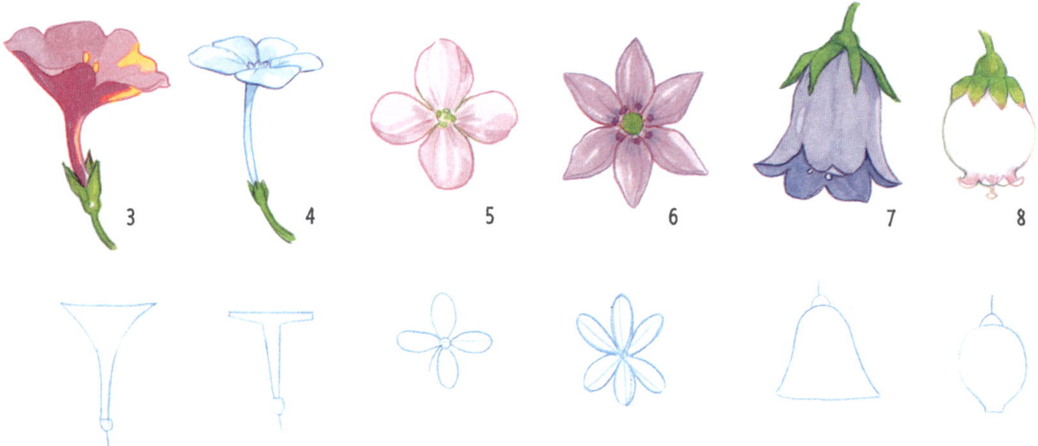

Petal shapes

Here are some of the more common petal shapes from the plant world. Besides a petal's basic shape, its tip or edges can be round, wavy, flat, lobed or elongated. The illustrations show some variations.

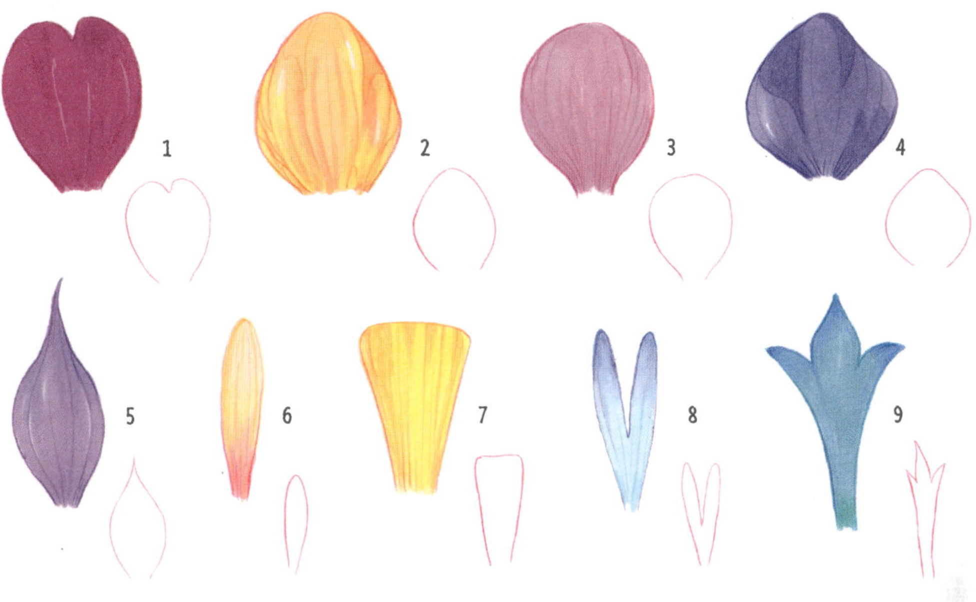

1. **OBCORDATE**: Heart-shaped; widest at the top.
   Example: dog rose
2. **OVATE**: Egg-shaped; widest towards the base.
   Example: single dahlia
3. **OBOVATE**: Egg-shaped; widest above the middle.
   Example: shrubby cinquefoil
4. **OVAL**: Resembles an elongated circle; widest at the middle.
   Example: water hyacinth
5. **ELLIPTIC**: Similar to an oval petal, but longer.
   Example: everblooming ixora
6. **ELONGATED**: The petal is visibly longer than it is wide.
   Example: Indian aster
7. **WEDGE-SHAPED**: Tapers towards the bottom; widest at the top.
   Example: cosmos
8. **BIFID**: Deeply divided into two parts.
   Example: snow-in-summer
9. **TRIFID**: Deeply divided into three parts.
   Examples: tropical chickweed

Inflorescence

Inflorescence - the way flowers cluster on a stem - can take many forms. The two primary types are racemose and cymose. The main difference between them is where the new flowers grow. In the outline sketches, circles represent flowers, where pink is the youngest and yellow the oldest. This knowledge can be useful when drawing flowers at different stages of growth.

Cymose

Cymose plants have the oldest flower at the top of the main axis. The top flower stops growing so that new flowers develop lower down the stem.

1. **HELICOID**: New flowers develop on one side of the stem only, often leading it to curl round to one side.
   Examples: 'Indian pink', day lily
2. **SCORPIOID**: New flowers develop alternately on both sides of the stem , causing it to wave like a scorpian's tale.
   Examples: forget-me-not, heliotrope, Virginia bluebells

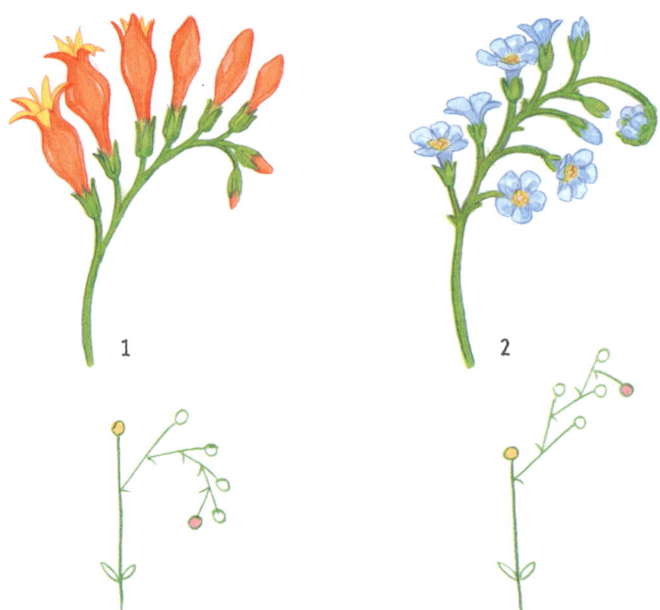

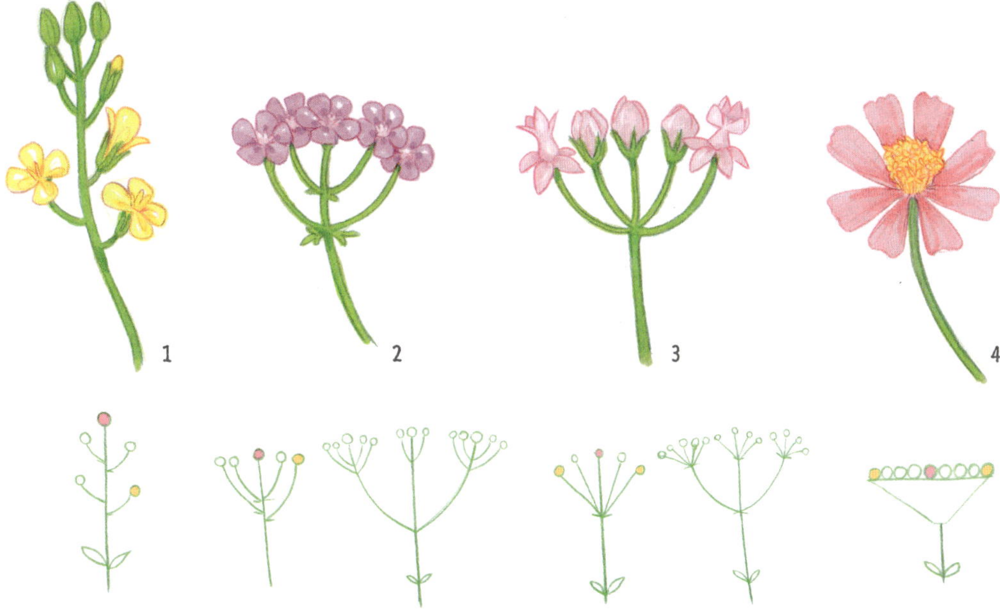

Racemose

Racemose plants produce new flowers at the tip, or centre, of a stem, with the oldest flowers closest to the bottom, or periphery.

1. **SIMPLE**: Flowers grow on either side of the main axis, connected by a stalk; each stalk is the same length. Examples: mustard, foxglove, lily of the valley
2. **CORYMB**: Flower stalks have different lengths - the lower they are on the stem, the longer they are; all flowers end on a similar height, creating dense flat-topped cluster.
   Examples: hawthorn, yarrow
3. **UMBEL**: Flat-topped or rounded inflorescence; stalks of individual flowers grow from one point. Examples: milkweed, carrot, coriander
4. **CAPITULUM**: A group of tiny florets that create compact, often circular clusters.
   Examples: *Zinnia*, sunflower, daisy

Flower studies

Practise drawing flowers at different stages of growth and from different angles.

From bud to full flower

In this sequence from bud to developed flower - in this case a daisy - notice how the petals become longer as the flower grows. The green parts of the flower (calyx and stalk) are more yellow at earlier stages and darken during development.

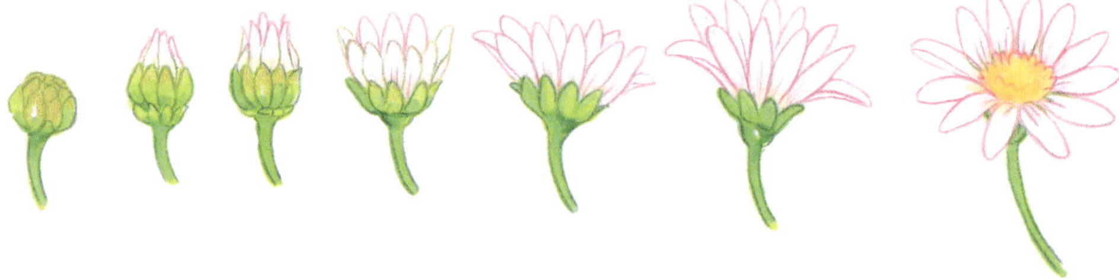

Different views

Each flower in this sequence starts with an ellipse intersected by lines. Where the lines meet marks the centre of the flower. When drawing a flower from an angle, the ellipsis is flatter and the middle of the flower is off-centre. When the centre is a bit lower, the petals closest to the viewer appear wider and shorter.

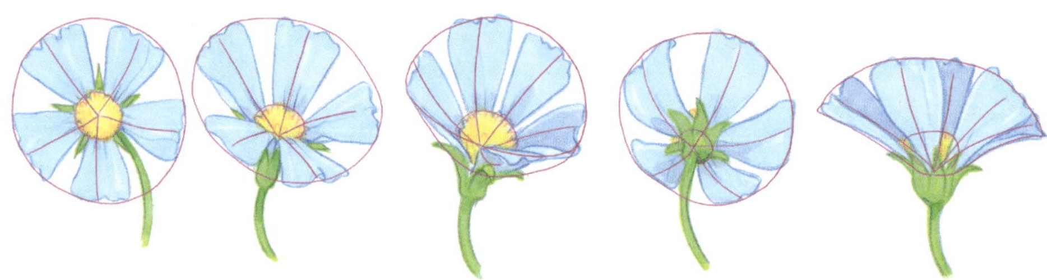

Basic flower

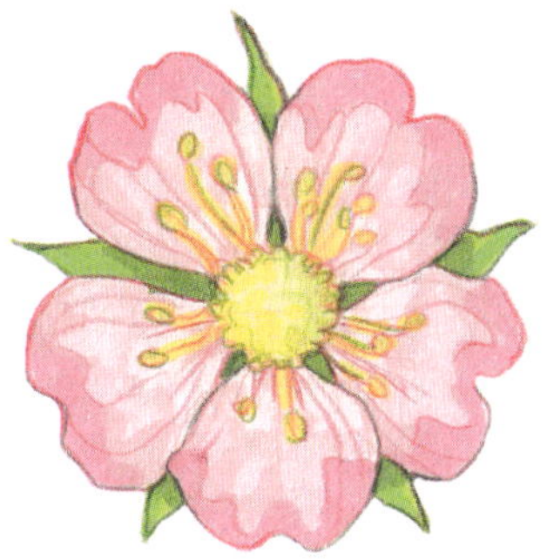

Flowers can be drawn by using simple shapes, such as ovals, circles and U-shapes. Use the centre point as a reference for the drawing, as every petal evolves from the middle. In this chapter we're going to draw a dog rose flower, but a similar approach can be used to draw any flower.

Materials:

- Acid-free paper
- Coloured pencils; I chose pink and green
- Alcohol-based markers

1. Start by drawing a rough circle using a pink pencil. Add two lines that cross at the centre of the circle to act as guidelines.

2. Draw a smaller circle where the lines cross at the centre. This will form the middle of the flower. Draw a series of short lines that radiate out from the smaller circle, equally spaced apart.

3. Using the larger circle as a guideline, start to draw the petals. The number of petals should equal the number of short lines you drew in Step 2. This flower has obovate heart-shaped petals, which means they are narrower at the flower's centre. Draw a pair of small circles or ovals either side of the short lines you drew in Step 2. These are the flower's stamens.

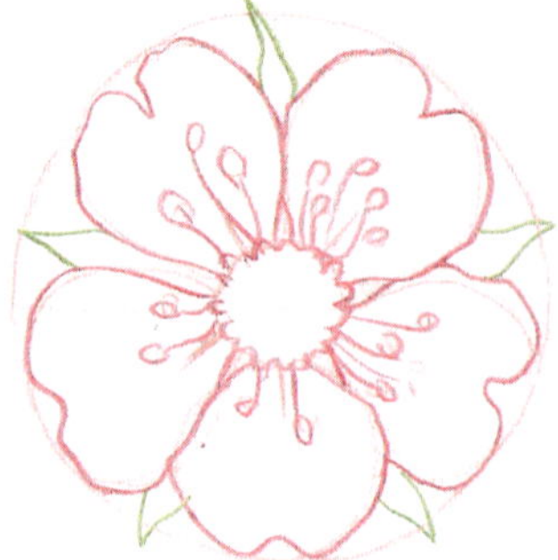

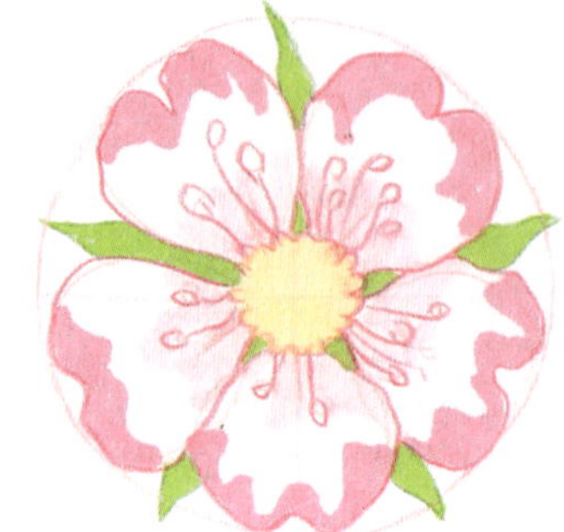

4. Refine the shape of the petals, drawing over your initial sketch. This flower is a dog rose with heart-shaped petals, so add a small dip at the top of each petal. Redefine the centre of the flower, making its contour irregular. Connect the stamens with the centre of the flower, using curved lines. These lines are the filaments. Add sepals by drawing five triangular shapes peeking between the petals, using a green pencil.

5. Lay down the base colours using the alcohol-based markers. Use yellow for the centre of the flower and green for the sepals. To colour the petals, use three different shades of pink. Use the darkest at the top edge of each petal and the lightest shade near the middle of the flower. Make the shapes irregular.

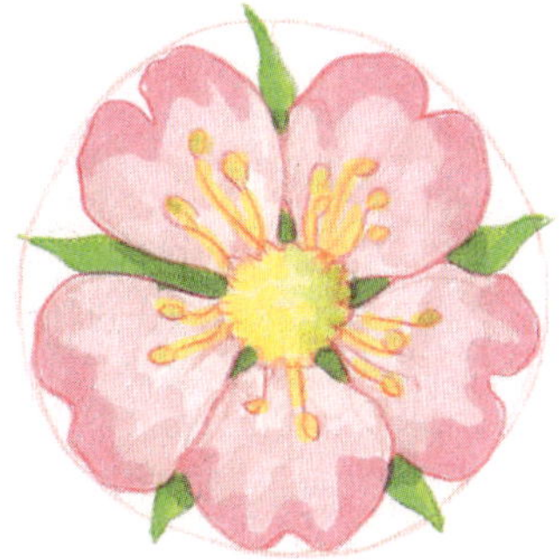

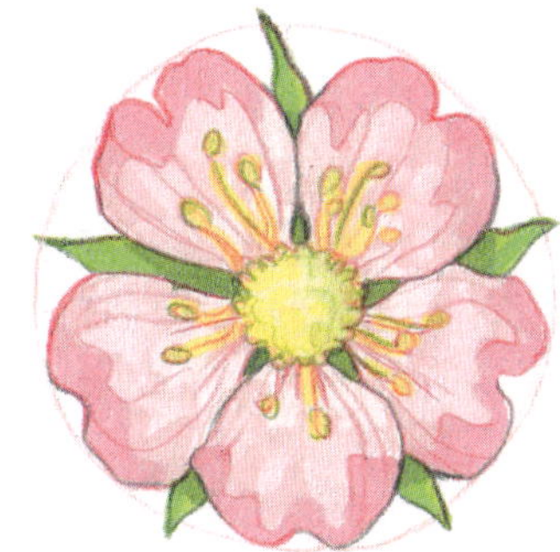

6. Finish off colouring in the petals by using the mid-tone in the middle of each flower. Blend the colours (see page 44). Add some shading to the centre of the flower by quickly tapping the nib of a darker yellow marker around the edge of the centre circle. Use the same marker to colour the stamens and filaments. Optionally, add some green details. To finish colouring the sepals, use a darker green marker in the places where the petals and sepals connect.

7. Add pencil outlines and details. First, outline the petals in a darker shade of pink. Using an olive-green pencil, outline the sepals and all of the yellow parts of the flower. To make the illustration look more organic add some green outlines to the petals. Keep these green outlines light, and add them in places where the petals touch the sepals. Finish by adding green outlines where the sepals touch the yellow parts of the flower.

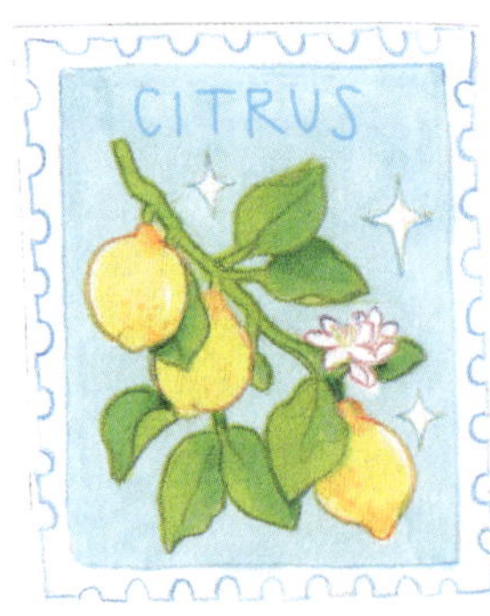
CITRUS
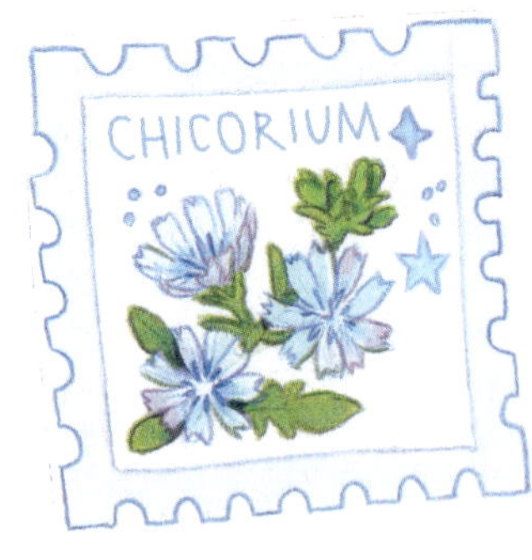
CHICORIUM
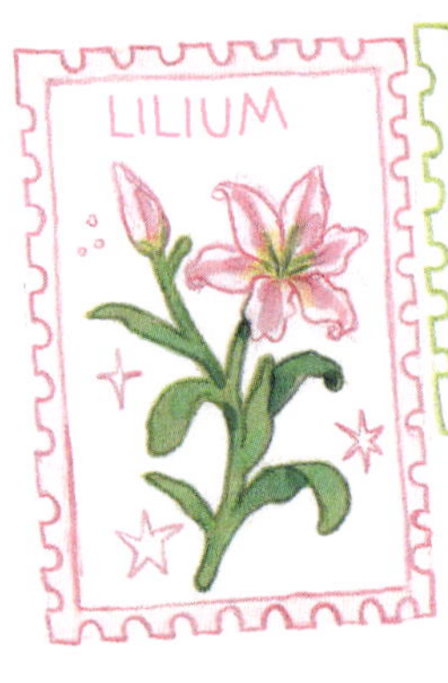
LILIUM
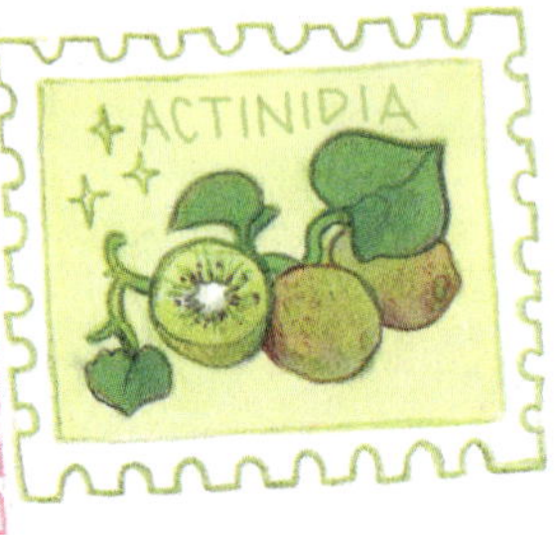
ACTINIDIA
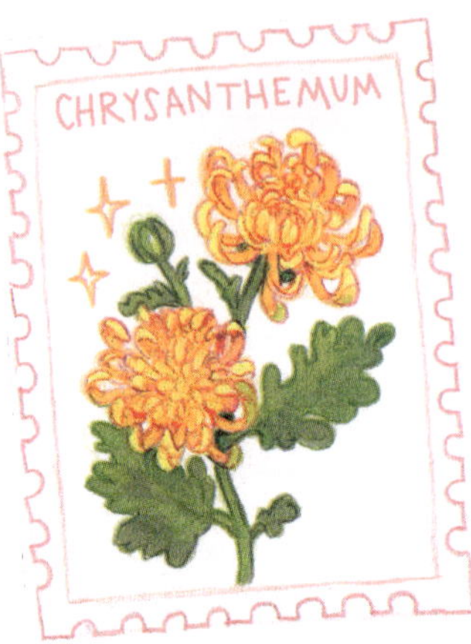
CHRYSANTHEMUM
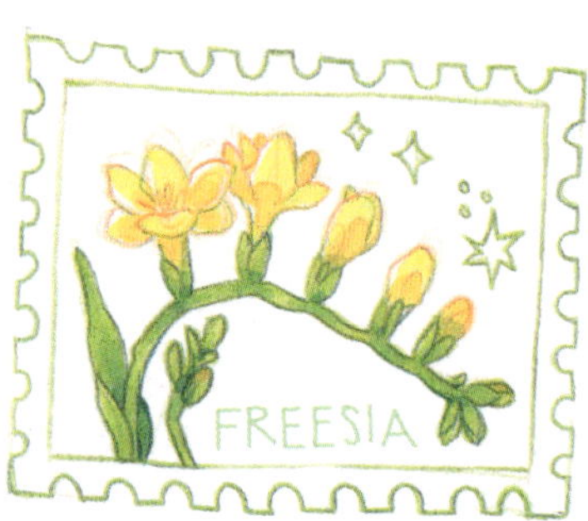
FREESIA
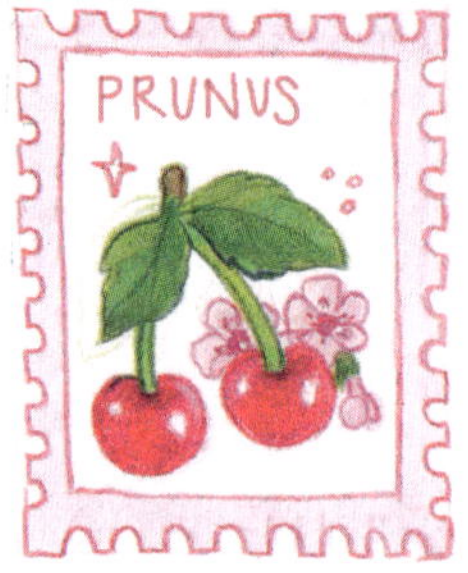
PRUNUS
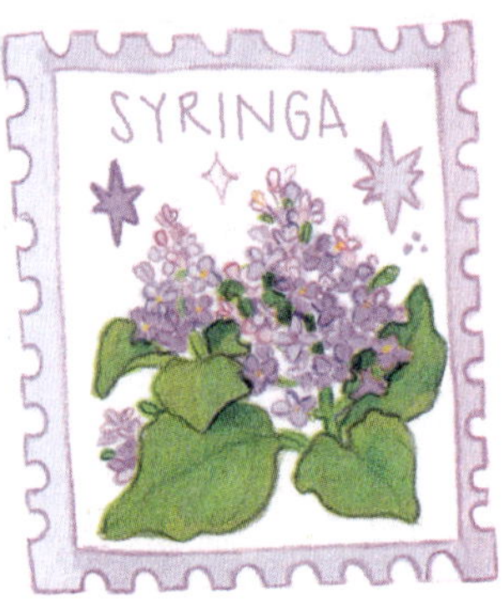
SYRINGA
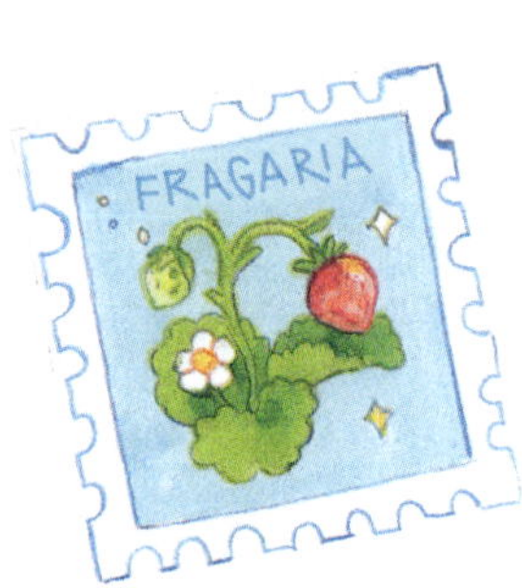
FRAGARIA

VIOLA
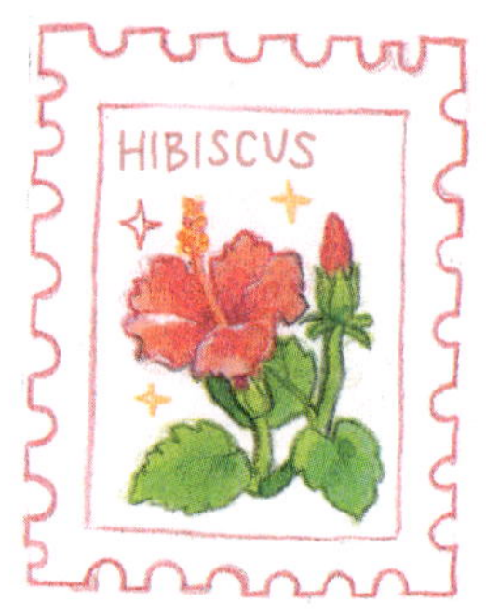
HIBISCUS

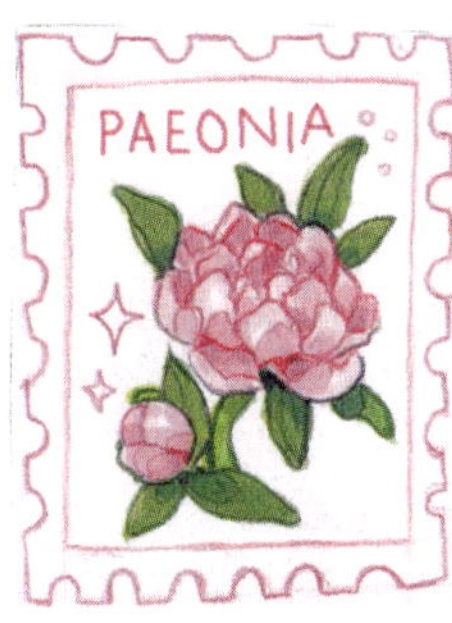

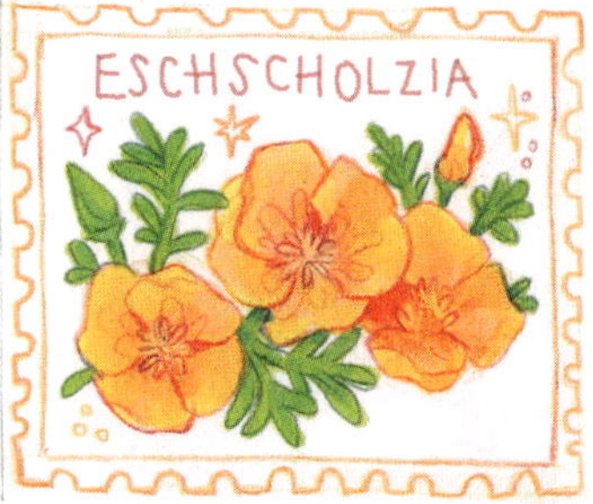

Create your own postage stamp collection

Creating an ongoing collection of postage-stamp-style illustrations is a great way to introduce new flowers into your repertoire. Working at this size allows you to study the general shape, form and colour of a plant without getting overwhelmed by details. You don't have to make complex sketches of a plant to gain an understanding of its anatomy. Study photographs of the plant first to see what kind of plant it is, what colour and shape it has, and what the leaves and flowers look like.

Materials:

- Acid-free paper
- Coloured pencils
- Alcohol-based markers
- Ruler (optional)
- Scissors (optional)

Postage stamps are usually portrait (with a 3:4 ratio), landscape (4:3) or square (1:1) but it's not a rule set in stone. If working on very small formats doesn't appeal to you, try this exercise at postcard size or any other size that works for you.

1. Draw a frame using a ruler if you want crisp lines. I've chosen a square format measuring 4 x 4 cm (1.5 x 1.5 in). For the outer border with the perforations, draw in only the corners.

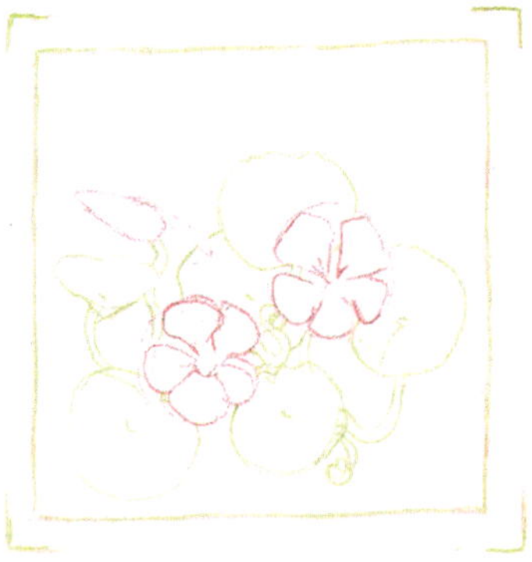

2. Using simple shapes, start sketching the plant using coloured pencils. I chose a nasturtium, a trailing plant that has round leaves attached to stalks at their centres and showy, funnel-shaped flowers with five petals. The two top petals are bigger than the other three. When thinking about the composition, remember to leave space for the plant's name and the stamp price.

All parts of the nasturtium plant are edible, including the leaves, flowers and seeds; they have a peppery, watercress-like flavour.

3. Trace over the lines in your sketch using darker coloured pencils, and add details such as the plant centres and major leaf veins. Keep in mind that this is just a simple illustration. There's no need to illustrate every vein on a leaf, for example. Add folds in a few leaves to make them three-dimensional and don't be afraid to exaggerate some features.

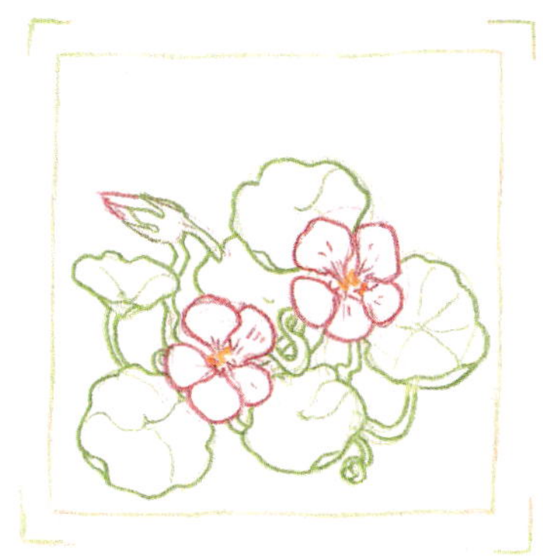

4. Using alcohol-based markers, add the base colours of the leaves, stems and petals, choosing a different shade of green to colour the undersides of the leaves. I left some small areas uncoloured for visual interest. Keep everything very simple.

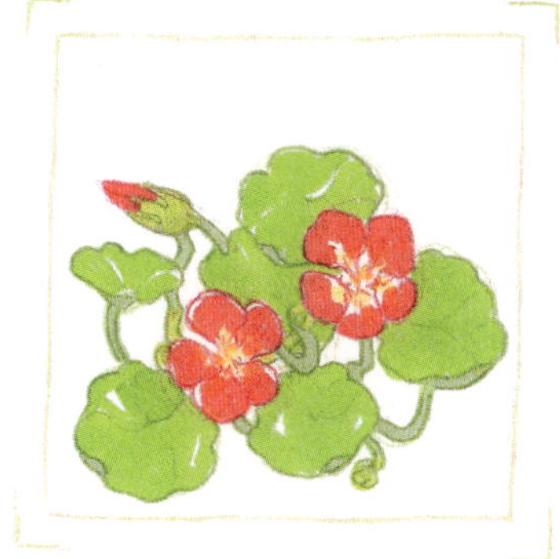

Nasturtium leaves have light-coloured veins, but I decided to not emphasize these. Making small illustrations really teaches you to simplify an object and decide which features to keep and which to skip.

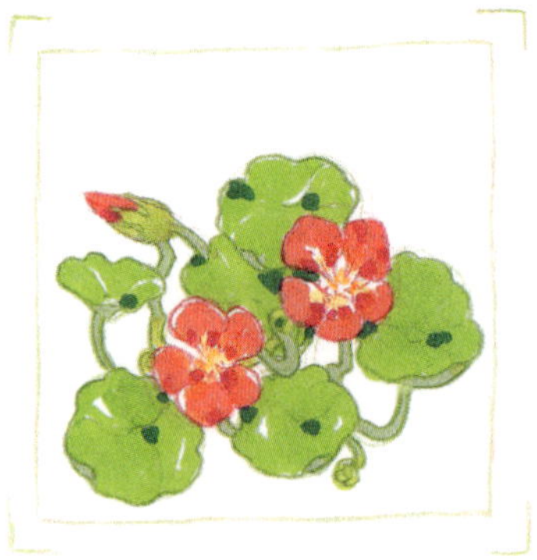

5. Add the darkest shades on the leaves and petals, barely touching the paper and using the nib of the marker or making very small circular motions.

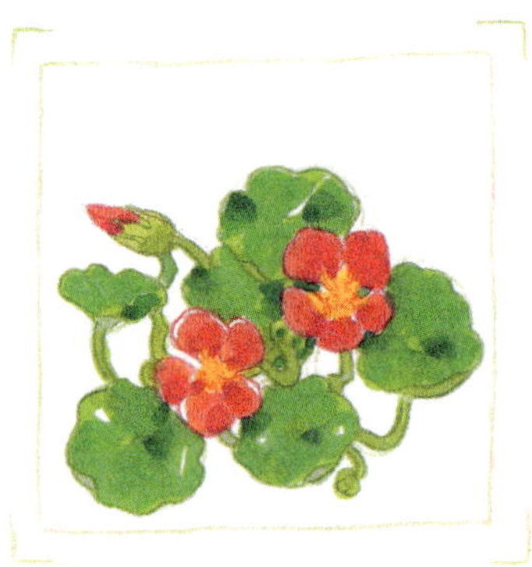

6. Use mid-tones to create balance, using circular motions. If you want to soften the darkest shades, work quickly, before the ink has a chance to dry out on the paper (see page 46).

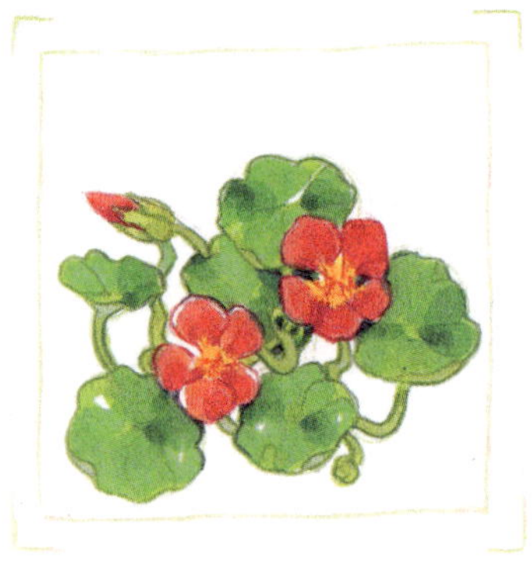

7. Give the outlines of the leaves and petals more definition. Use pencils and start with the darkest colours. Darken any areas that need more shading using the markers.

8. Use a coloured pencil to add the perforated border. Use straight lines and half-circle shapes to do this - don't worry too much about them being evenly spaced. If they look a little wonky, it only adds charm.

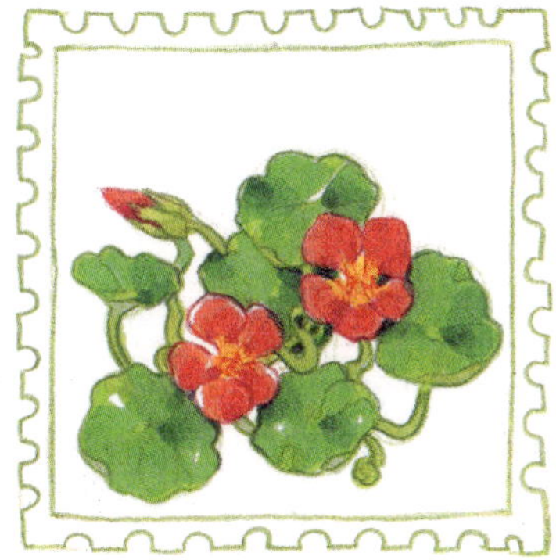

9. Now it's time for any final touches - all using coloured pencils. Add the name of the plant and the price. You can use the scientific or common name - it's up to you.

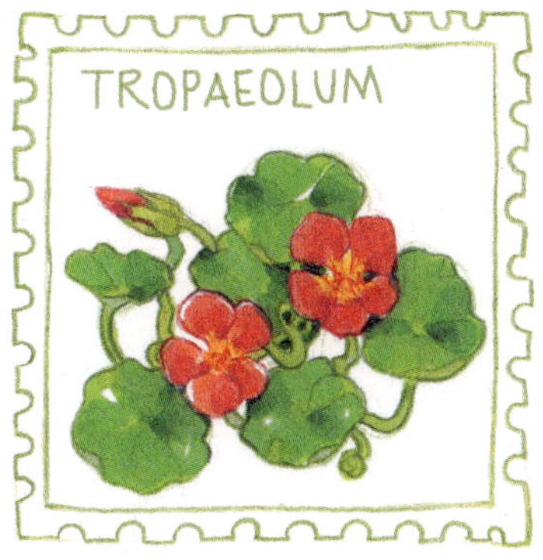

10. For a more cohesive look, use a marker to fill in the perforated border in a colour that complements the illustration. I couldn't resist adding some sparkles too! Cut out the stamp or leave it in your sketchbook as it is.

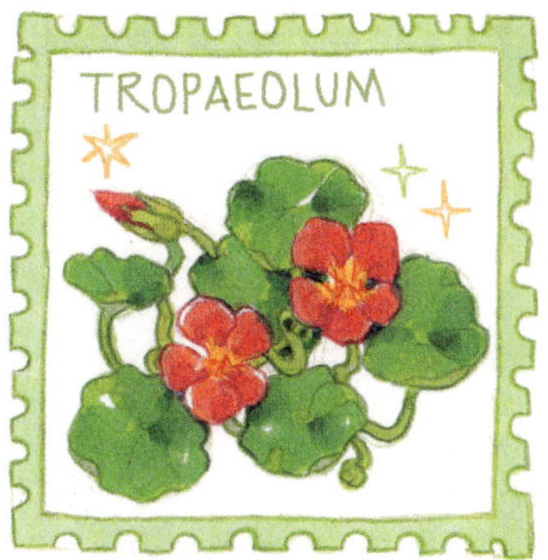

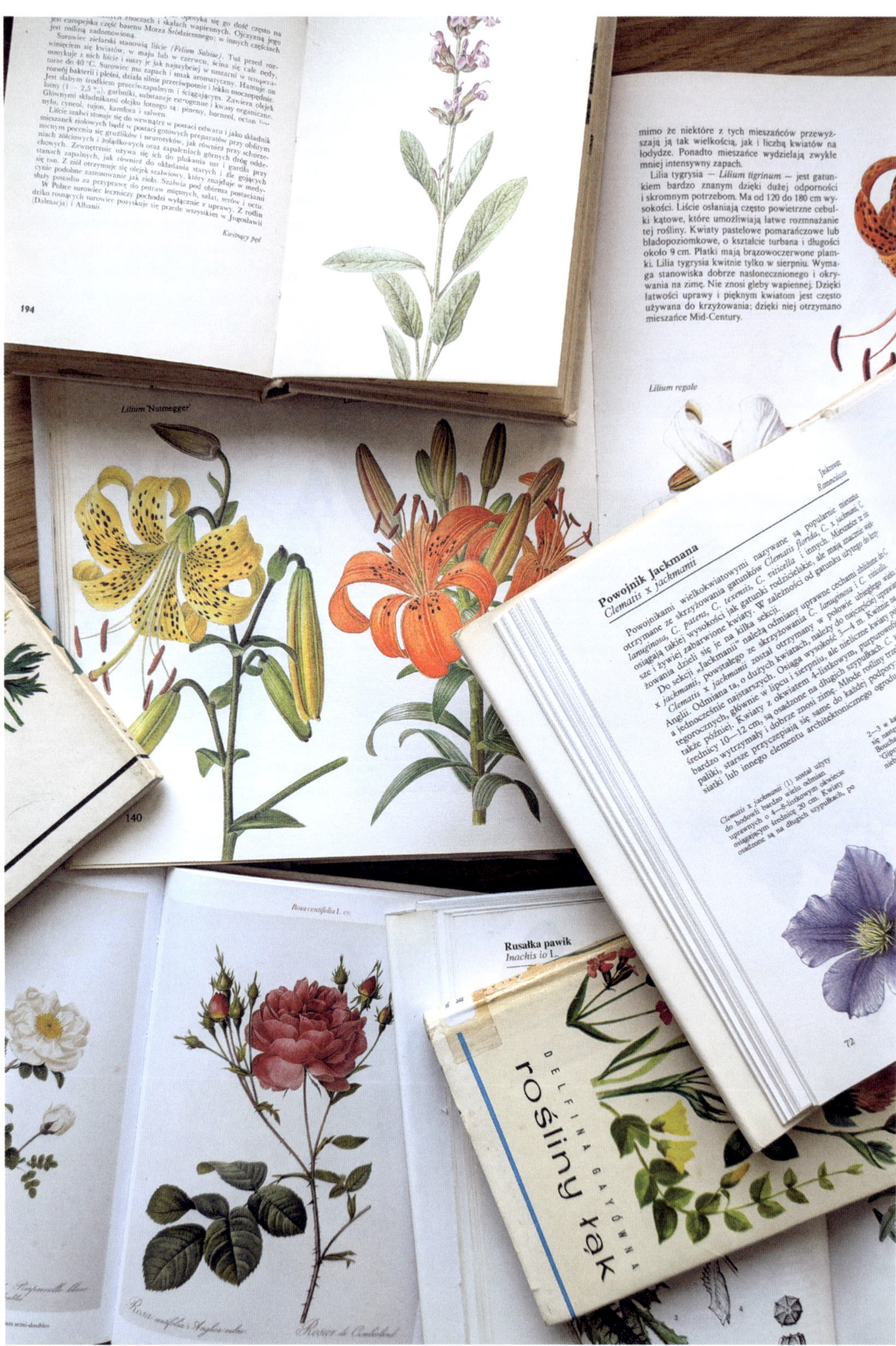
194
mimo że niektóre z tych mieszańców przewyższają ją tak wielkością, jak i liczbą kwiatów na łodydze. Ponadto mieszańce wydzielają zwykle mniej intensywny zapach.
Lilia tygrysia — Lilium tigrinum — jest gatunkiem bardzo znanym dzięki dużej odporności i skromnym potrzebom. Ma od 120 do 180 cm wysokości. Liście osłaniają często powietrzne cebulki kątowe, które umożliwiają łatwe rozmnażanie tej rośliny. Kwiaty pastelowe pomarańczowe lub bladopoziomkowe, o kształcie turbana i długości około 9 cm. Płatki mają brązowoczerwone plamki. Lilia tygrysia kwitnie tylko w sierpniu. Wymaga stanowiska dobrze nasłonecznionego i okrywania na zimę. Nie znosi gleby wapiennej. Dzięki łatwości uprawy i pięknym kwiatom jest często używana do krzyżowania; dzięki niej otrzymano mieszańce Mid-Century.
Lilium 'Nutmegger'
Lilium regale
140
Powojnik Jackmana
Clematis x jackmanii
72
Rosa centifolia L. cv.
Rusałka pawik
Inachis io L.
DELFINA GAYÓWNA
rośliny łąk

INSPIRATION

Finding inspiration

Having worked through the tutorials on the previous pages, you will have learned all you need to know about drawing basic leaves and flowers. Now you can start to draw them for yourself. Inspiration can come from many places.

- Take a look in your garden or in a local park and draw plants and flowers that interest you.
- Draw plants that are native to your region.
- Look for plants that have strong connections to your favourite historical era - for example, those used by medieval healers or flowers used for bouquets in the Victorian era.
- Every month has a flower associated with it. You could draw flowers that link to your birth month. Maybe create a composition of the flowers that represent the birth months of your family members.
- Draw plants specific to an environment that interests you. Which plants grow near rivers and ponds? Which ones could survive the heat of the desert? Get curious!
- Use botanical albums from the local library. Old botanical books are a great source of inspiration.
- Source images online using plant identification platforms or the websites of botanical gardens.
- If you're not really into doing any kind of research, you can always draw made-up plants! Just choose the shapes of leaves and flowers that you like most and use your imagination.

Finding your style

Finding an art style is something all artists think about and it can take time. The most important skill in any discipline of art is the art of noticing. Look for common threads in the art that you like. Are the colours vivid or muted? Is blending smooth or are there visible strokes? Do you like more realistic illustrations or more stylized ones? Look at the line art - is it bold or minimal, is it colourful or black?

Try applying these things in your own artworks. Learn from other artists by copying their techniques. Try having a few sources of inspiration and take something from each of them. Developing your own style doesn't have to be an organized process. If you know that you like colourful outline, that's a great starting point - you can take things from there. In many ways, it is best not to think about it too much and just let the things unfold as you practise and discover new ways of drawing.

You might also choose to stylize an illustration, to exaggerate some shapes and details, whilst ignoring others. Here are some examples:

Bellflower

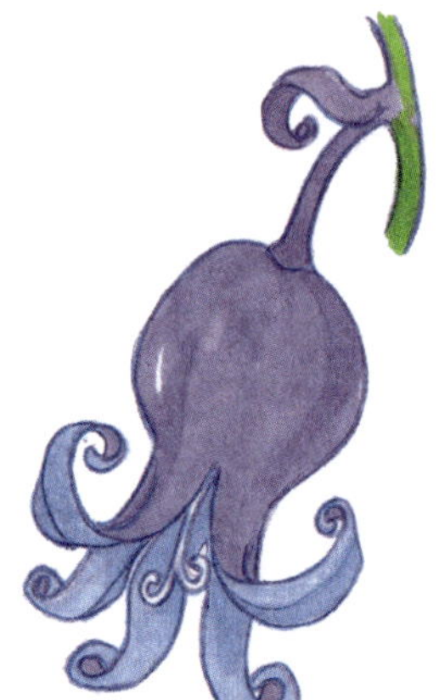

The flower on the left has slightly exaggerated features. The petals are longer and more geometrical than in a real bellflower. Multiple colours were used for the shading and some small details were added using coloured pencils. The flower on the right has much more exaggerated features. The petals are curled up and the bell shape more pronounced. It was drawn using just three colours and no blending. Using different colours for inner and outer parts of a flower is a great way to simplify colouring.

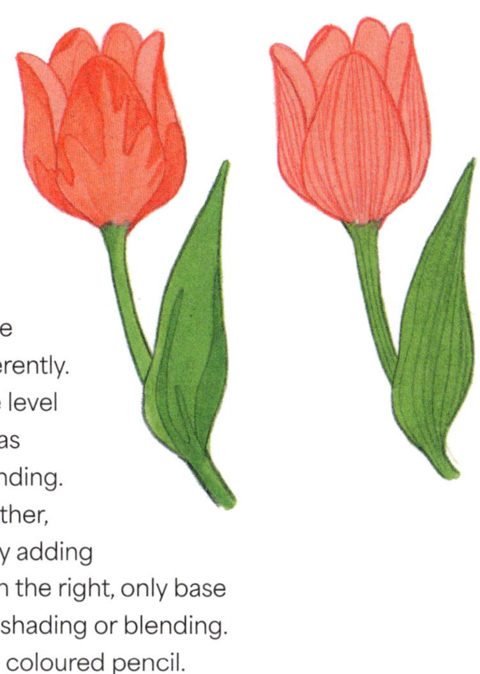

Tulip

The two illustrations are the same shape and form but stylized differently. This time it's about changing the level of detail. The flower on the left has minimal shading and limited blending. Instead of blending colours together, areas of colour are highlighted by adding a pencil outline. For the flower on the right, only base colours are used and there is no shading or blending. Detail is added simply by using a coloured pencil.

Leaf

Stylizing can also mean simplifying. Here, instead of drawing a fully serrated leaf with pinnate venation (see page 62), just a few 'teeth' on the leaf margin and minimal veins have been added. This style signals that the leaf has these features without the need to draw them in fully.

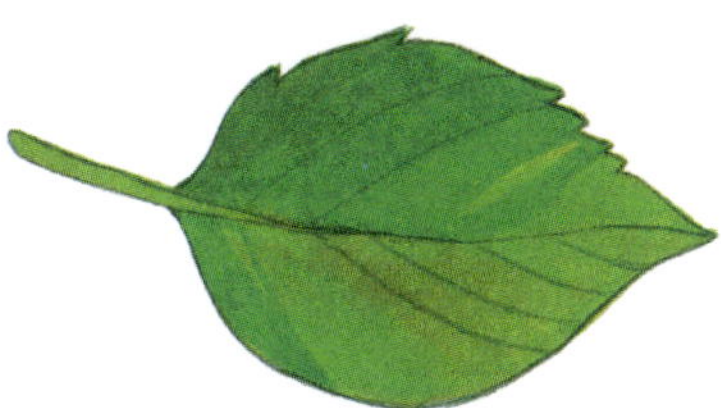

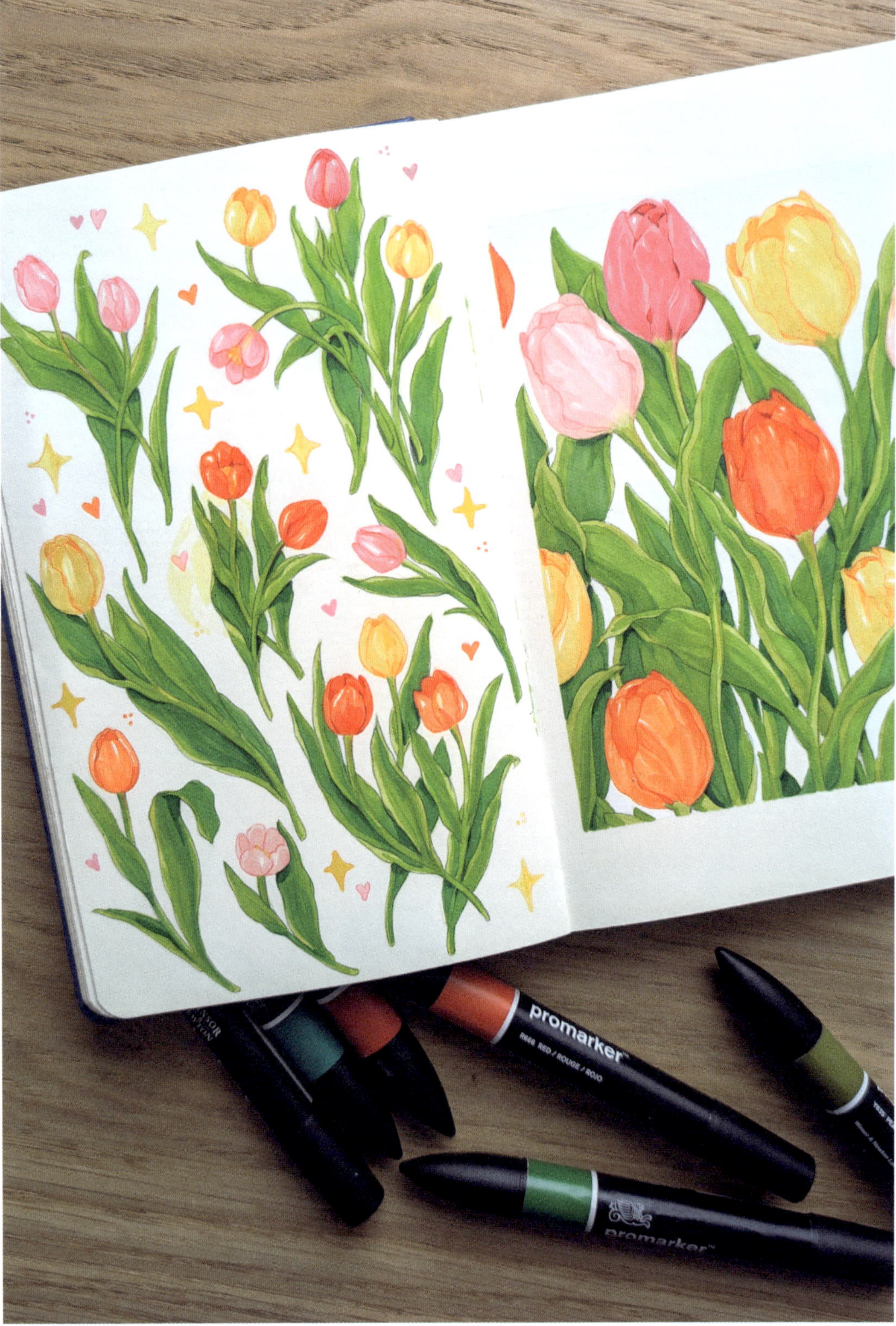
promarker
promarker

TROUBLESHOOTING

Alcohol-based markers are quite an unforgiving medium. It may take a while to get used to the effects you can create, but also to the ways in which the markers behave - their quirks and limitations. Mistakes are easily made and difficult or impossible to correct cleanly. Below are a few notes and tips on dealing with common issues that arise and fixing any mistakes you might make.

Ink stains

There are times when red ink used in a drawing creates staining on the facing page. It happens because the red ink tends to oxidize, and this causes a yellow stain. It also happens with some oranges or browns that have a red undertone. When you finish an illustration, leave the sketchbook open for at least a day, allowing the ink to dry out completely. Keep it somewhere away from light and heat sources. As an extra precaution, perhaps keep a sheet of loose paper between the pages.

Accidental use of the wrong colour

If you accidentally apply a wrong colour when halfway through a drawing - say a blue on top of a green leaf - quickly grab the green marker you have been using and apply the colour over the entire leaf. The blue ink might blend with the green, rendering it unnoticeable. This is a technique that works best using colours that are close to each other on a colour wheel.

Erasing colour

Small areas of colour can be erased using a colourless blender (usually included in a set of markers). Simply use it to run over the affected area several times. Be sure to protect other pages of your sketchbook as the page will become wet from using the blender. Ideally, place several pages of paper or wax paper between the pages before using the blender.

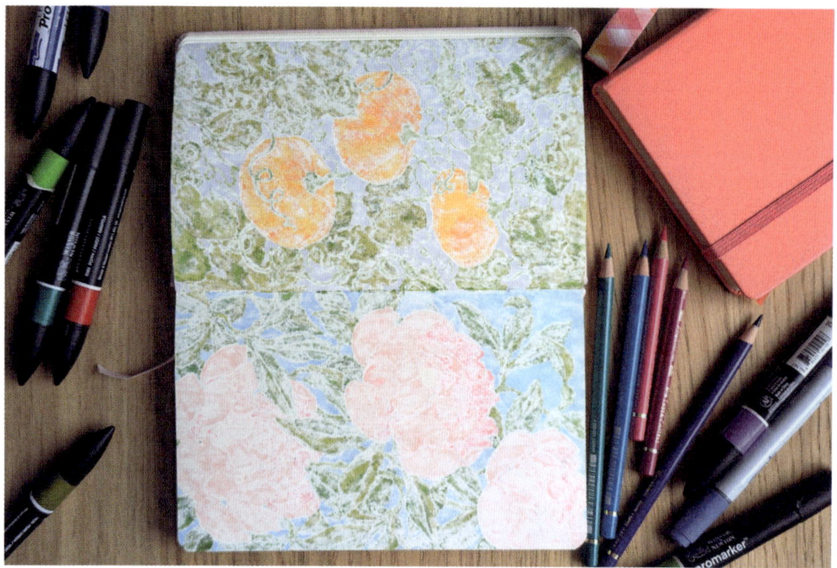

Fading ink

Illustrations made using alcohol-based markers fade with time because the ink is not resistant to light in the way that natural pigments are. There are also certain colours that fade or change tone more quickly than others - this is especially true for purples and blues, which tend to fade or change hue within weeks. Most of my illustrations are made in an acid-free sketchbook and aren't exposed to light, yet even these fade with time. Personally, I find it pretty romantic; everything in life fades with time. Whilst you cannot prevent this from happening, there are ways to slow down the process:

- Avoid placing your artworks in direct sunlight and exposing them to strong light in general. If you plan to display your marker art, place it behind UV-resistant glass.
- Use acid-free paper. A lot of paper made from wood pulp contains a natural substance called lignin. Exposure to light makes this substance break down and form acids, which can cause the inks to fade.
- Use UV-resistant spray on top of the artwork. Be sure to use a non-alcohol-based varnish first to prevent a reaction between the marker ink and the spray, as both are alcohol-based.
- Avoid placing your work where there is a lot of humidity or high temperatures.
- Take a photograph or scan your artwork and have it printed for display.

Bleeding ink

If you work using a sketchbook - even one with very thick pages - you will quickly become aware that the ink from these markers bleeds through the paper. Sometimes, if you are using very dark colours or building many layers, it may even bleed through more than one page. Here are some useful tips for dealing with this:

- Always work on alternate spreads of your sketchbook, leaving two blank pages between each artwork. Alternatively, work only on the right-hand or left-hand pages of the book.
- To avoid ink bleeding through multiple pages, place a loose sheet of paper directly beneath the page you are working on.
- Once you have filled an entire sketchbook, go back and glue the 'blank' pages together so that they become invisible.
- Work on loose paper and stick the finished art into your sketchbook. That way you don't need to waste any pages at all.

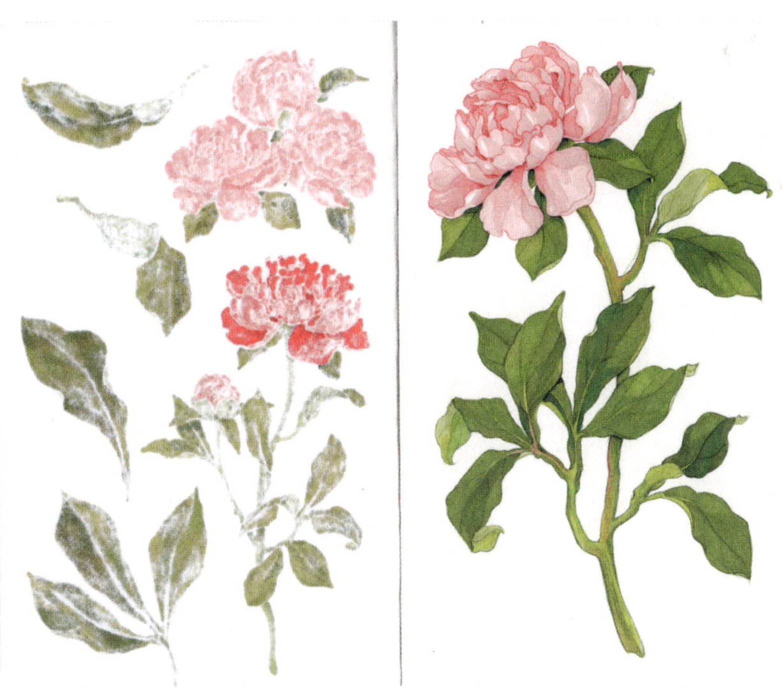

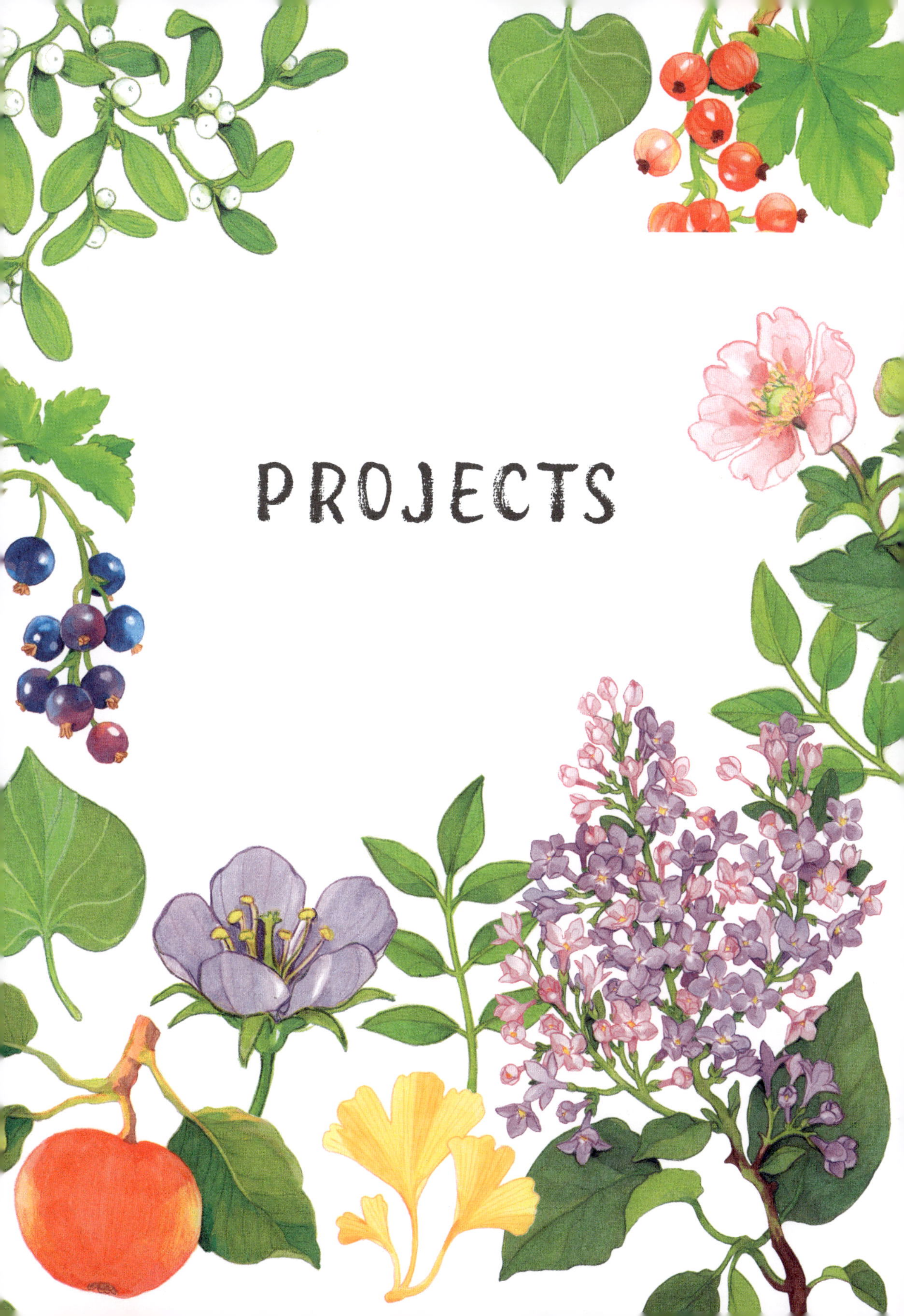

PROJECTS

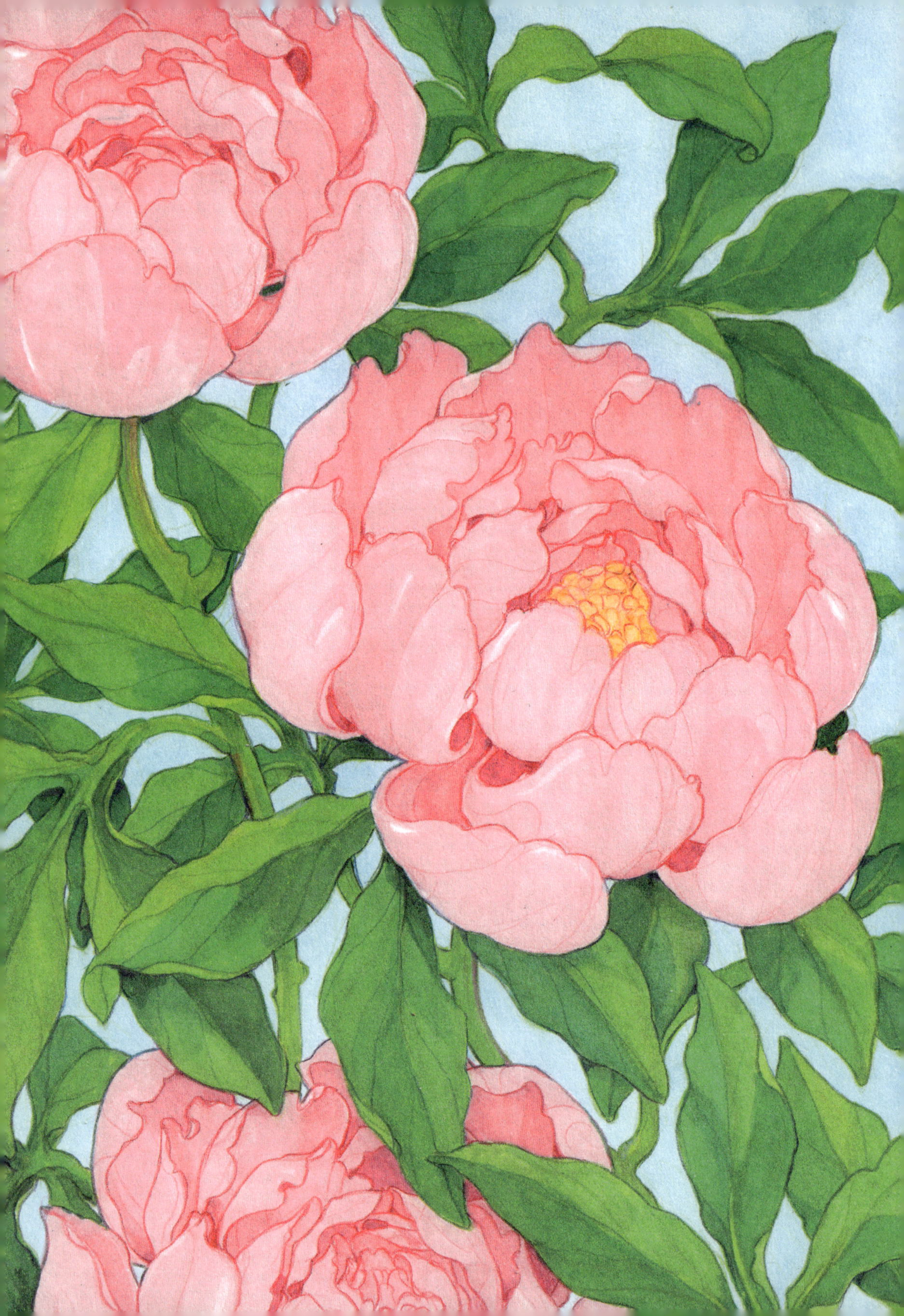

SPRING

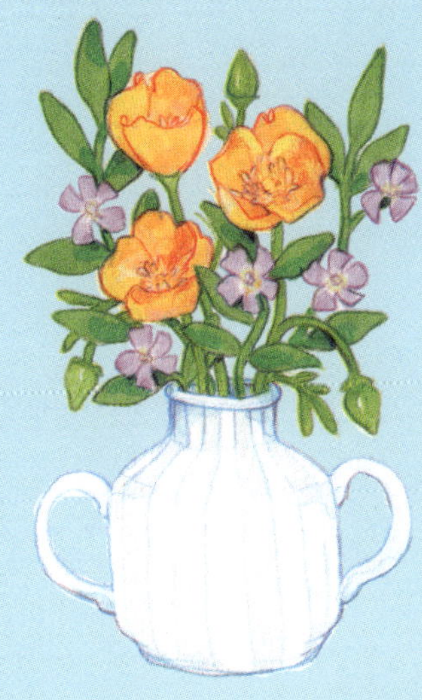

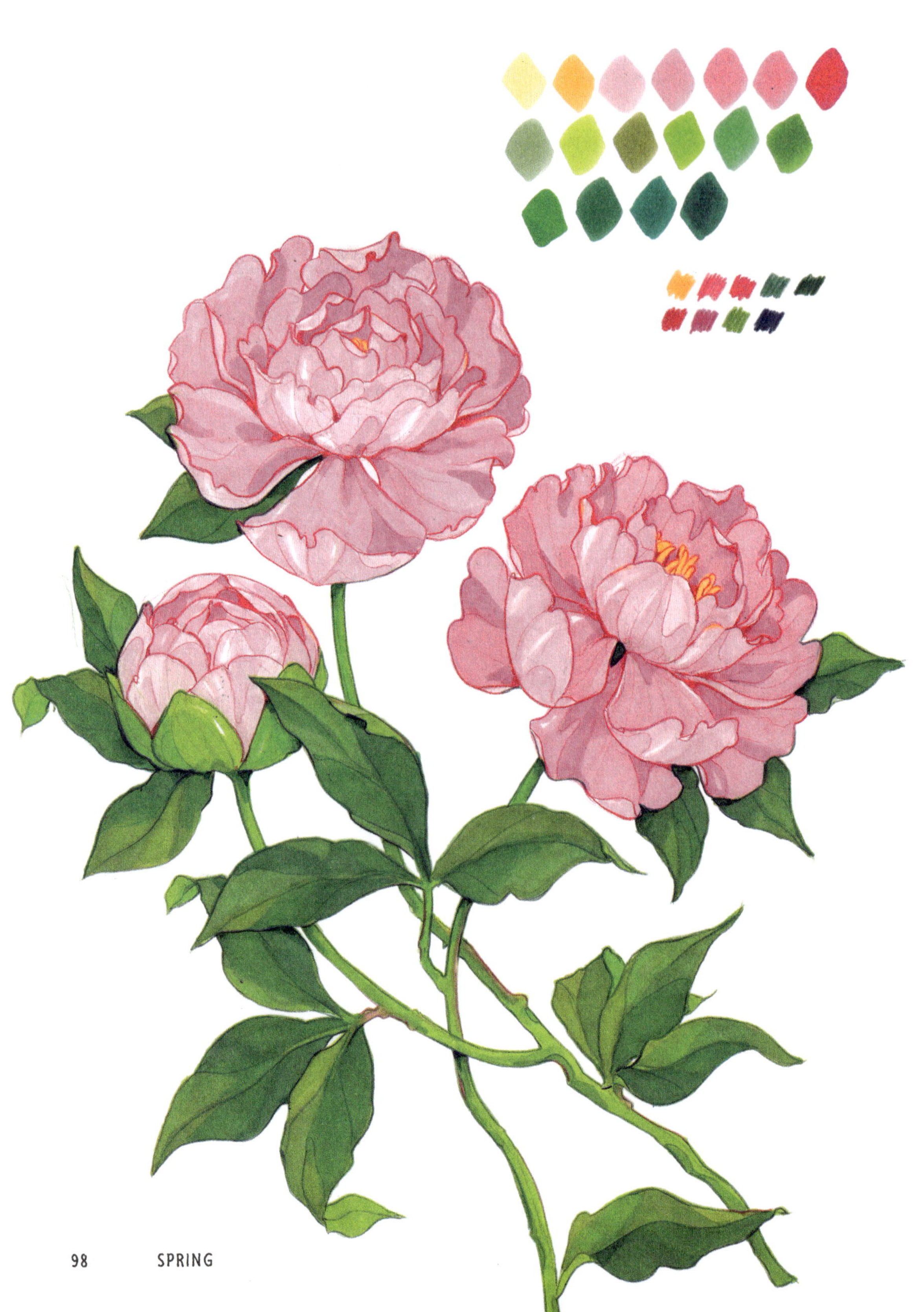

Peonies

Who doesn't love beautiful bushy peonies? Whilst they are one of the more challenging flowers to draw due to the many layers of petals, with the skills covered in this book you'll soon be able to draw them. They just require some patience. I encourage you to practise sketching this flower first, to really understand its anatomy. Feel free to come back to this project later, if you don't feel confident enough to give it a go yet.

Materials:

- Acid-free paper
- Coloured pencils
- Alcohol-based markers

1. Choose two coloured pencils for the sketch: green and pink. Sketch three flowing lines for the stems. Next draw three big circles or ellipses to form the flowers. The centre of each flower should be the point at which it meets the stem; draw smaller ellipses around these points. Now, decide on a more precise shape for each flower: draw a sphere for the bud, two bowl-like shapes for the central flower and half a sphere and ellipse for the third flower. Think of teacups, bowls or side plates!

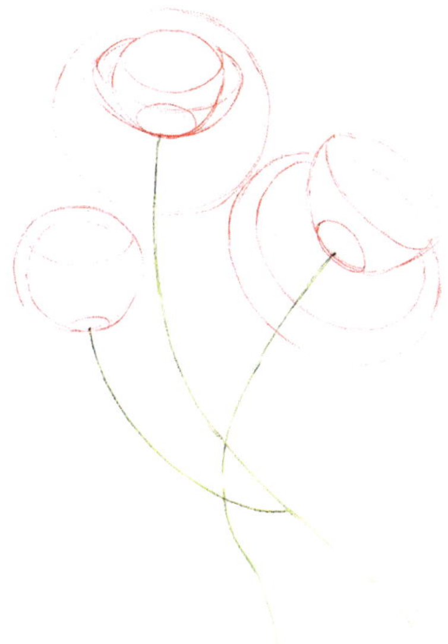

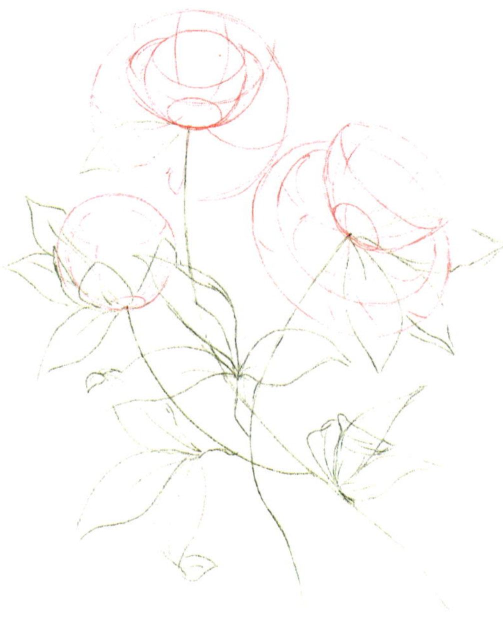

2. Using curvy lines, mark the direction of the petals. Imagine petals folding around the spheres. Be careful not to put too much pressure on the pencil. Draw three narrow leaves coming from one stem, slightly touching each other at their bases.

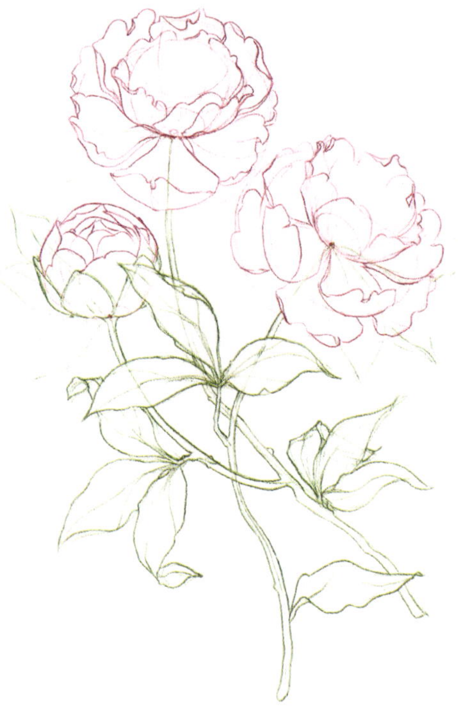

3. Draw the petals for each flower, starting at the centre. It's up to you how ruffled or detailed they are. The petals should fold around the spheres - be mindful of their directions and use the middle of the flower as the reference point. Decide which overlapping parts of the illustration should be in front and leave the sepals (see page 70) coming from the bottom of the flowers for later.

4. Refine your sketch. Use darker colours in the folds, to emphasize the darkest spots and to guide your choices for future shades. Outline the stamens in yellow.

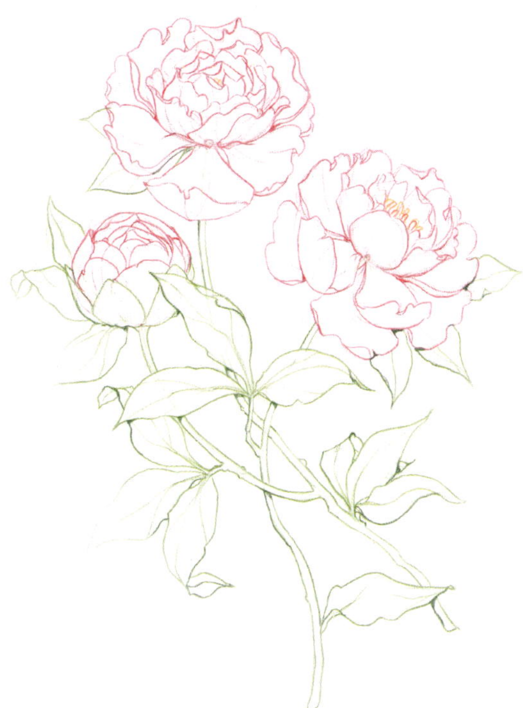

5. Lay down basic colours with the markers. Lime green for stems, neutral green for the undersides of leaves, olive green for the tops of the leaves. For the petals use pink, choosing a lighter shade for the outer surfaces. Leave some spots uncoloured for highlights; highlights should follow the direction of the petals and leaves.

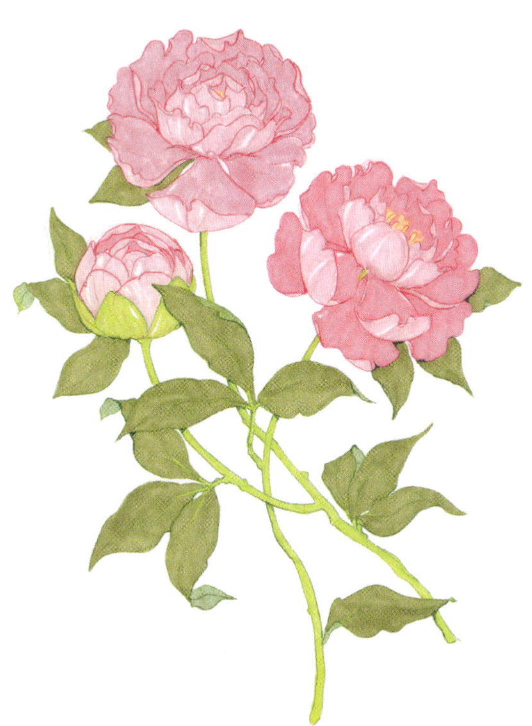

6. Blend the colours (see page 44) then step away from the paper at least once, to check that you're happy with the colour blending. Add more colour if necessary.

7. Finish the illustration by outlining the flower using coloured pencils.

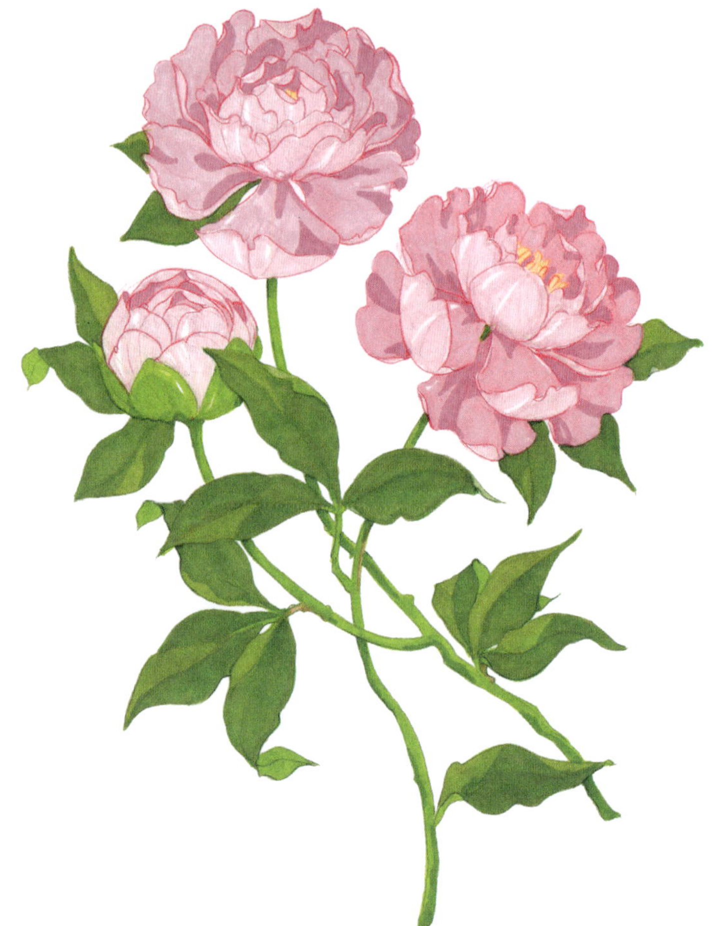

Peonies are long-lived plants that can live for over 100 years.

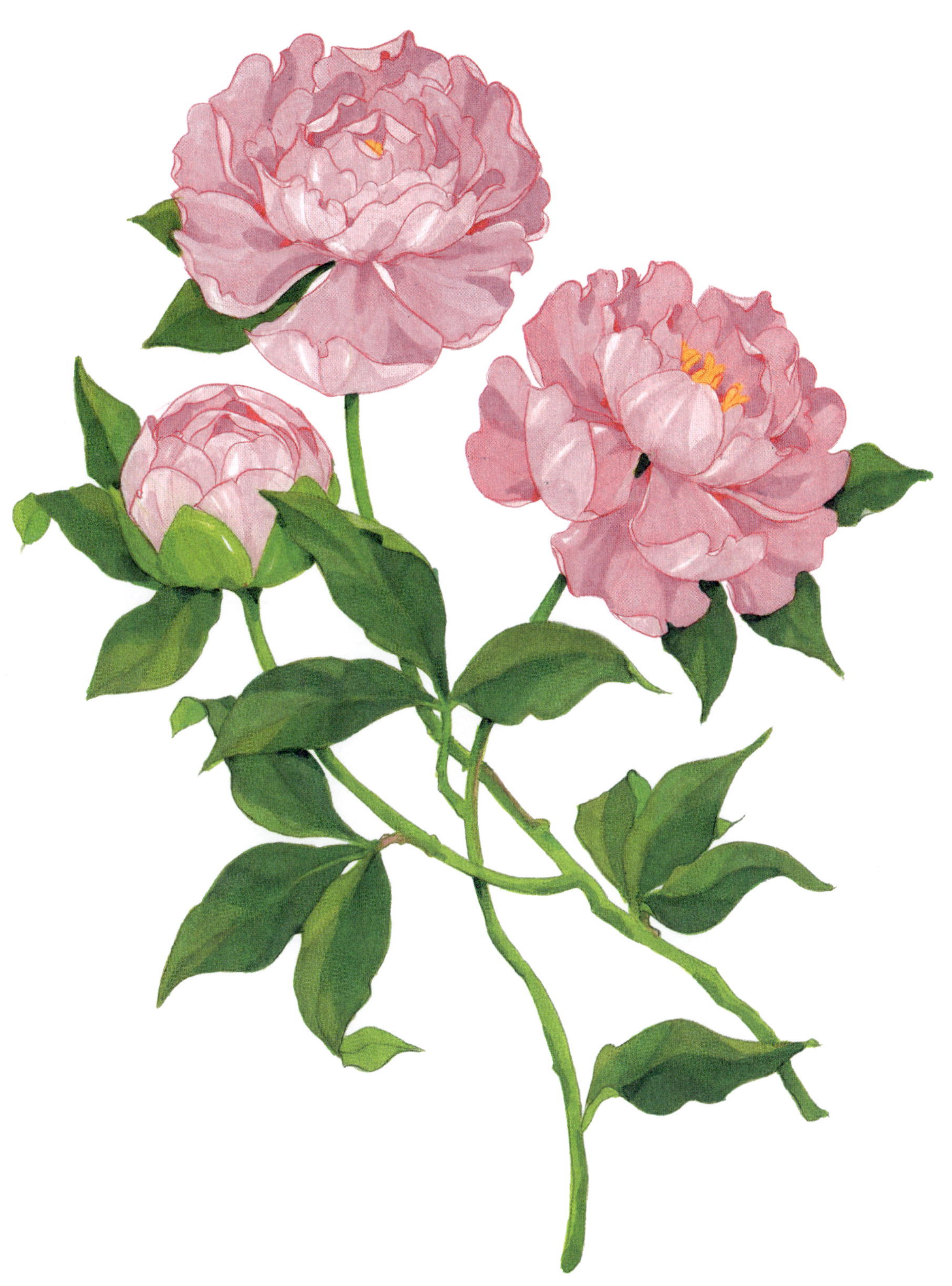

Meadow

When drawing botanicals you can capture the beauty of just one plant, but you can also play with creating a composition of multiple plants species. Flowers of various sizes, shapes and colours can be found in meadows and drawing meadow flowers is a great way to practise your composition. In this project we're going to use different undertones when colouring the leaves to make the plants distinct and add some interest to the illustration.

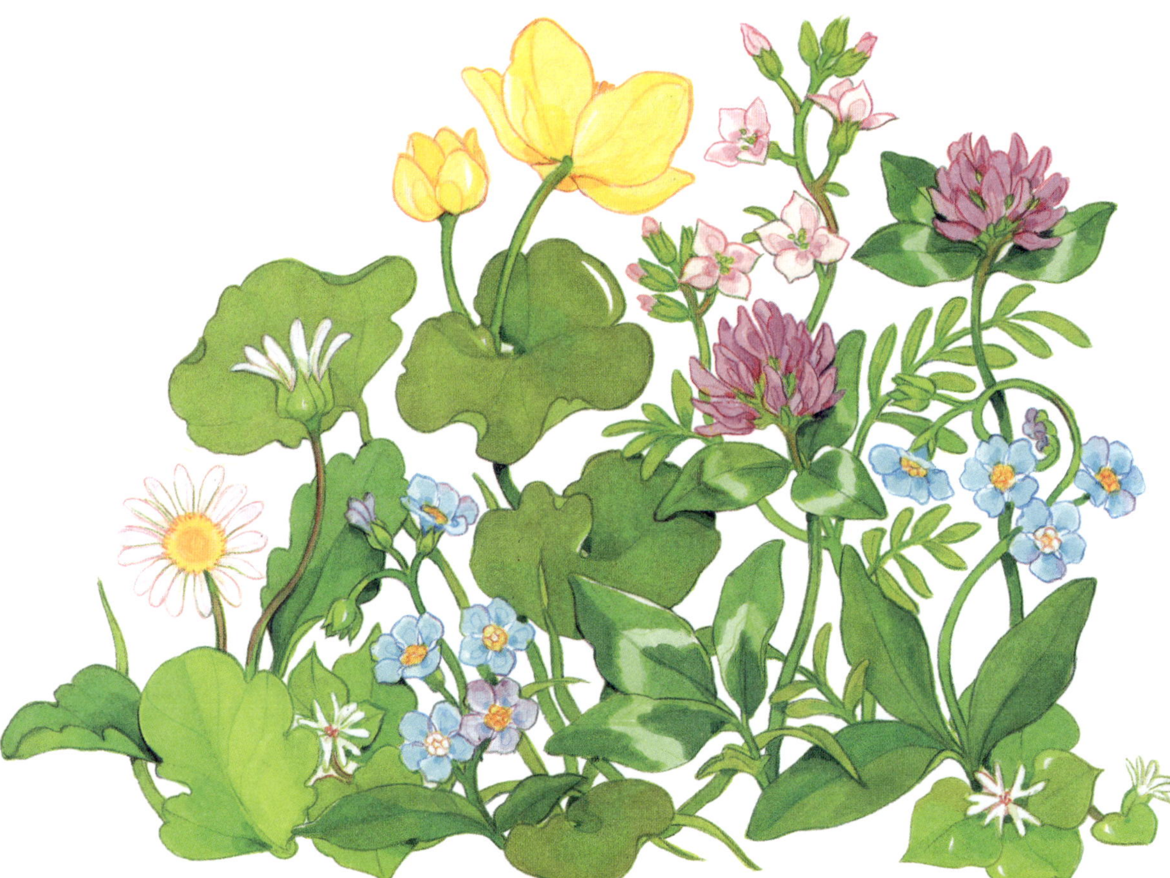

Featured flowers

- Red clover (*Trifolium pratense*) • Forget-me-not (*Myosotis arvensis*)
- Marsh marigold (*Caltha palustris*) • Lawn daisy (*Bellis perennis*)
- Chickweed (*Stellaria media*) • Cuckoo flower (*Cardamine pratensis*)

Materials:

- Acid-free paper
- Coloured pencils
- Alcohol-based markers
- White gouache paint (optional)
- Small paintbrush (optional)

1. Create a composition of wildflowers in coloured pencil. Pick flowers of different sizes and colours.

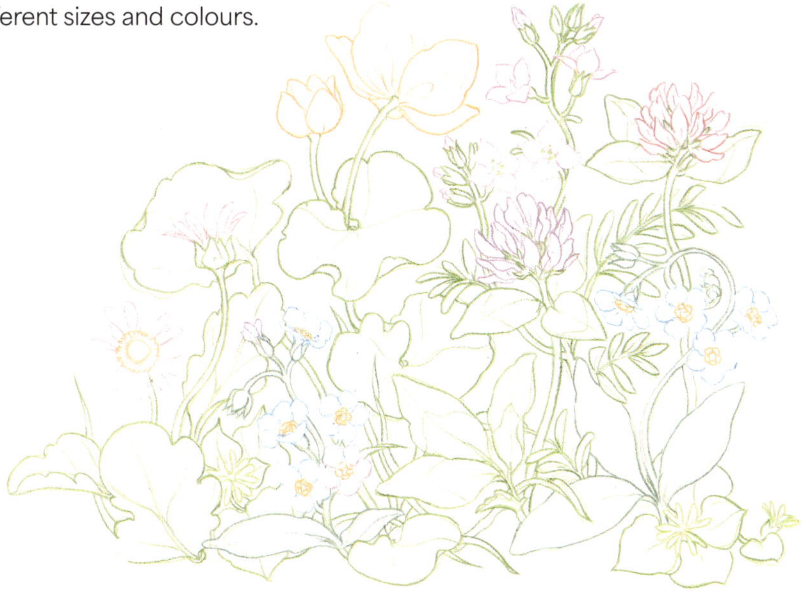

Red clover was traditionally used for medicinal purposes.

2. Lay down base colours using alcohol-based markers. Use different shades of green for the foliage. Leave some spots uncoloured for highlights; highlights should follow the direction of the petals and leaves.

If the paper you are using is not pure white you can use white gouache paint to colour any white flowers (see page 57), just remember that colours layered on top of the white paint will appear lighter.

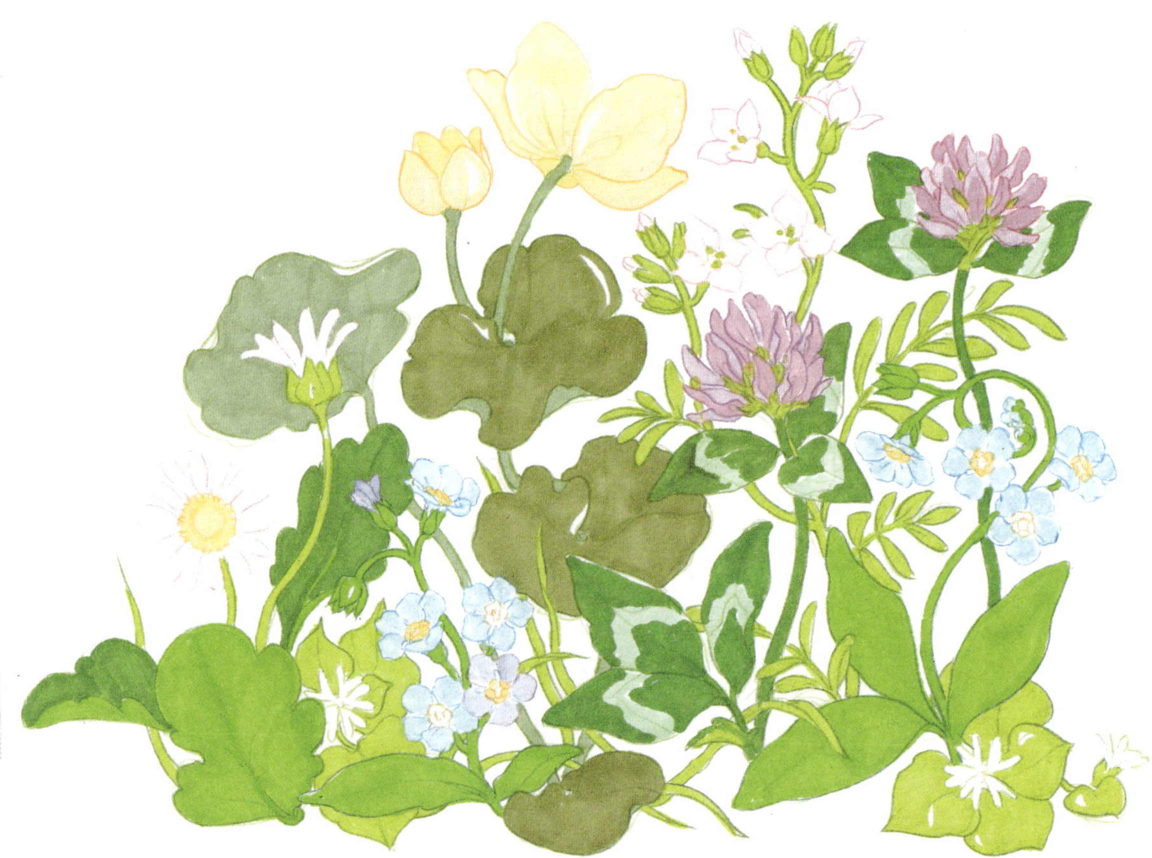

3. Blend the colours (see page 44). Pick three or four green tones to colour all of the stems and leaves. Start with the lighter shades and build up different tones from there (see page 48). Notice how the different green base colours affect the final appearance of the foliage.

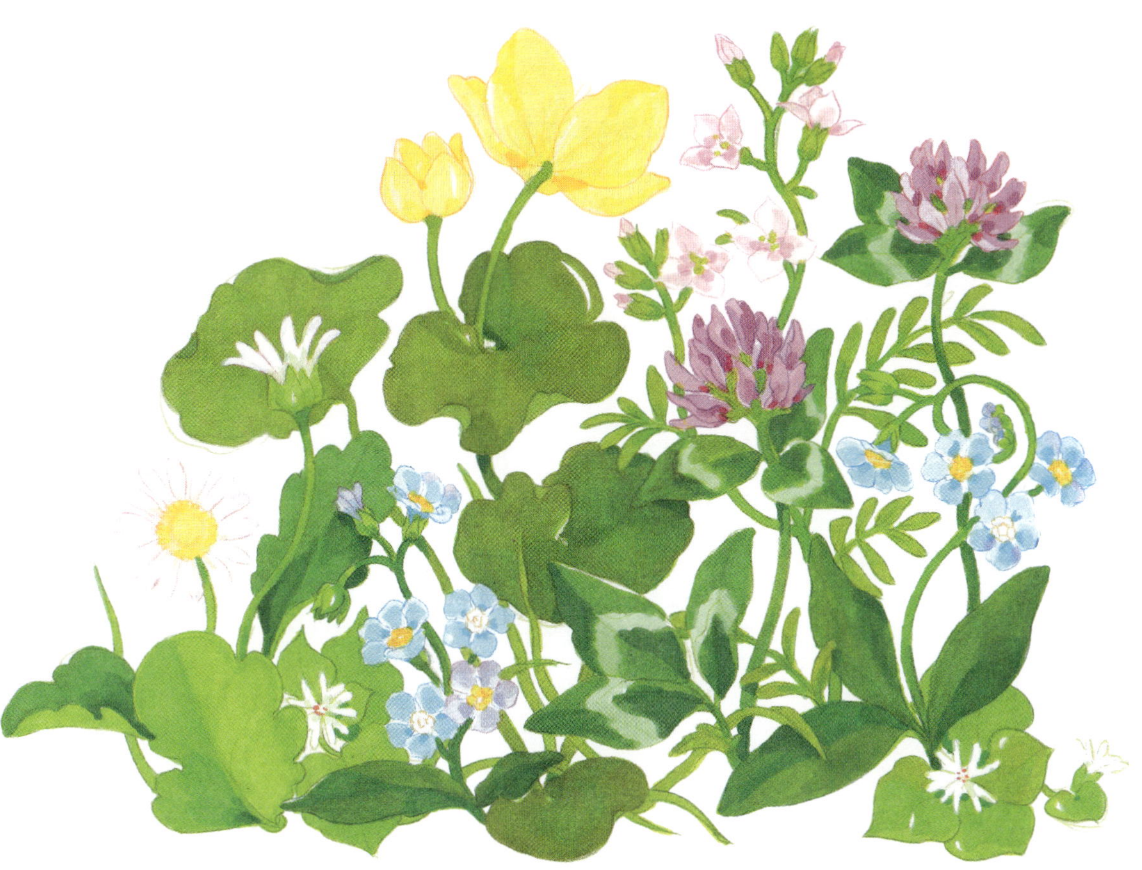

Chickweed got its name for being a favourite snack of birds, especially chickens.

4. Let the greens dry completely. As they dry, the colours may change slightly in appearance. Darken some areas and add extra shades if needed.

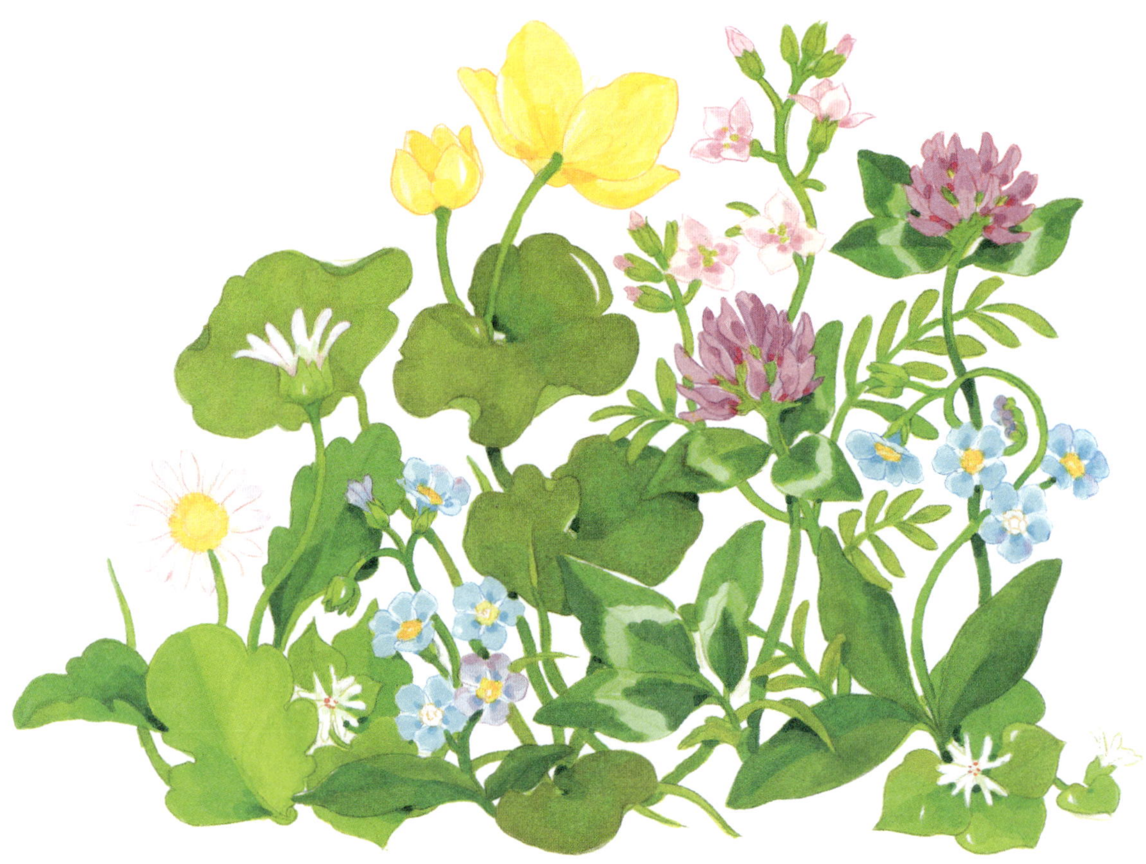

5. Apply pencil to complete the illustration. Use darker colours for the outlines and add some details using lighter colours. The amount of detail you add is up to you. I like to draw in a few veins and outline a few shades, but you can add more. Use pink and yellow markers or pencils to add some colours to stems.

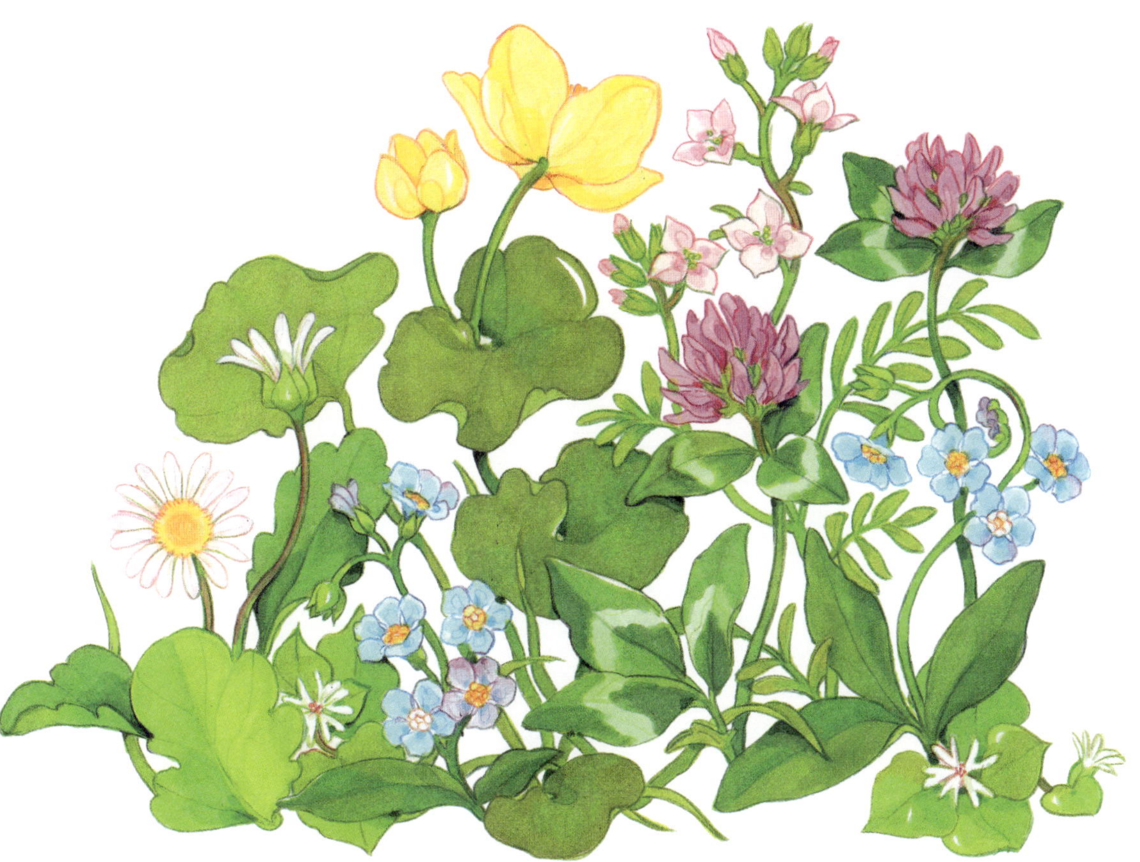

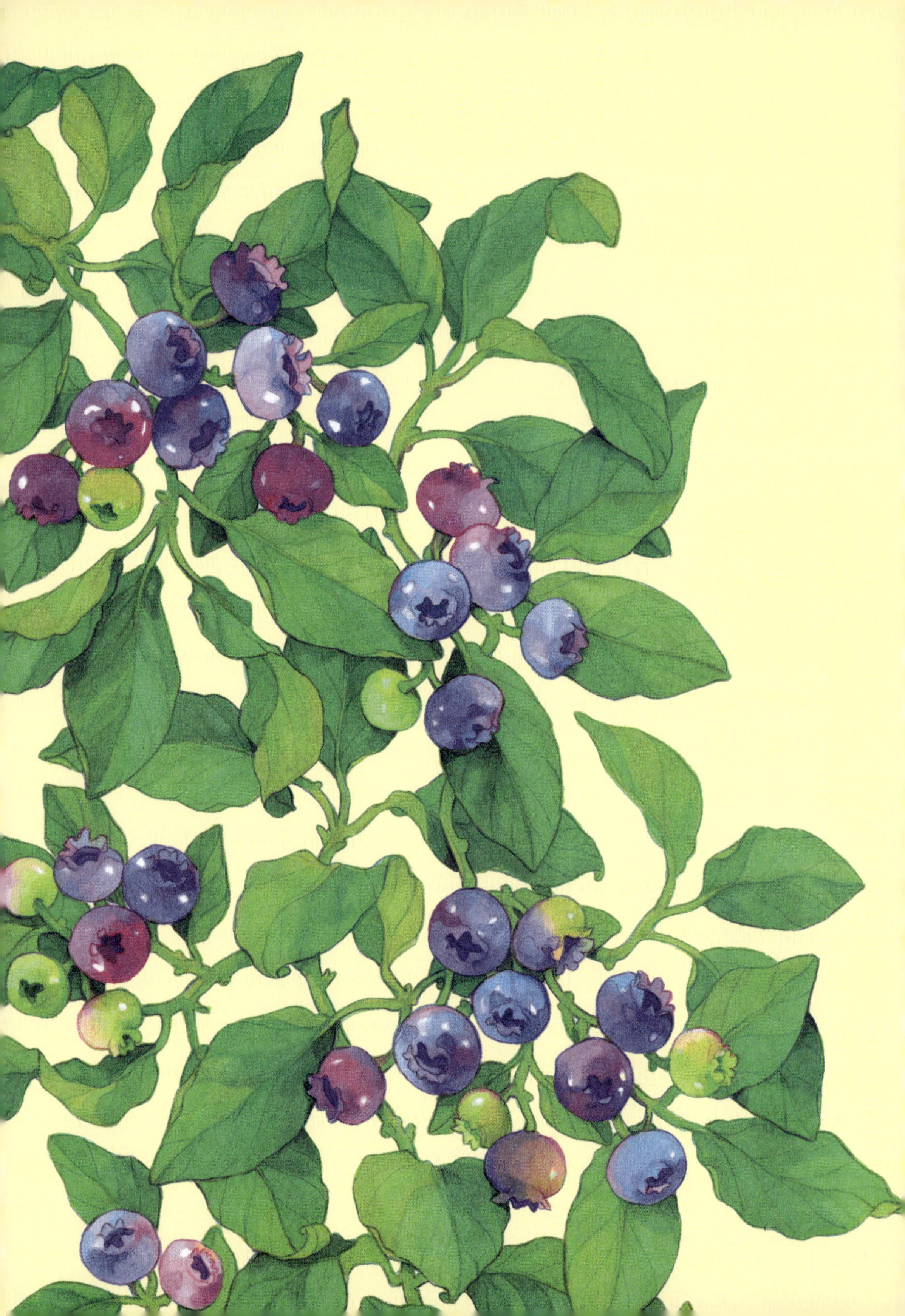

SUMMER

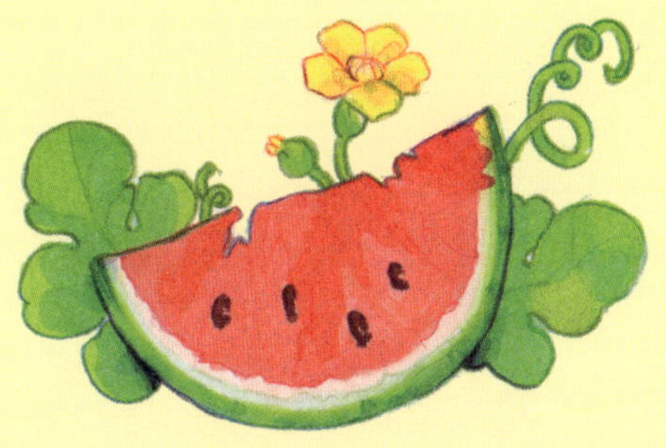

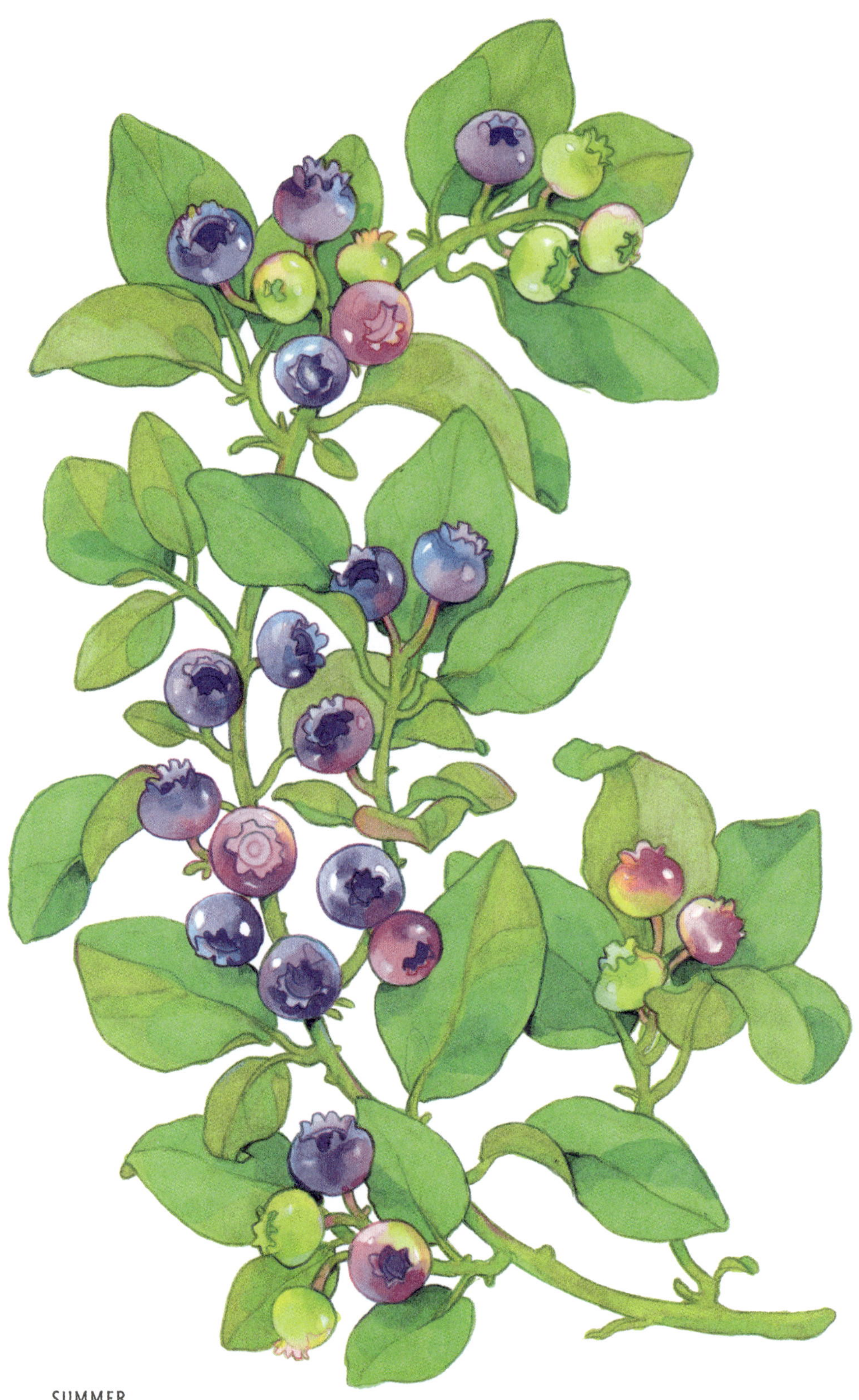

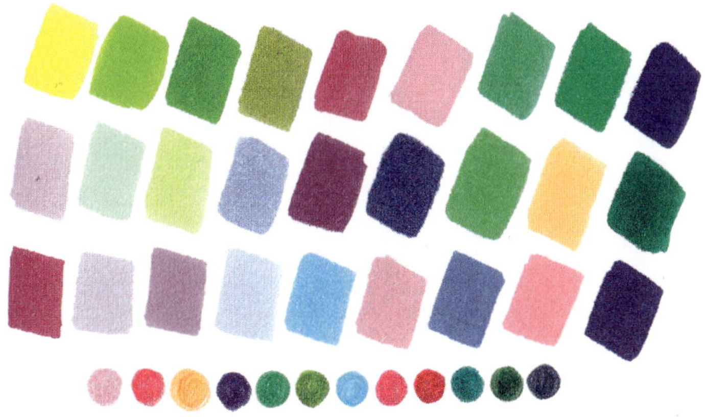

Blueberries

Blueberries make an amazing subject for studying colour and for improving your blending skills using markers. Feel free to use many colours for this project and just have fun with them - it's a project in which you get to use some of the lesser-used colours, such as fluorescent pink and deep, dark purple. Practise drawing a smaller cluster of blueberries first, as a warm-up exercise, if you like.

Materials:

- Graphite pencil
- Acid-free paper
- Sketchbook
- Coloured pencils
- Alcohol-based markers

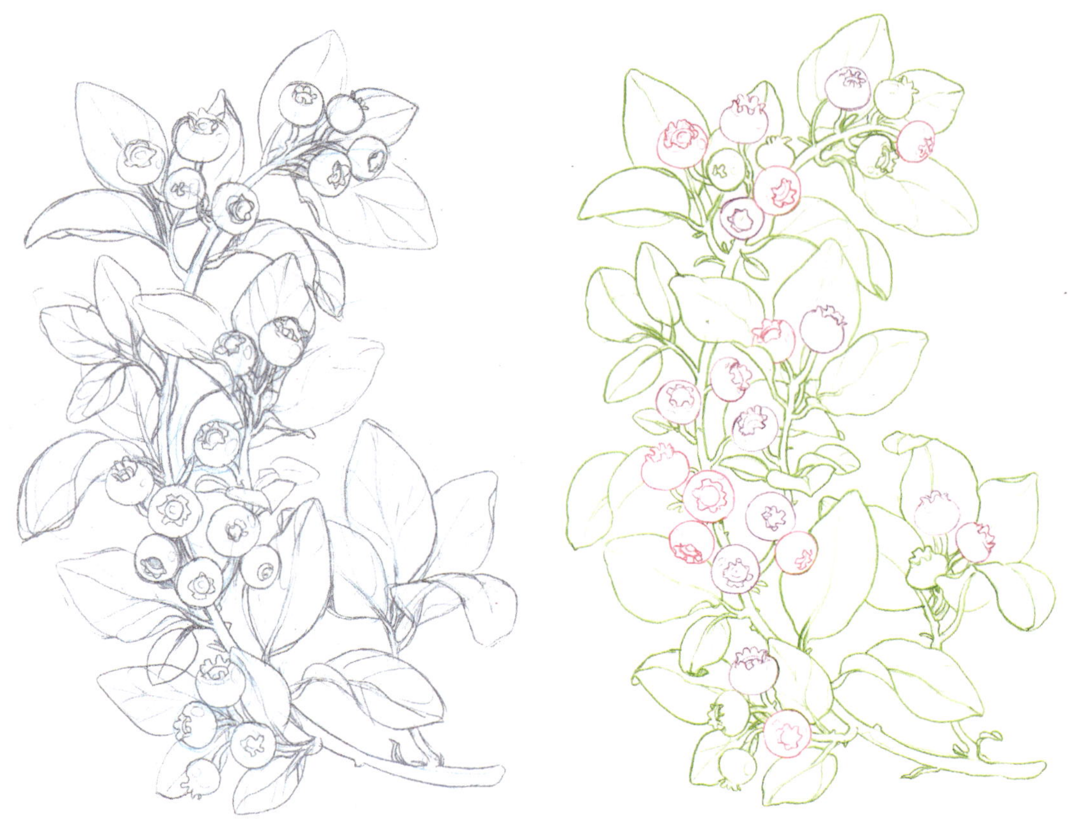

1. Decide on your composition (see pages 28-31). Make a pencil sketch on a loose sheet of paper and trace it into your sketchbook (see page 36). You can make changes to the sketch as you trace it. Follow the tutorial on page 67 to draw the leaves at different angles.
2. Use green, purple and pink coloured pencils to refine the lines of your illustration.

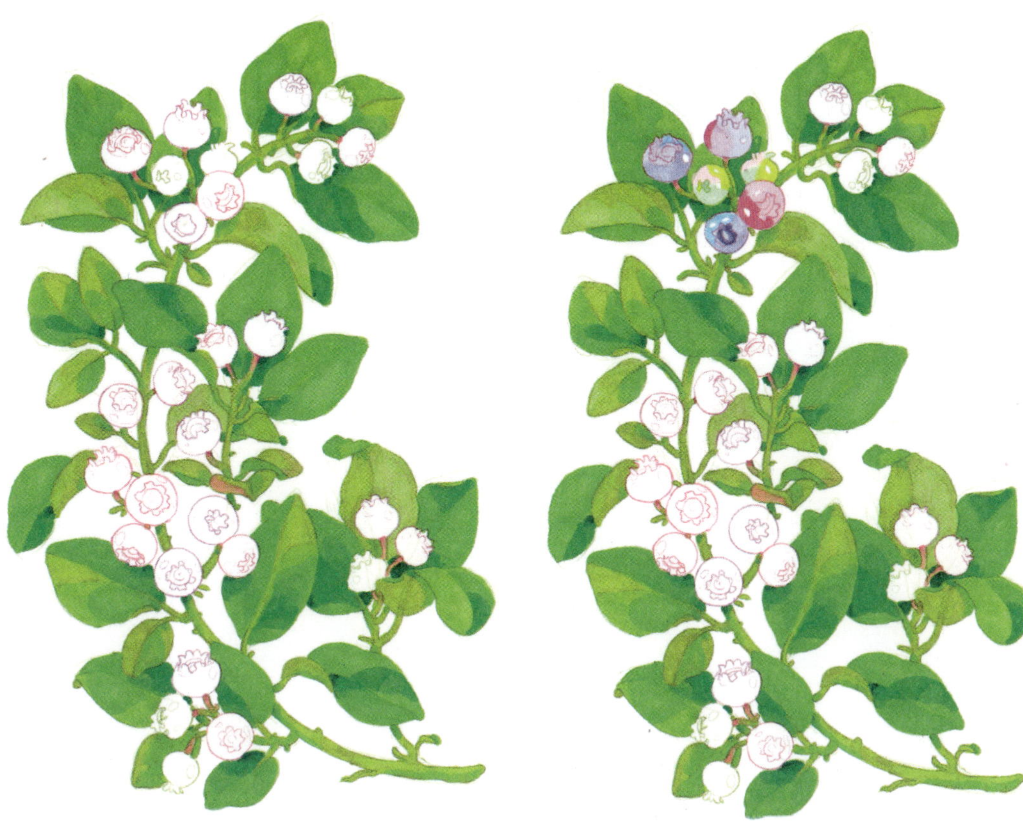

3. Follow the tutorial on page 69 to paint the leaves. For any fruit study, it is good to have all of the foliage in place first so that you can then focus on the fruit (or vice versa). This makes for a much smoother process.

4. Use markers to lay down some base colours for the berries. Blueberries have blue, purple, pink and green hues; it's up to you how colourful you make them. Keep some of them unripe, using green and pink, and be sure to leave some spaces uncoloured for the highlights. Timing is important when colouring round objects with markers, as you want the colours to blend together smoothly (see page 44). It is a good idea to work on a cluster of blueberries one at a time.

Blueberry bushes can produce fruit for more than fifty years.

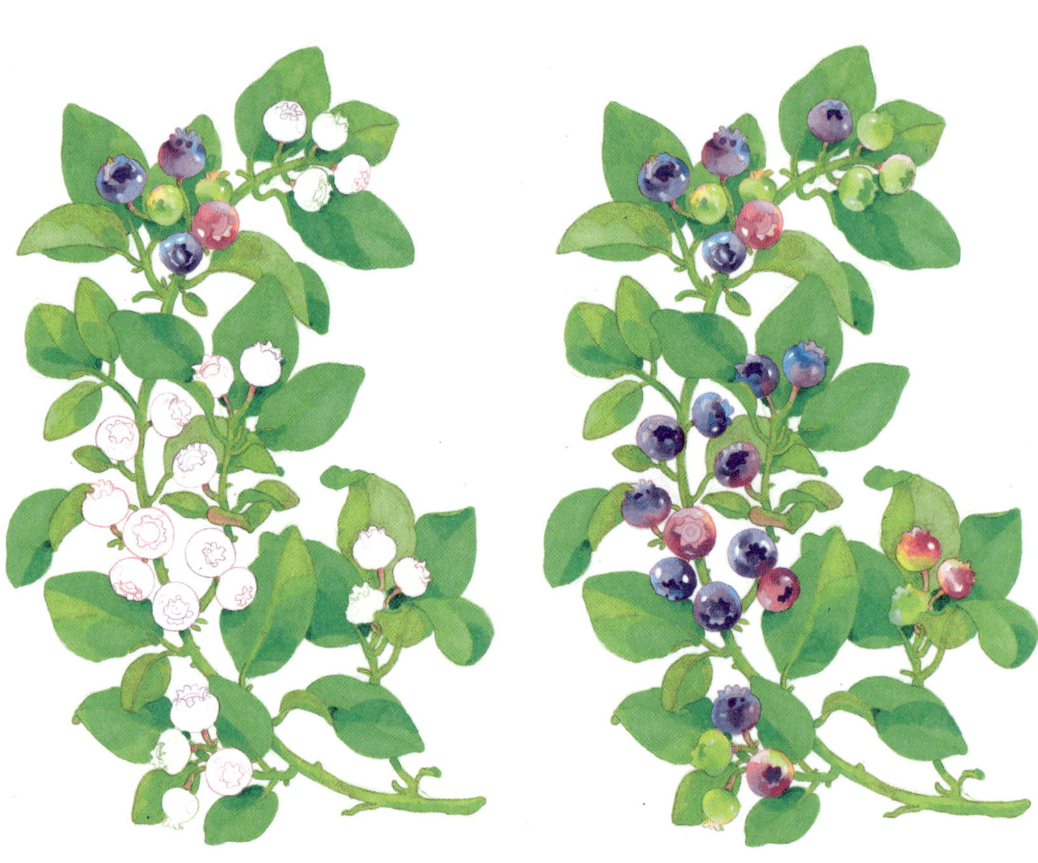

5. Blend colours by adding layer upon layer, using a circular motion.

6. Repeat Steps 4 and 5 to colour all of the berries.

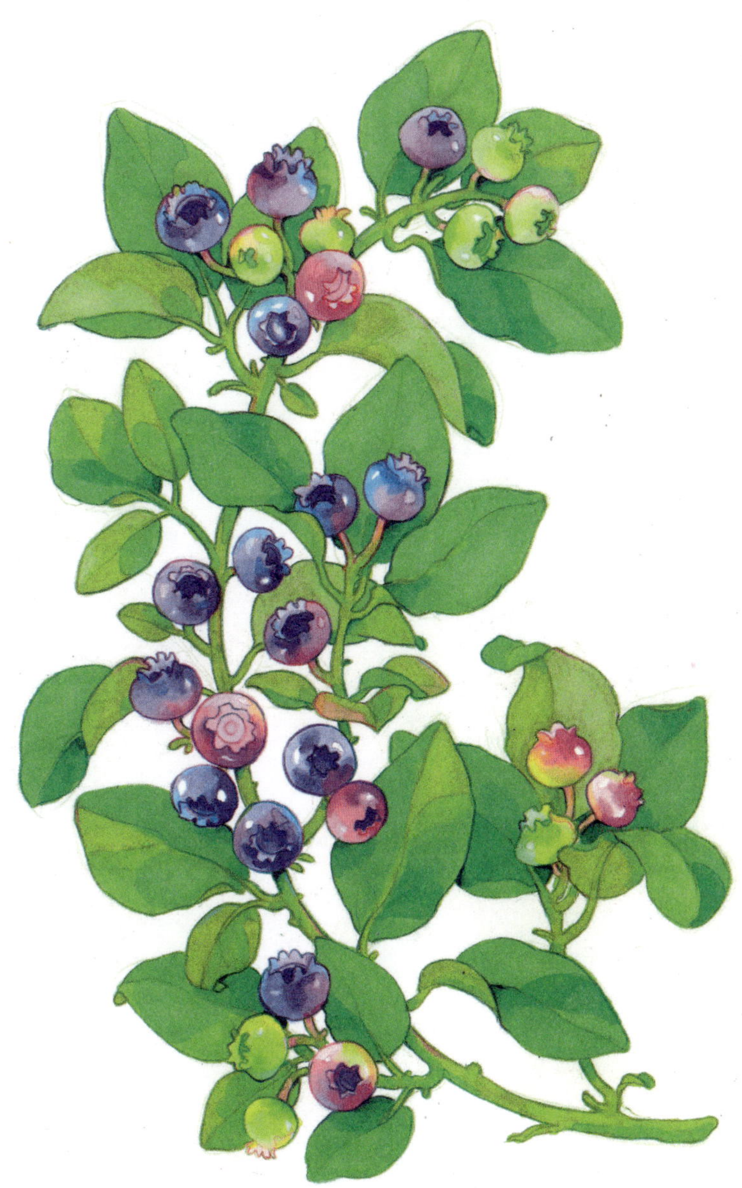

7. Add an outline to your illustration. Since this is so colourful, play with the colours a little, using green tones to outline some of the berries and purple or blue for some of the leaves. To make it look more organic, add a few purple, yellow and lilac details to the stems and edges of the berries and the leaves.

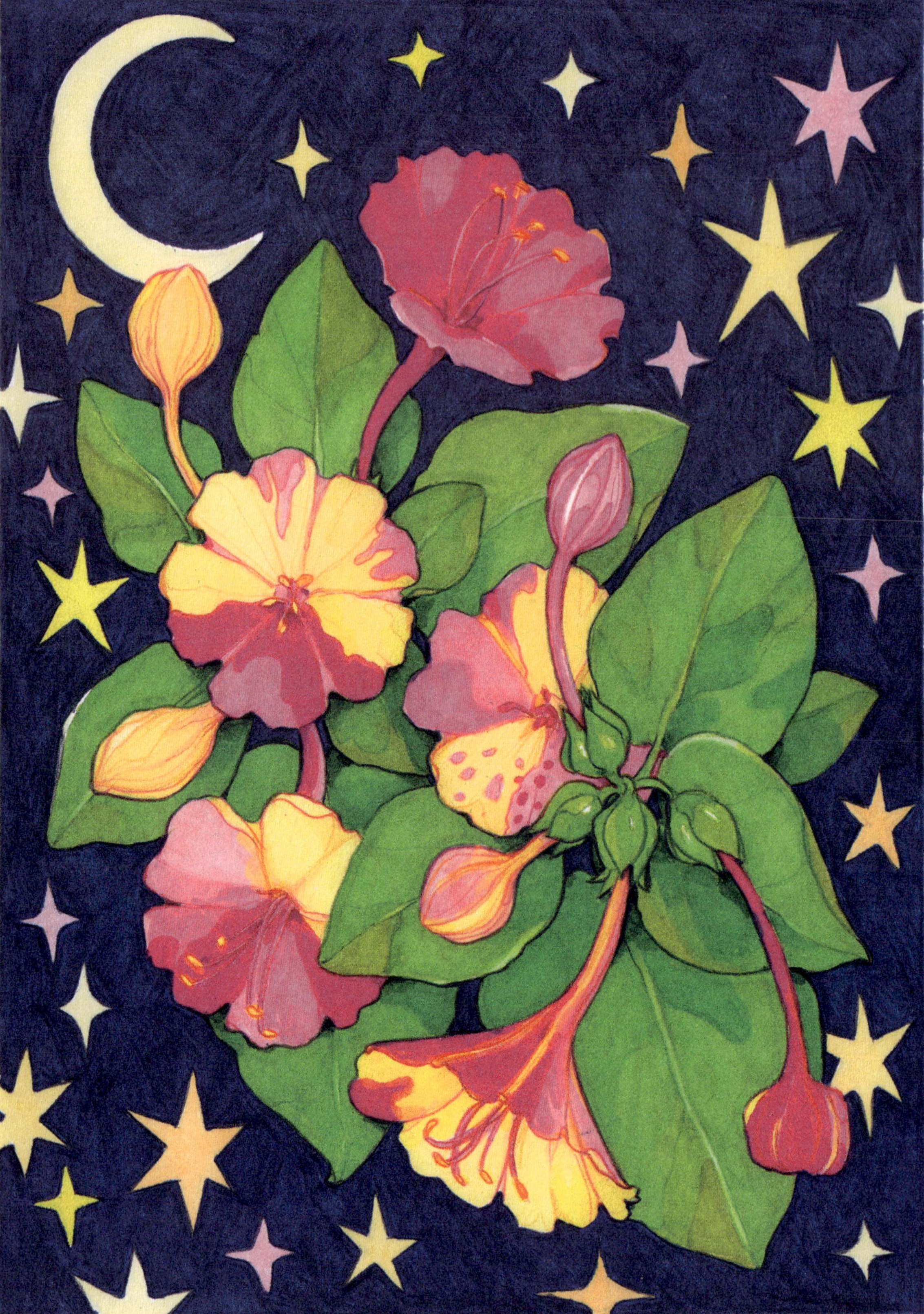

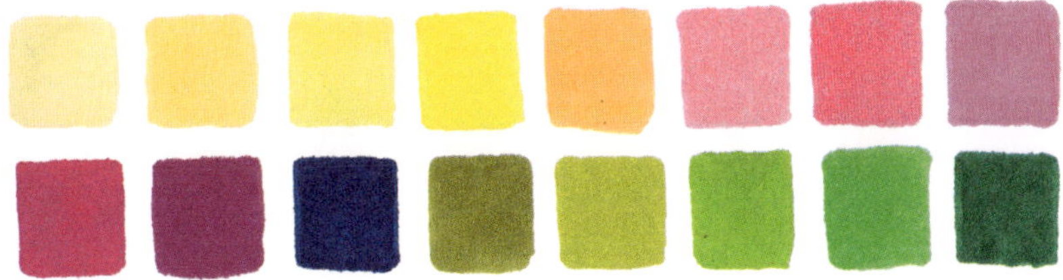

Nighttime bloom

At the height of summer, nature is in full bloom. The days are long, and spending time outside on warm evenings is one of the biggest joys of the season. Once twilight sets in, night-blooming flowers come to life, releasing sweet fragrances to attract moths and other night pollinators. One such flower, and the subject of this project, is *Mirabilis jalapa*, commonly known as the four o'clock flower or marvel of Peru. This project is a great one for practising using washi or masking tape and introducing dark colours into your backgrounds (see page 53). Tape creates a frame so that you can work up to the edges (see page 32).

Materials:

- Acid-free paper
- Washi or masking tape
- Coloured pencils
- Alcohol-based markers
- Gouache paint (optional)
- Small paintbrush (optional)

This plant gets its common name from the fact that its flowers open in early evening.

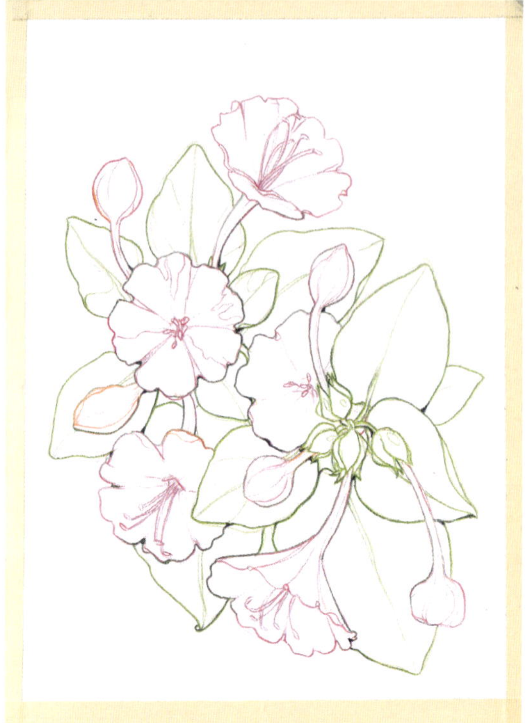

1. Use washi or masking tape to create a frame for your illustration. Start building your composition using simple shapes such as circles for flowers and rectangles for leaves. Use a light-coloured pencil to avoid having to use an eraser later on.

2. Use coloured pencils to give your sketch more definition. Use green for the leaves. The flowers are multicoloured, so alternate your colours to create pink, orange and yellow outlines. Use an indigo blue pencil in some corners to give more dimension and depth to the sketch.

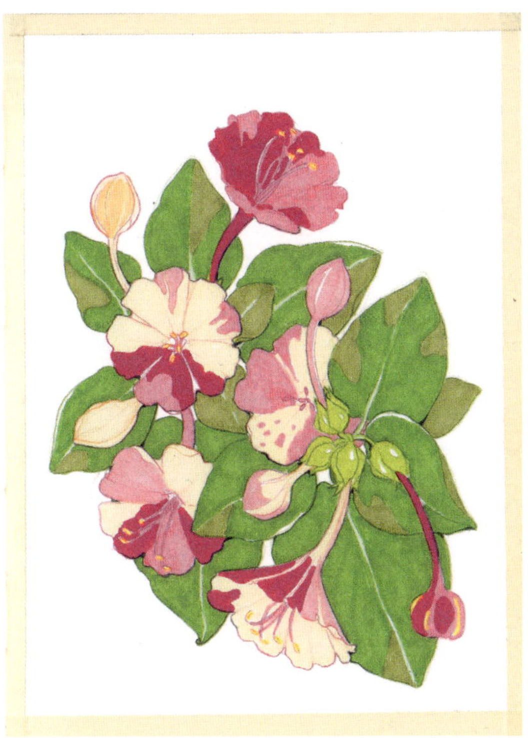

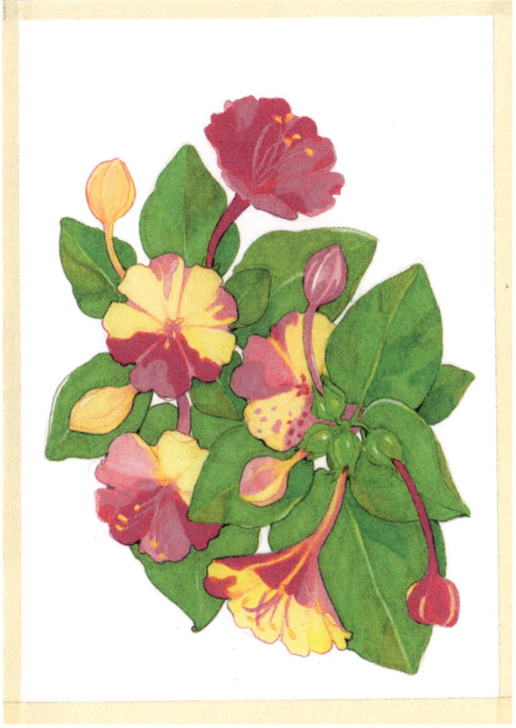

3. Start adding base colours, using the markers. Use various shades of green for the leaves (yellow, lime, neutral), and yellow and pink for the flowers. Always start with lighter tones, as you will build the colour with additional layers. This stage is just about base colour and patches shouldn't overlay yet.

4. It's time for shading. First, use bright green on top of the yellow-green tones added in Step 3. Darken some areas, by adding another layer of the same colour. Have fun combining yellows with pinks on the petals, just remember to always use more saturated or darker colours on top of lighter ones for the best results (see page 48).

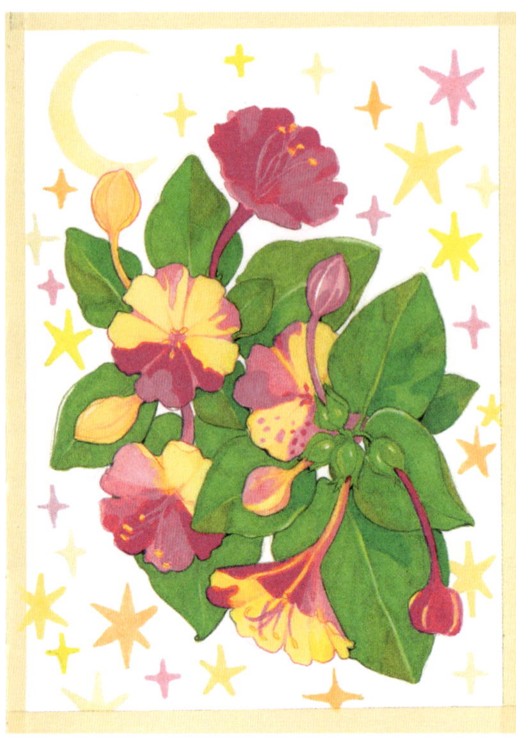

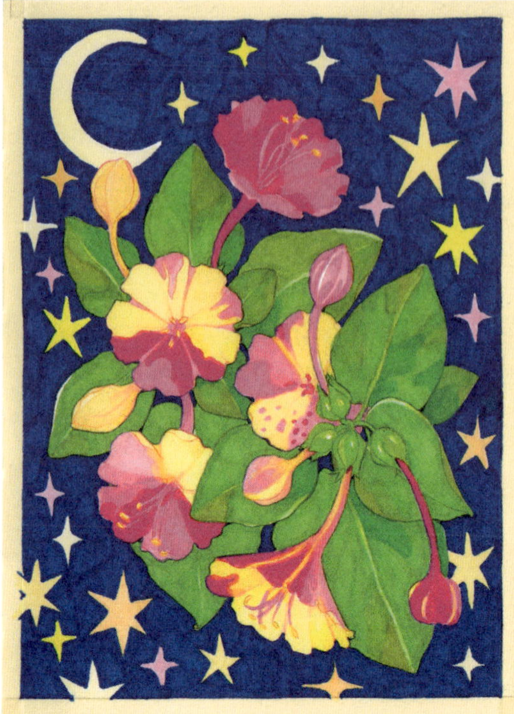

5. To fully embrace the night garden vibe, draw some stars, sparkles and the moon. Use colours that feature in the illustration for a more cohesive look. Avoid colours that are too dark or oversaturated, as they might overpower the drawing.

6. Colour the background, using a navy blue or indigo blue marker. Use circular motions and colour one small area at a time. This is your chance to cover any 'imperfections' and visible sketch lines. If you'd prefer a more polished look, try using gouache paint for this step.

7. What's a marker illustration without a pencil outline? Add the outlines using multiple colours - the more, the merrier. For the background elements use a dark blue. Add more shading to the flowers with markers if needed.

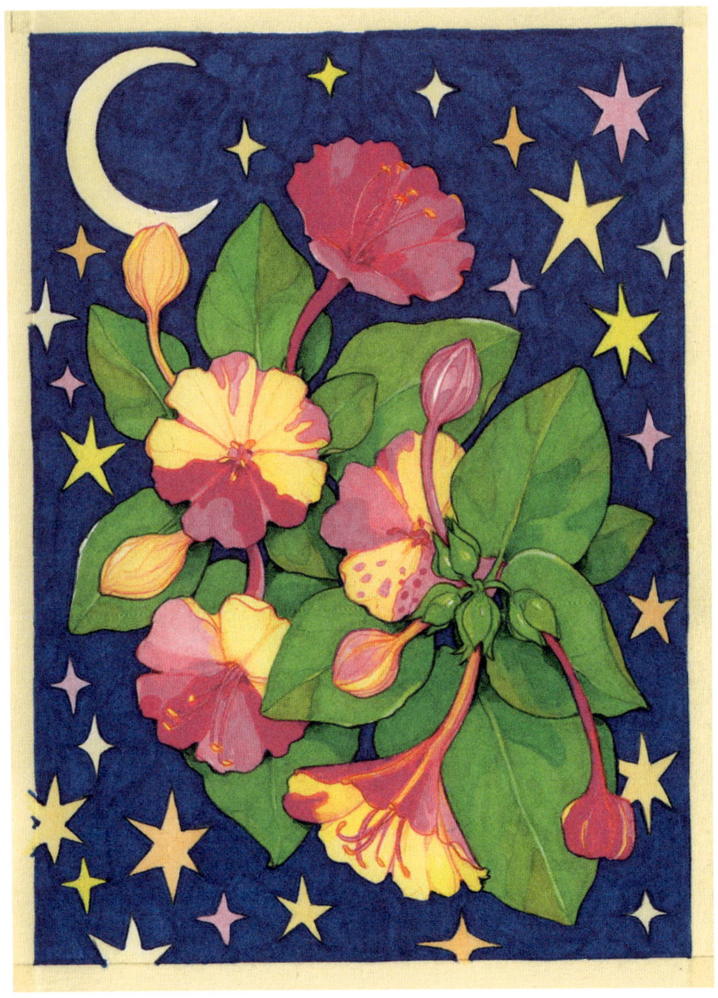

Darken the background colour further if it needs it. Apply another layer of whichever medium you used in Step 6 or a coloured pencil for a more organic look.

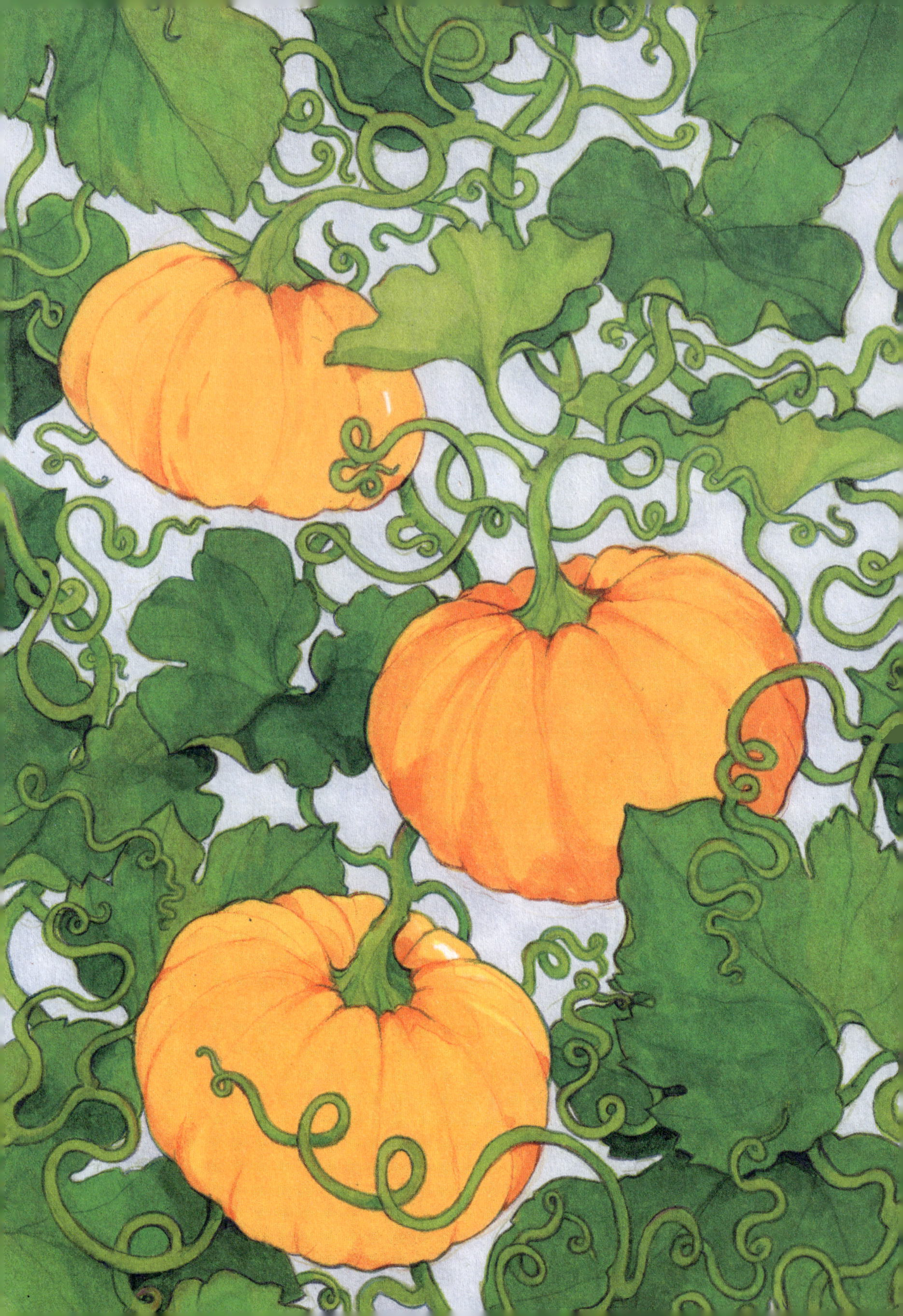

AUTUMN

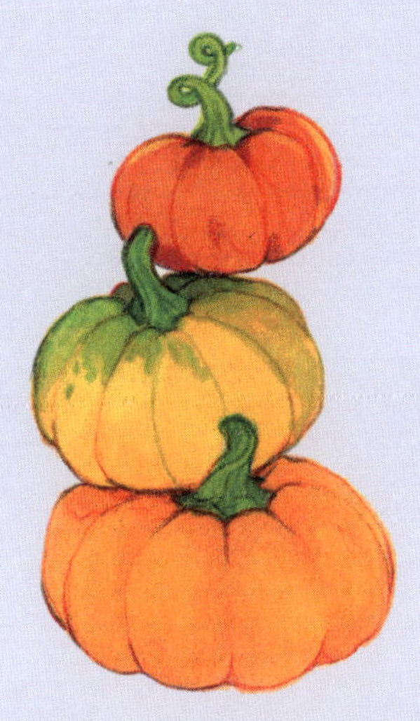

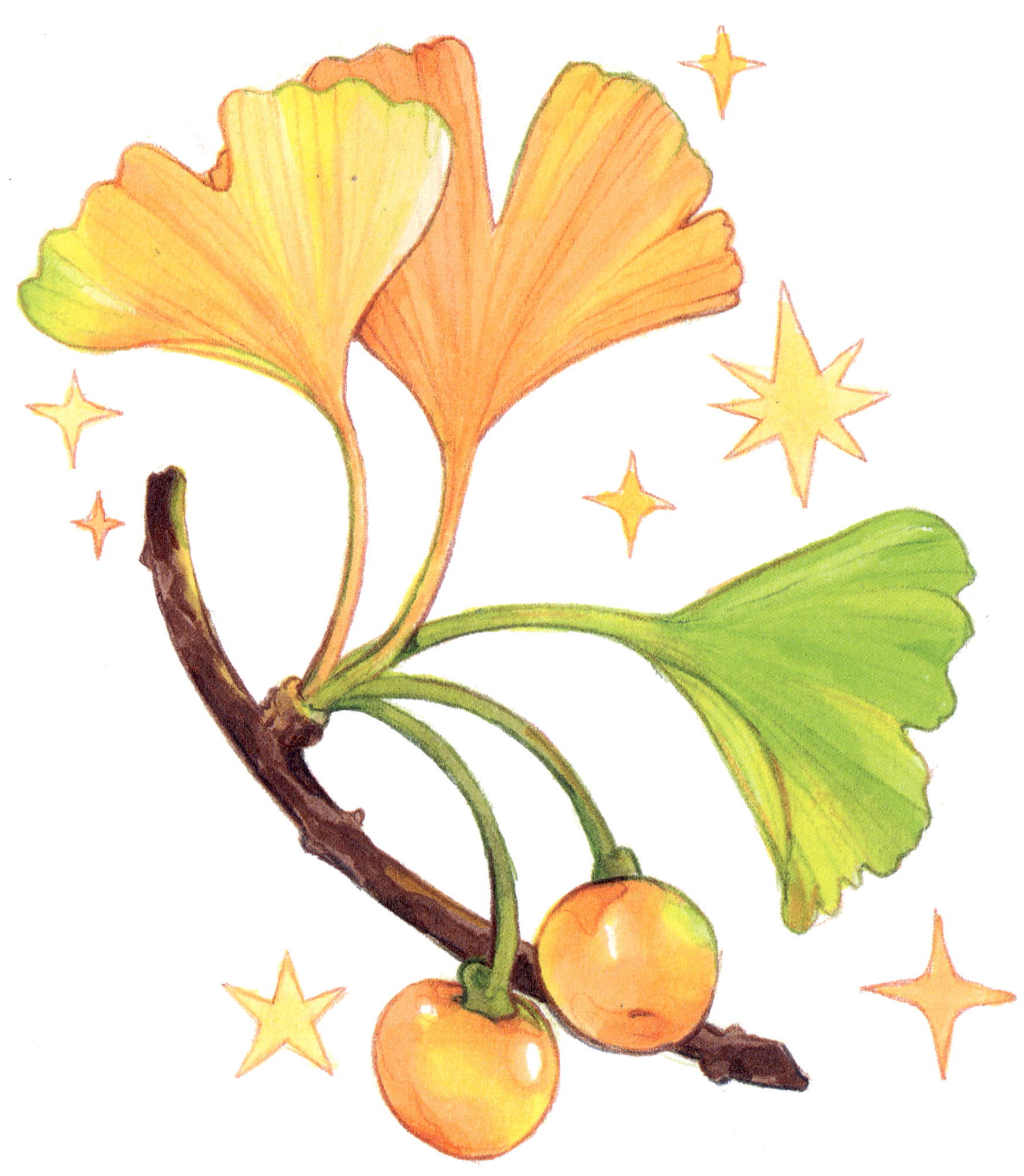

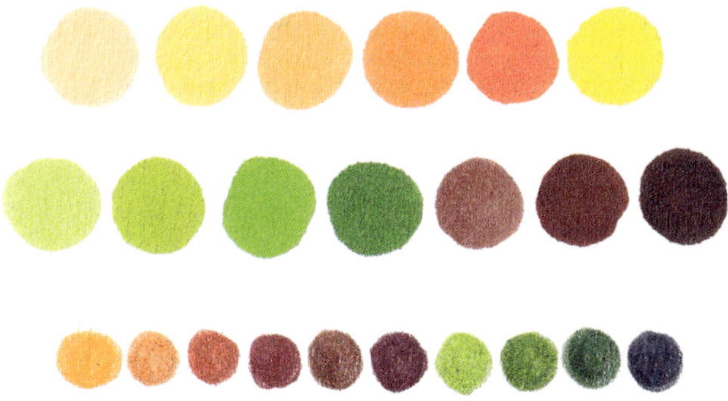

Ginkgo branch

During autumn, as nature prepares itself for rest, many leaves change colour. One of the most striking trees at this time of year is *Ginkgo biloba*, which turns a vibrant golden yellow. This project involves drawing a single ginkgo branch and makes for a good exercise in capturing the tree's unique, fan-shaped leaves as they turn from apple green to gold.

Materials:

- Acid-free paper
- Coloured pencils
- Alcohol-based markers

Ginkgo is one of the most ancient and resilient species on this planet; it's the sole survivor of a group of trees that was on Earth before the dinosaurs.

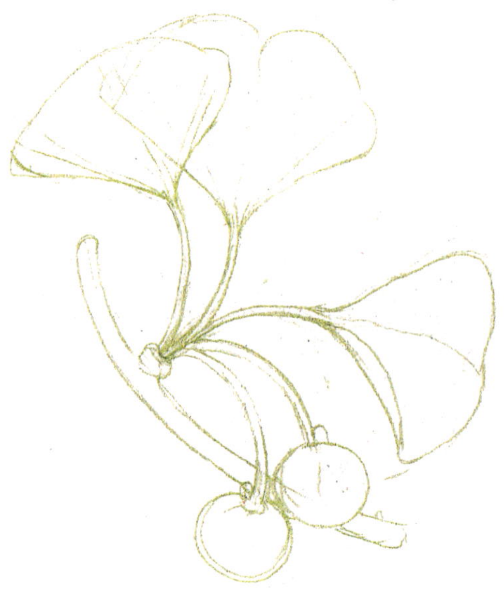

1. Sketch out the basic shape of the ginkgo branch using a light-coloured pencil. I used olive green. Sketch lightly, so you can erase any lines you don't like. Draw the curved shape of the branch first, then add the fan-shaped leaves and round berries. Mark the centre of each leaf.

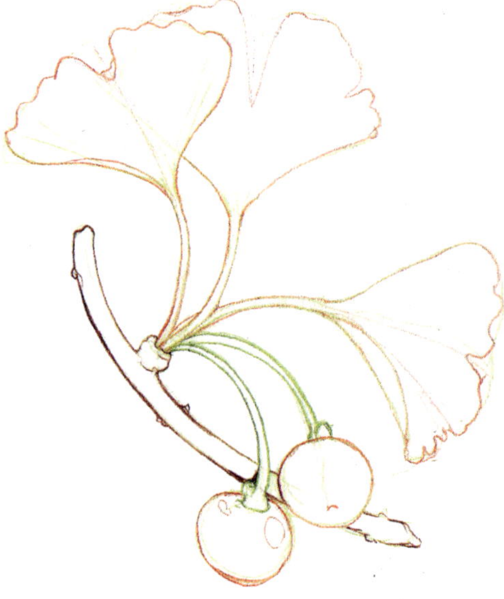

2. Draw over your initial sketch using burnt sienna, olive green and terracotta pencils - all earthy, autumnal colours. Define the shapes of the leaves. Ginkgo trees have very distinctive leaves, their shapes varying from one to the next. Some are deeply grooved at the centre, whilst others are almost flat.

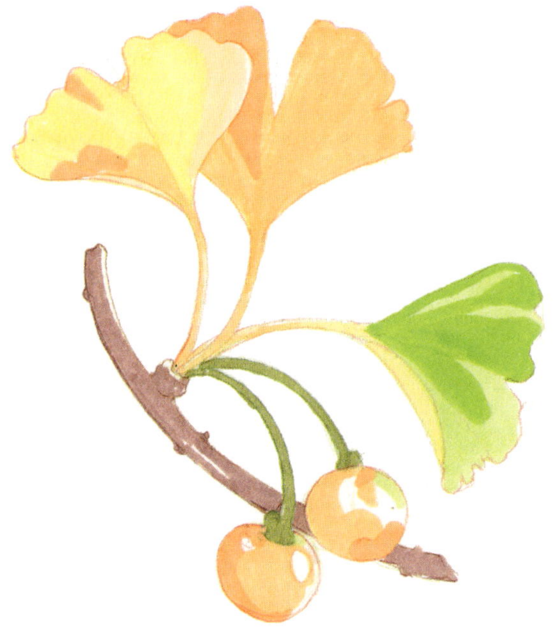

3. Use alcohol-based markers to lay down the base colours, working in a circular motion, but don't overlay any colours yet. Leave small areas near the edges of some leaves and the highlights on the berries uncoloured. In autumn, ginkgo berries are yellowish-tan or orange and the leaves turn golden. For more variety, colour one leaf green and add yellow shading to indicate the upcoming change.

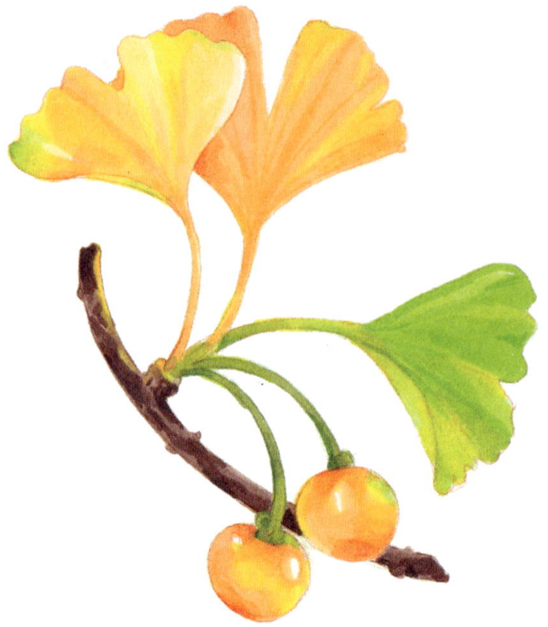

4. It's time for shading and blending colours. First, add shades using the same, or similar, colours to those used in Step 3. Add the darkest tones first, then go over them quickly with mid-tones, especially on berries (see page 46). Add a hint of green to the berries and at the top of the yellow leaf to add visual interest. Once the shading is done, use a yellow marker for the distinctive ginkgo golden glow. Pick a saturated vibrant tone.

You can always add a few details using coloured pencils. For example, you can gently outline areas of shading or add a few more shades, like the green I added at the top of the branch.

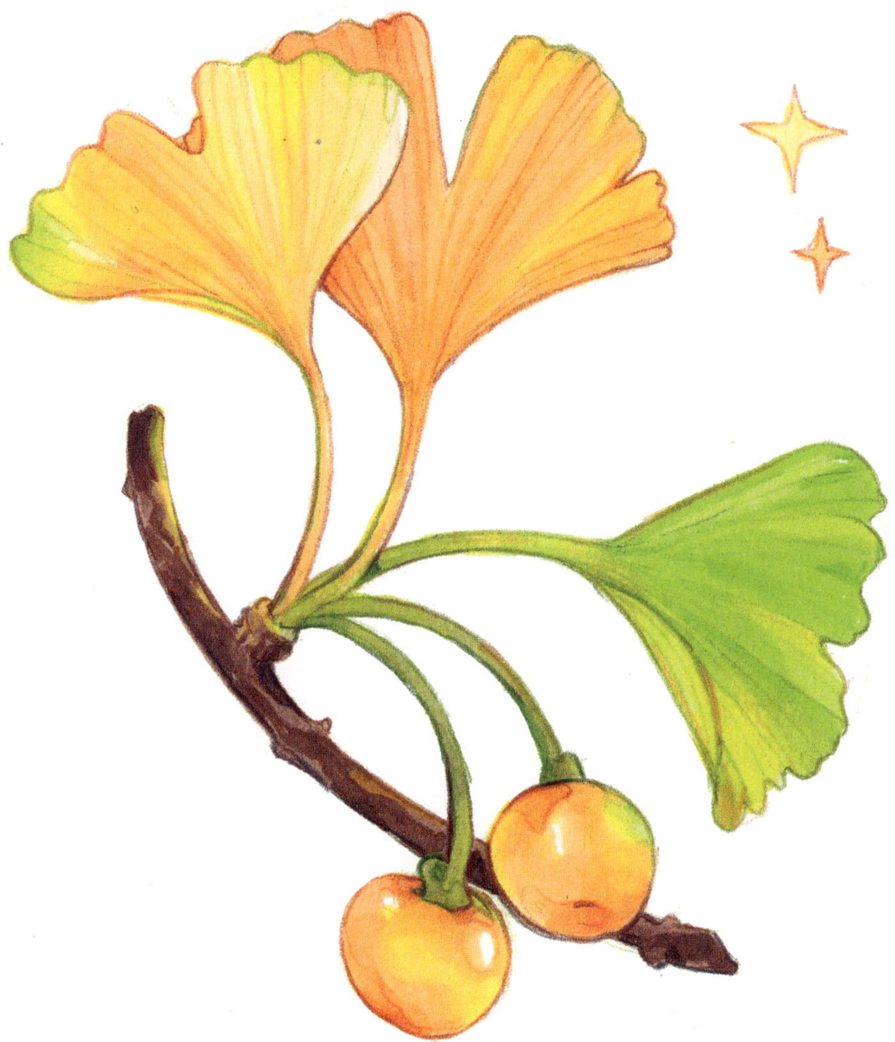

5. Use coloured pencils to add an outline. Play with the colours, using green on some parts of the golden leaves and brown on some parts of the berries. Draw veins on the leaves using very thin lines. Make some of the lines go all the way from edge of the leaf to the petiole and keep others a little shorter - the more variety, the more organic the look. Add stars and sparkles to finish your illustration, if you like.

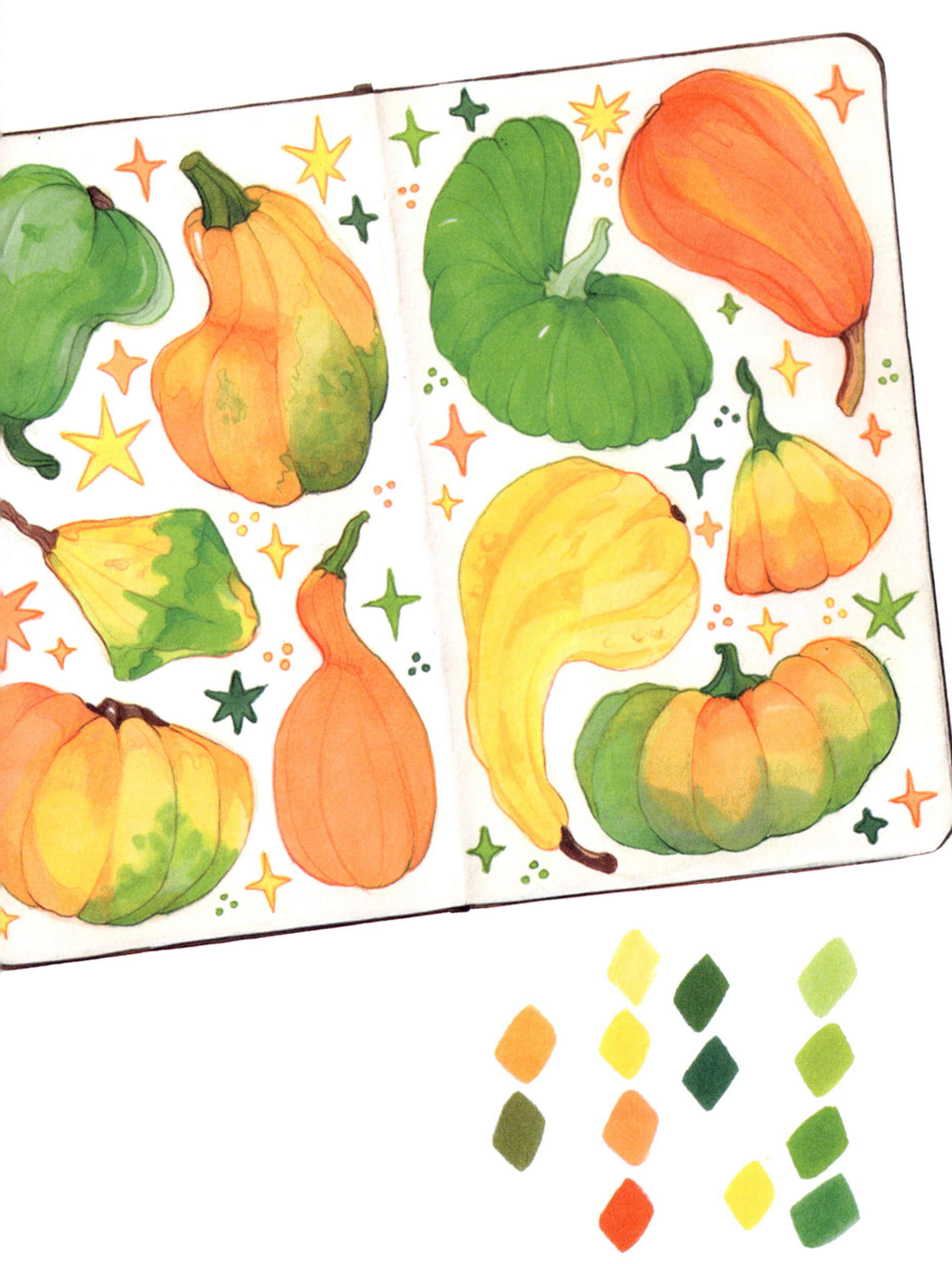

Colourful pumpkins

Is there a more iconic symbol of autumn than the pumpkin? This gorgeous centrepiece of the season is used for making delicious seasonal dishes and decorating the home. There are many types of pumpkin, each a different size, colour and texture. This project offers a great way to play with shapes and colours. Whether you'd like to draw a classic orange pumpkin or a group of ornamental pumpkins, make it fun! Bumpy texture? Wonky shape? Unusual colouring? It's up to you!

Materials:

- Acid-free paper
- Coloured pencils
- Alcohol-based markers

1. Using a yellow pencil, draw a blob-like outline for your pumpkin. Mine resembles a bean. Draw a hexagonal shape somewhere on the blob - this is the base of the pumpkin's stem. Draw a short curved line upward from each point of the hexagon and draw an elliptical shape. On the main body of the pumpkin, draw vertical lines running from the top to the bottom. These are the ribs of the pumpkin. Use curved lines to connect one to the next.

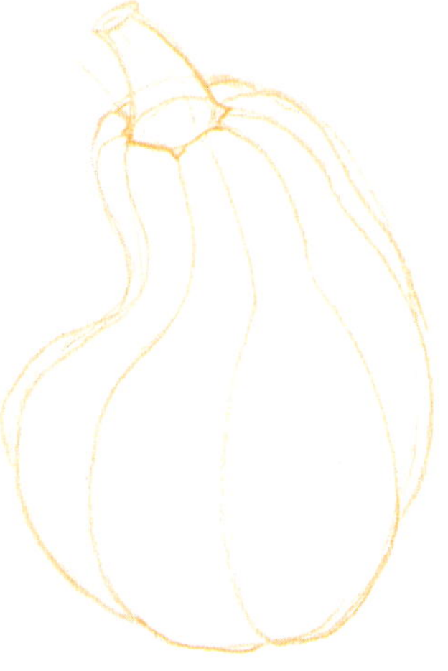

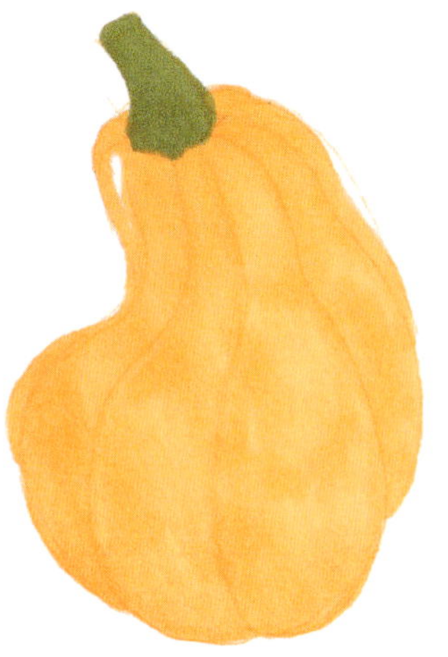

2. Lay down the base colours of the pumpkin and its stalk, leaving a small area of the pumpkin uncoloured for a highlight.

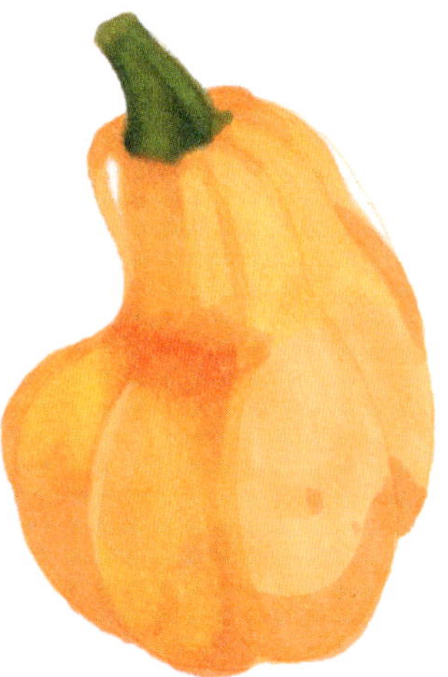

3. Add more depth to the illustration with shading (see page 43). I like to shade each section between the ribs of the pumpkin individually, rounding the shapes at both the top and the bottom.

If you blend enough colours together, they'll turn brown. This is not such a bad thing for a pumpkin, making this a great exercise to just experiment!

4. For the green areas, start with the darkest shade and add patches of colour by drawing small shapes or dots (see page 49). Blend these using lighter shades of green. Use yellow to blend the orange and green together more convincingly.

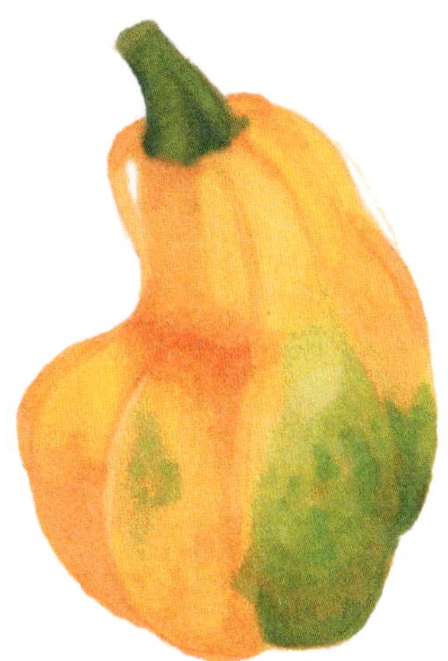

5. Add pencil outlines to the pumpkin. Use them to define the ridges on the stalk as well as the ribs on the pumpkin. Outline some coloured patches, too. Have fun with colours and line weight!

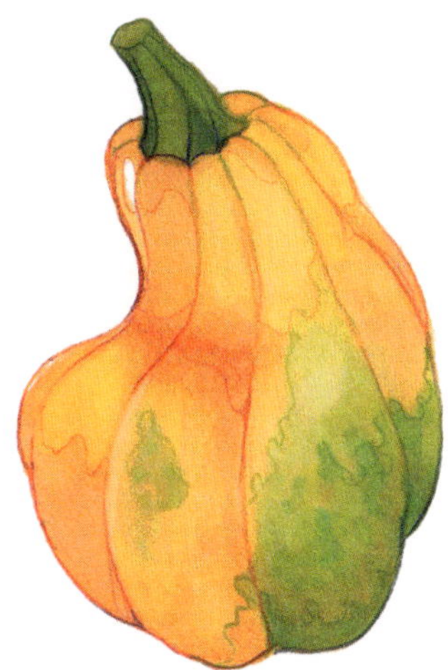

If you'd like to draw a pumpkin that has ripened unevenly, colour top half of it green and the other half orange and blend the two together using yellow.

6. Repeat Steps 1 to 5 for more pumpkins. Once you're done, you can fill the spaces between the pumpkins with stars and sparkles, colour swatches or whatever comes to mind. A plain, complementary colour background would also look great for a project like this (see pages 52–53). Make it yours!

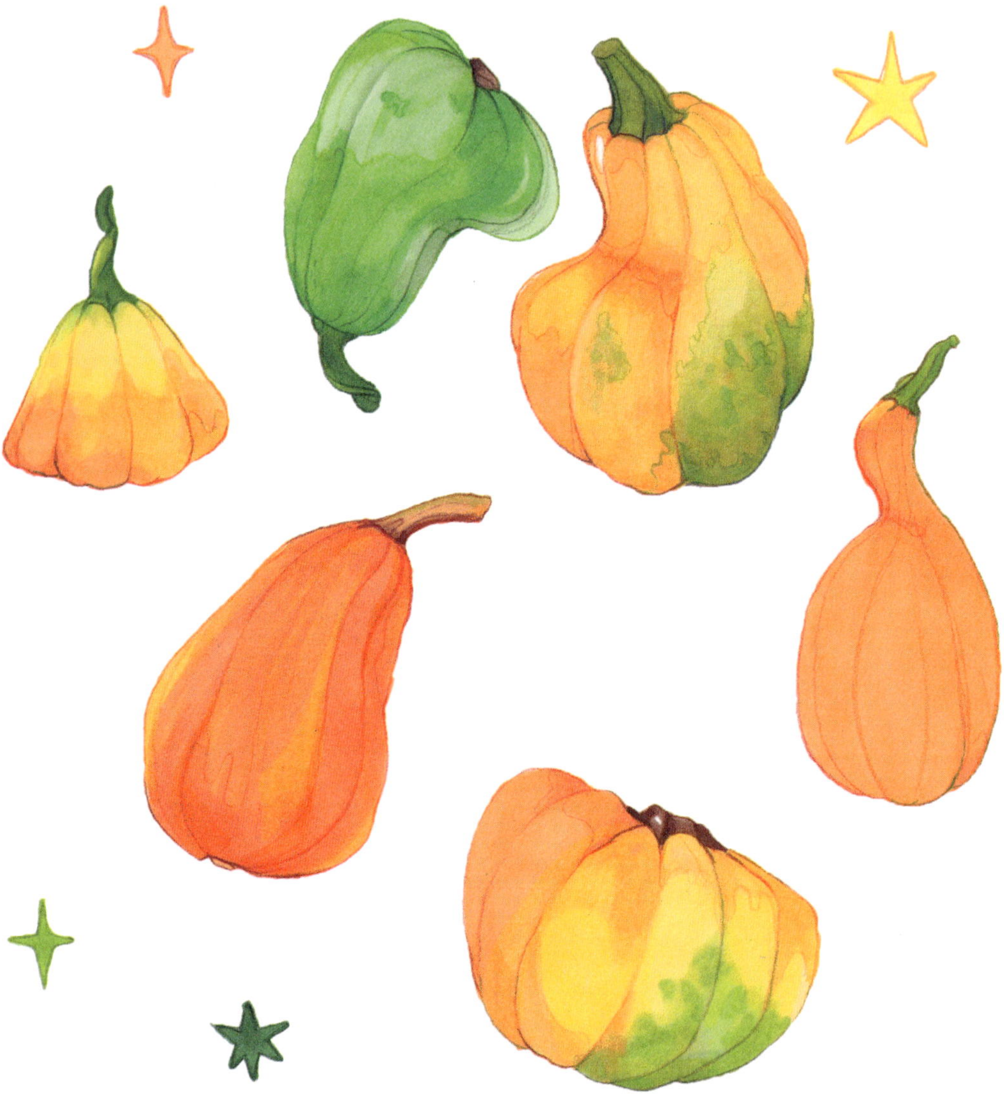

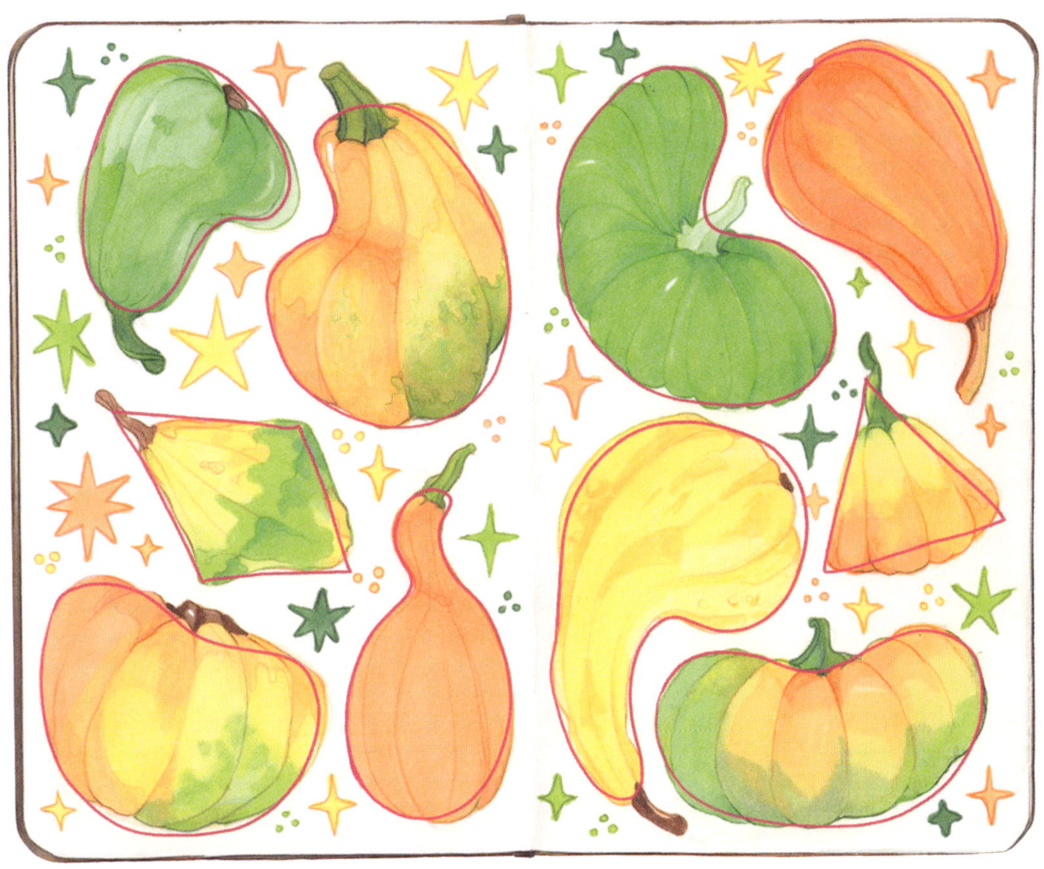

If you're planning to fill the whole page with pumpkins, think about the shapes they might have. They can be based on any geometrical shape – a triangle, a rectangle or a parallelogram – or they can be pear-, peanut- or bean-shaped.

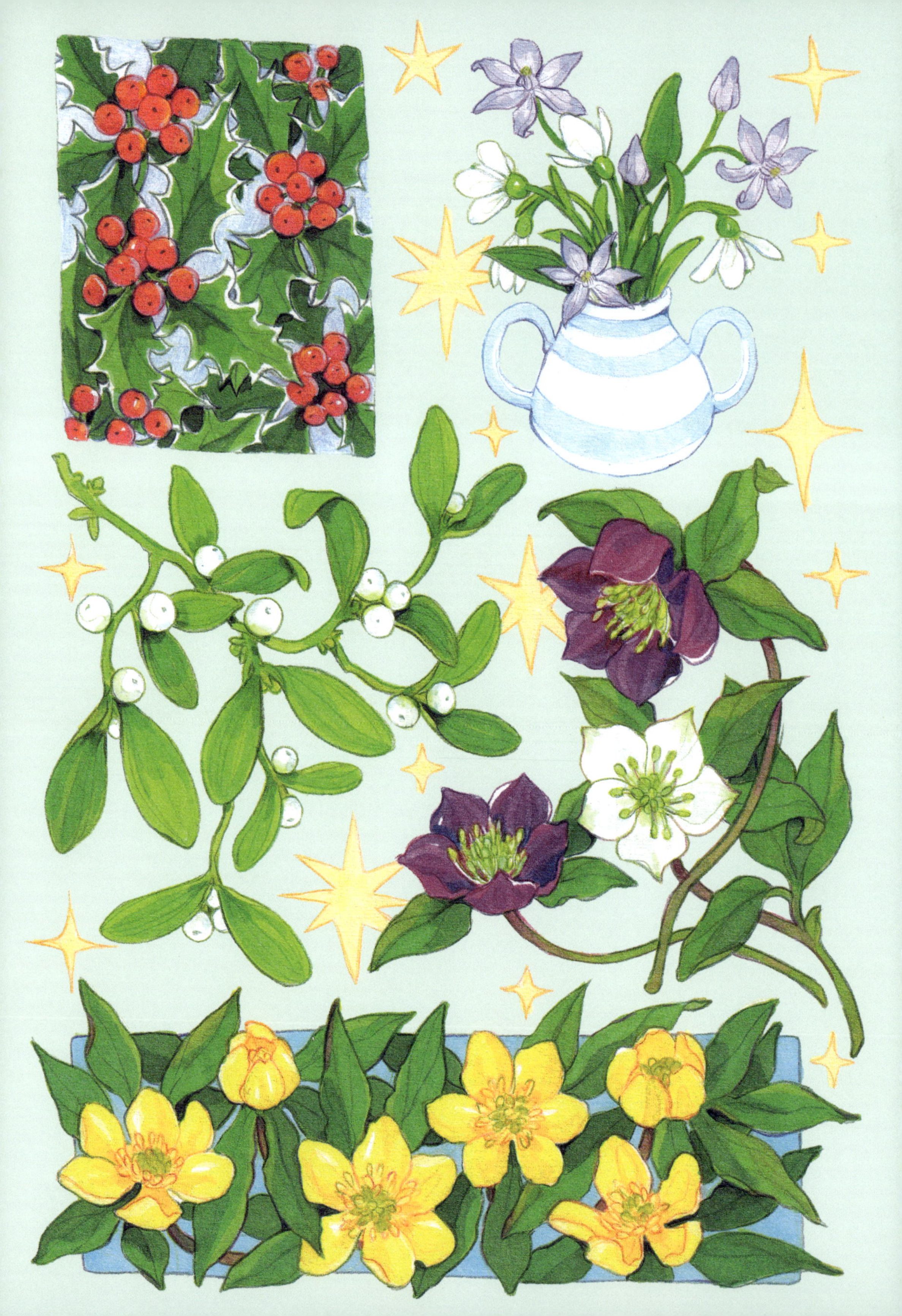

WINTER

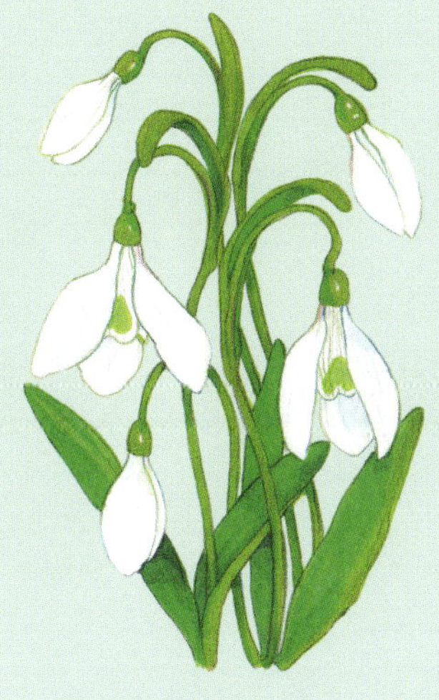

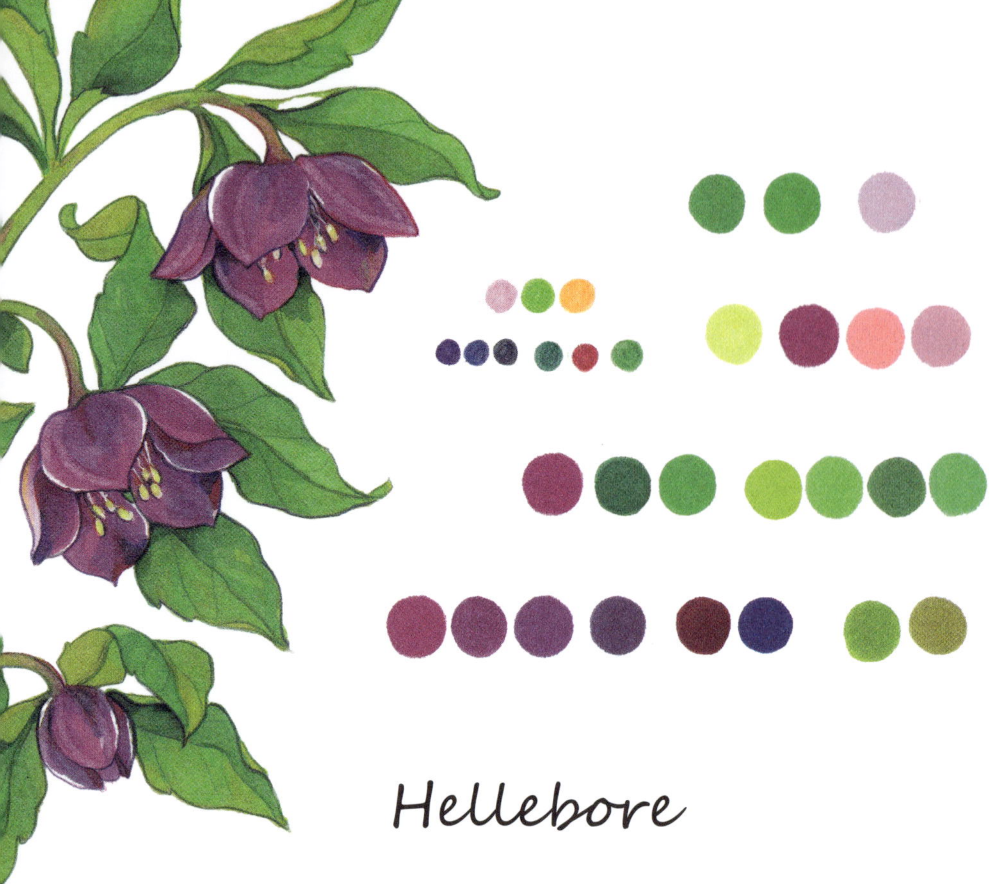

Hellebore

When the rest of nature seems to be sleeping deeply in late winter, the beautiful hellebore flower comes into bloom, showcasing its gorgeous colours. There are many different varieties, from white and pink, to purple and even black. In this project you'll learn how to draw darker flowers and the art of using a colourless blender in botanical illustration.

Materials:

- Acid-free paper
- Coloured pencils
- Alcohol-based markers
- White gouache paint and brush size 0 or white gel pen
- Colourless blender (optional)

The common name of this flower is Christmas rose but it's not related to roses at all. It belongs to the buttercup family!

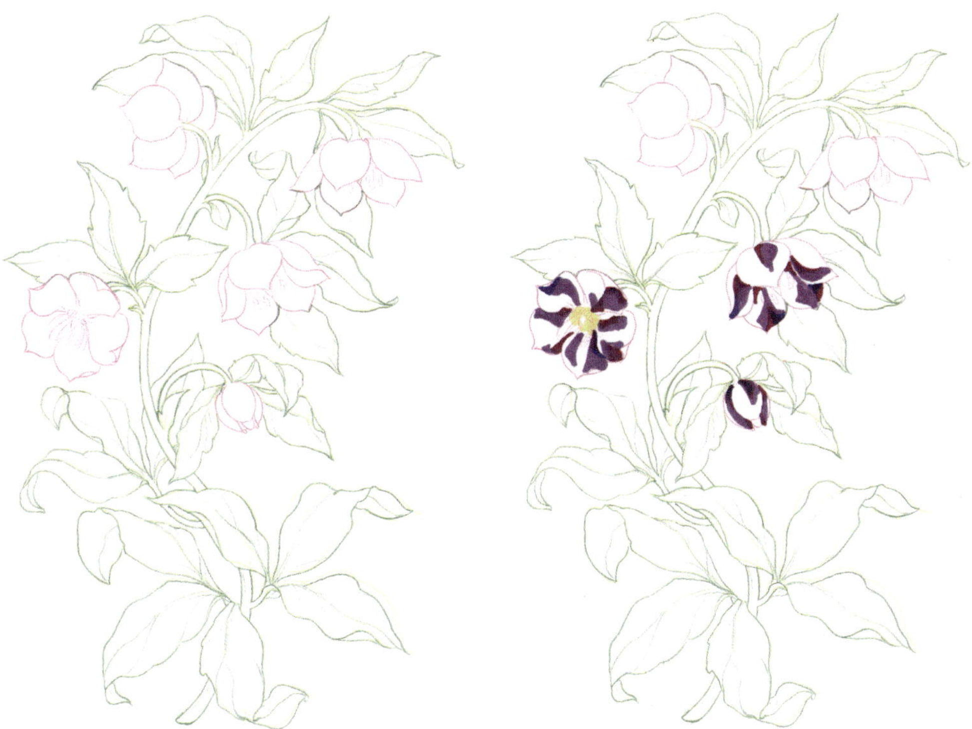

1. Starting off with the stem, make a sketch of the plant. Hellebore stems are quite chunky and mostly straight, but I have given mine a flattened 'S' shape. The flowers face downwards, making a kind of umbrella shape. Each has five petal-like sepals that are wide and teardrop-shaped. Be sure to make the tops of the sepals pointy. Refine your sketch using coloured pencils.

2. Steps 2 and 3 are time sensitive, so my example shows only a few flowers. If you don't feel confident in your skills, colour each flower individually, following these two steps. First, using a light green or yellow marker, colour the centre of the flower . Then, add the darkest shading to the flowers. Use one or two very dark colours, such as burgundy, plum or navy blue. Areas where the sepals meet should be the darkest. Use a slightly lighter colour such as deep purple to work on top.

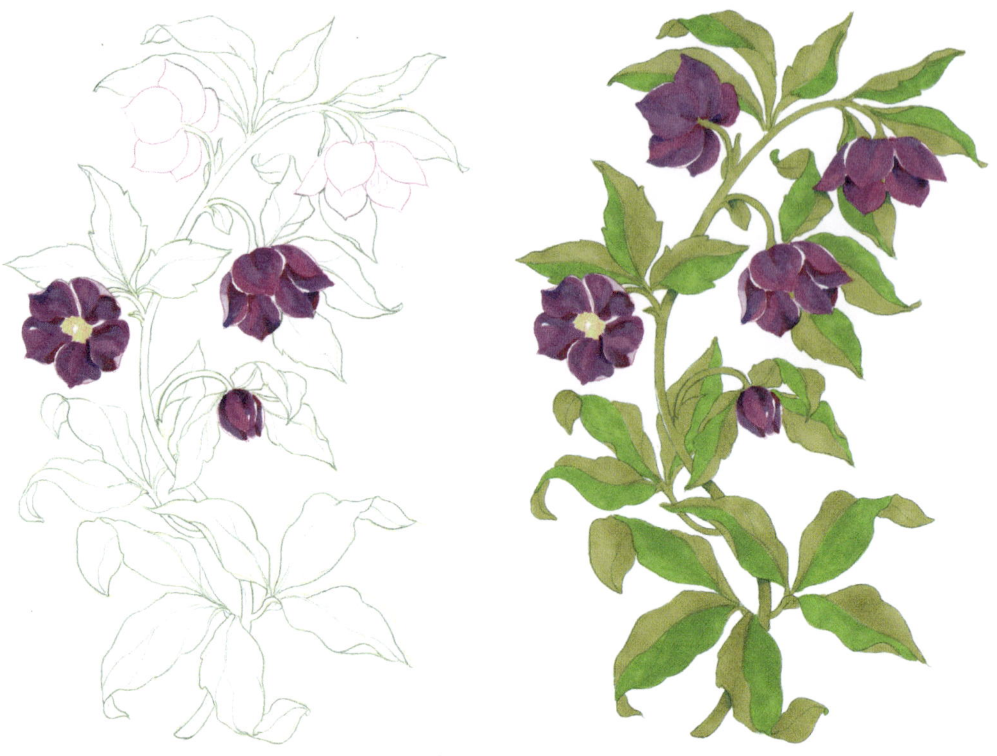

3. Fill in the rest of the flower using purple and maroon, leaving some areas near the edges of the sepals uncoloured to create clean highlights. Don't worry if you add too many or too few highlights, they can be changed later. Repeat the process until all the flowers are coloured, let them dry for a moment.

4. Colour the green parts of the plant, starting with the base colours (see page 69). Use yellowish green for the stem, the undersides of the leaves, the main vein and one half of the leaf. Use a neutral or warm green for the other half of the leaf. Hellebore leaves are mostly emerald but some of them have a warm undertone and this effect is captured beautifully using this simple technique.

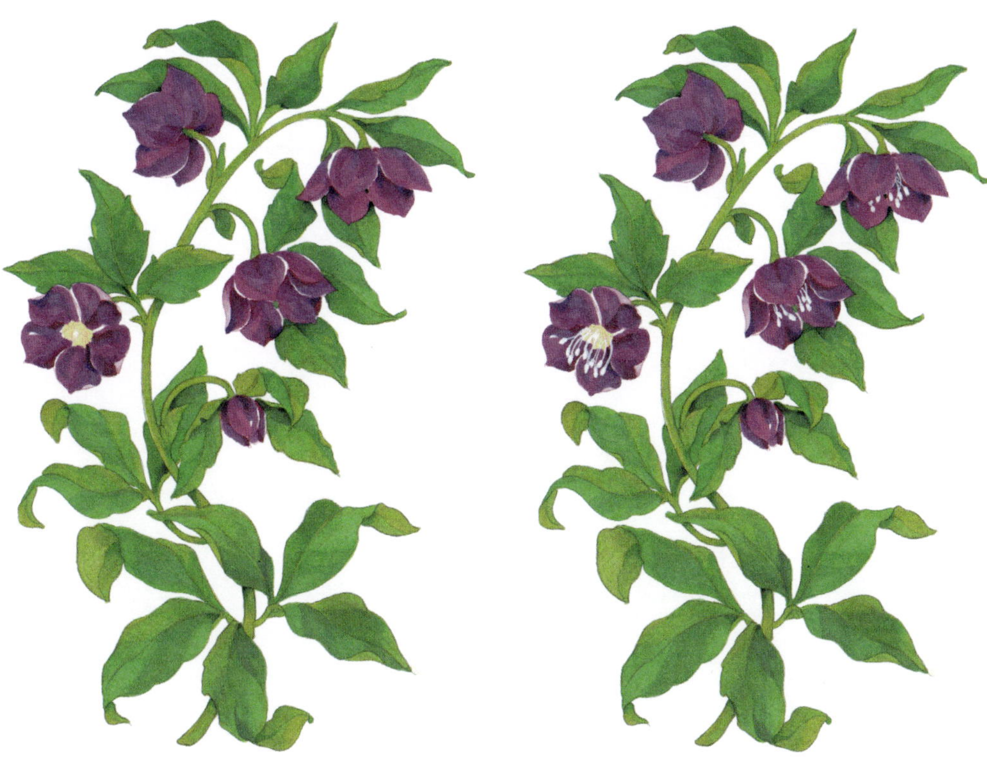

5. If you feel any areas of the plant need more colour, add more layers of the shades already used. If you'd like to significantly darken some areas, repeat steps 3 and 4.

6. Using white gouache or gel pen, draw the stamens. Try your best to use fine, flowing lines - ideally a single stroke for each one. If you are using paint, use as little water as possible and don't put too much pressure on the brush. Repeat this step if necessary, allowing the paint or ink to dry before applying a new layer. Depending on how dark the flower is, you might need a few layers. Let them dry.

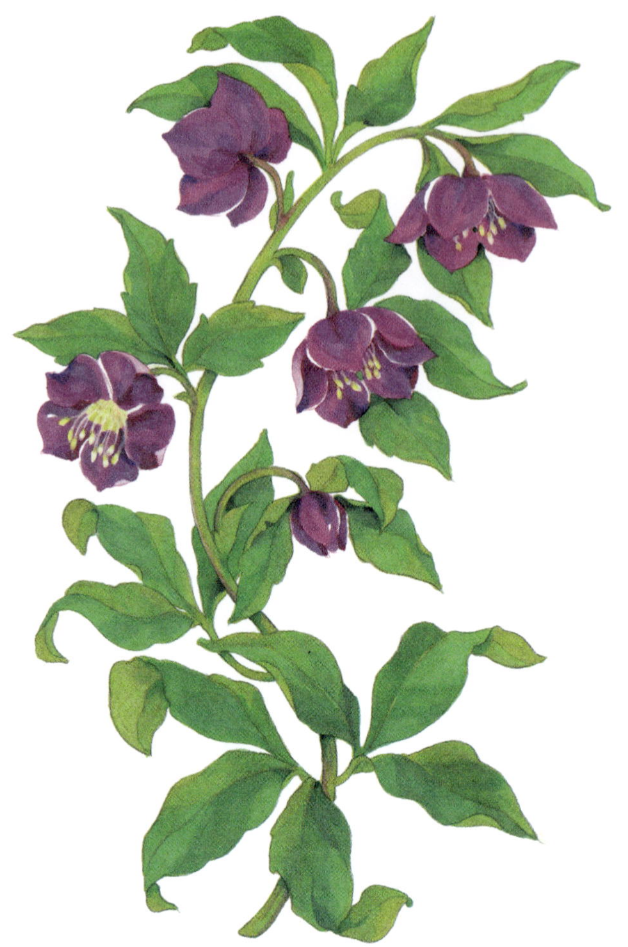

7. To make the illustration look more natural, add some pink and maroon on the stems. Since pure white doesn't exist in nature, colour the white stamens using lime green.

8. Add a pencil outline and any fine details. You can add more highlights on the flowers or to the stamens, preferably using white gel pen. Since the flowers are quite dark you can play with highlights. I encourage you to use some brightly coloured pencils - yellow, bright green, lilac - on the edges of flowers, to add some interesting visual effects.

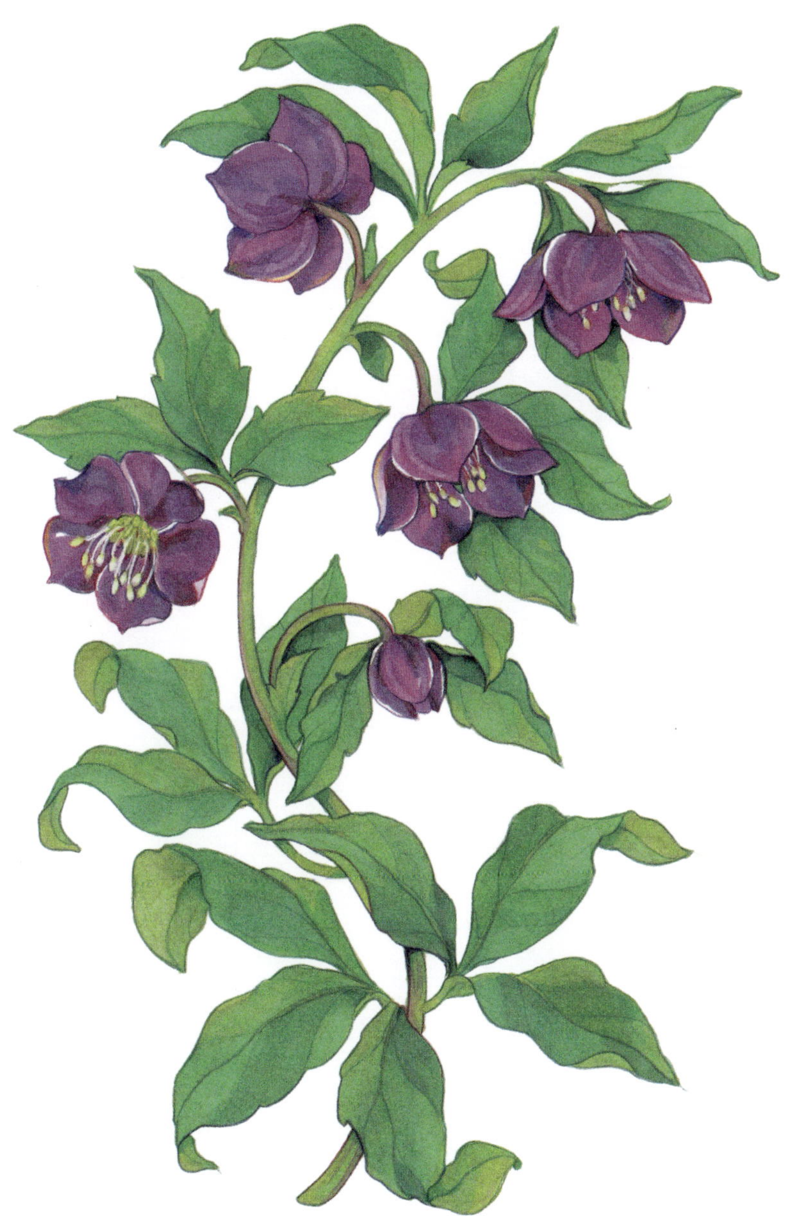

9. It's time to use a blender. I used a pale pink marker for this. Following the shape of the sepals, add a few highlights on the outside parts of the flowers. If the flower is dark, go over one area two or three times. Wait a few seconds to see how it turns out. It's easy to overdo this step so be cautious.

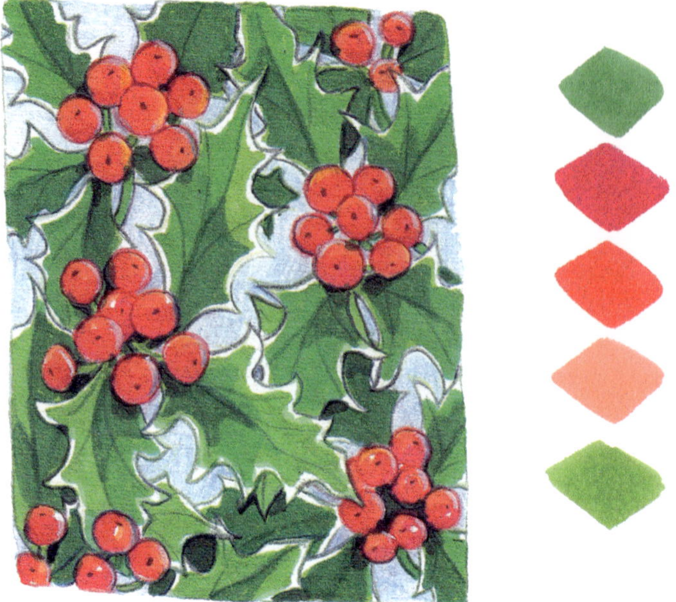

Holly

Nature doesn't look particularly abundant during winter in the northern hemisphere and the landscape is rather grey, but if you're lucky, you may spot some beautiful red berries. Holly is a classic winter decoration, and you'll almost certainly see it on greeting cards or as part of festive decorations. In this project you'll learn how to make an illustration on a smaller scale. Using holly leaves, you'll apply the techniques of glazing and adding a simple background colour.

Materials:

- Acid-free paper
- Coloured pencils
- Alcohol-based markers

1. Use a light green pencil to sketch the outline of the holly leaves so that they fit into a rectangular frame. Make sure some of the leaves continue 'beyond' the edge of the frame. Draw berry clusters keeping in mind the 'odd numbers' rule (see page 31)

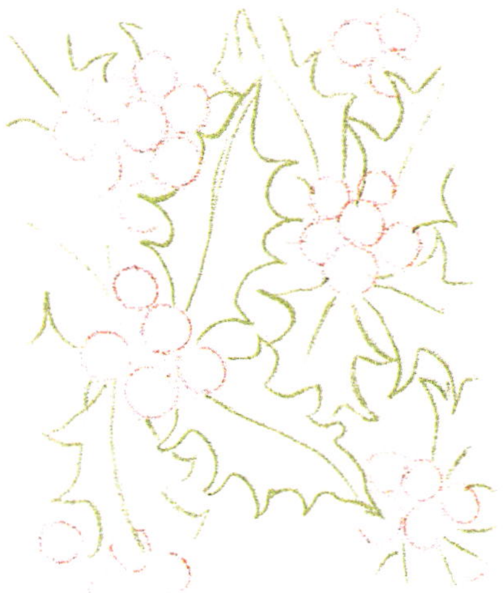

2. Refine your sketch using a range of greens for the leaves and outline the berries in red. Give the frame an outline.

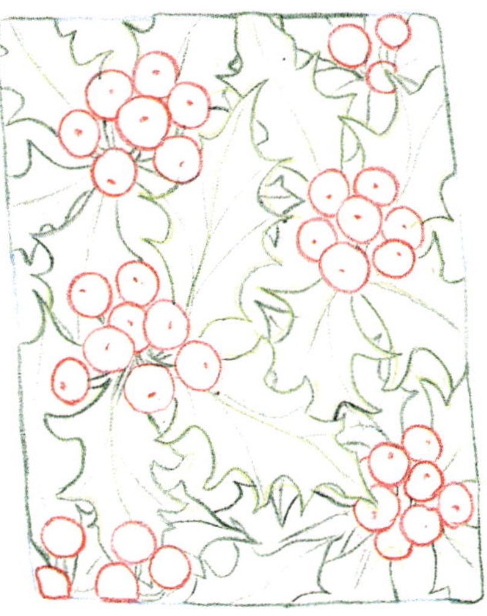

Ancient druids believed that holly had protective powers against evil spirits.

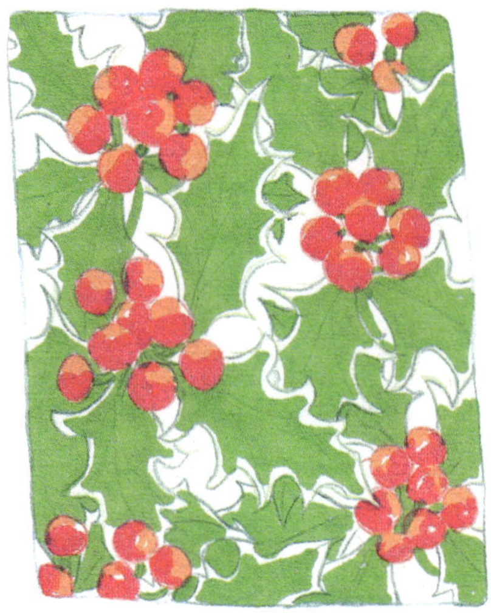

3. Start to lay down some base colours using alcohol-based markers. Add a hint of orange or yellow to one area of each berry and colour the rest in red. Leave areas of uncoloured paper as highlights. Colour the leaves green, but keep the outer edges uncoloured to capture the natural variegation.

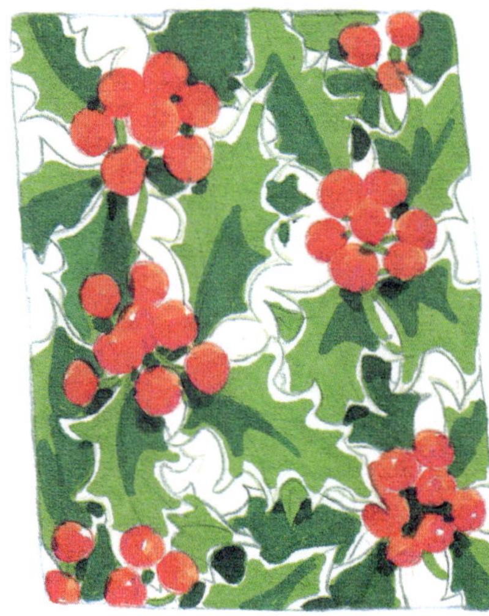

4. Blend the colours of the berries by adding a layer of red over the top of the whole berry. Next, add some shading to the leaves. Where the leaves overlap, use a darker green for shadow on the background leaves. Build on the leaf colour, adding lighter tones and blending them.

5. Use a coloured pencil to go over the outlines and to add details, such as the venation on the leaves. I used dark blue since this is a winter project and this cool colour fits with the season (see page 49).

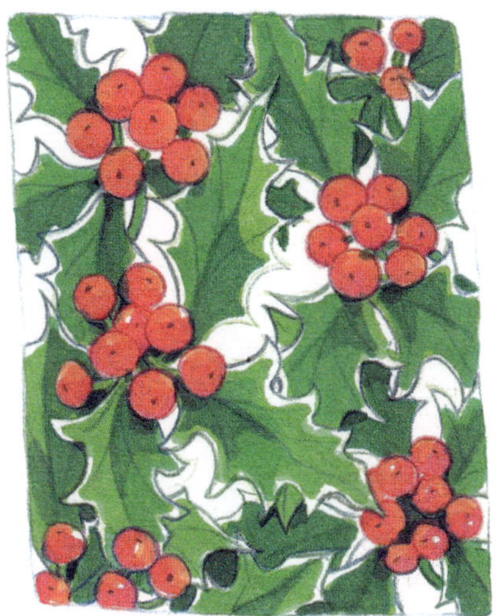

6. Use a white pencil and some other light pencils such as yellow and pale blue to add highlights. Finish by colouring in the background with a cool-toned coloured pencil (see page 52).

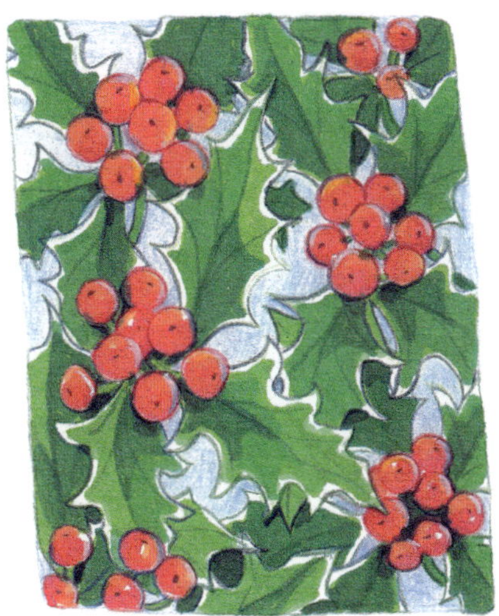

Add an additional layer of light blue marker on top of the existing background for more polished look.

Plant lore

It is always fascinating to learn about the plants you choose to study. Here are some things to know about the plants in all of the projects in the book.

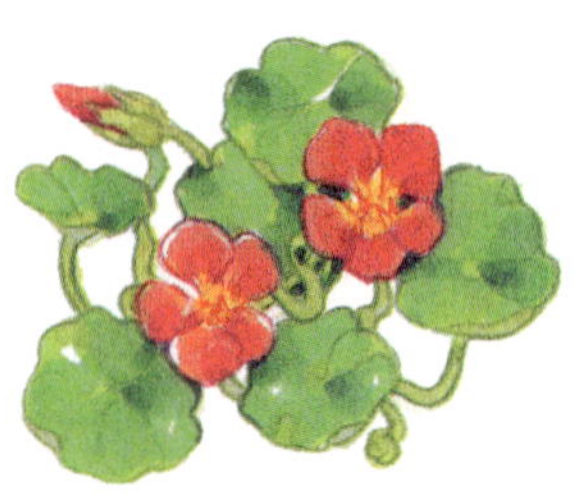

NASTURTIUM (*Tropaeolum*)

- All parts of the plant are edible, including the leaves, flowers and seeds; they have a peppery, watercress-like flavour.
- Nasturtiums are high in vitamin C and were used historically to help prevent scurvy.
- In the garden, these plants act as a natural pest deterrent and are often planted as a companion plant to repel aphids and squash bugs.

PEONY (*Paeonia*)

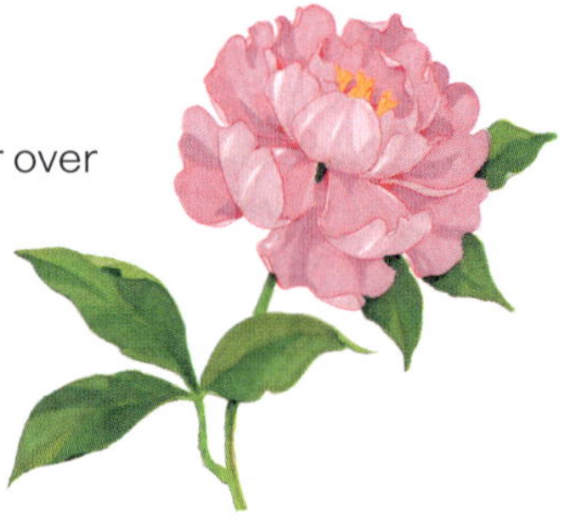

- Peonies are long-lived plants that can live for over 100 years.
- They are protected by ants but disliked by deer and rabbits.
- Native to China, peonies are used in traditional Chinese medicine to this day.

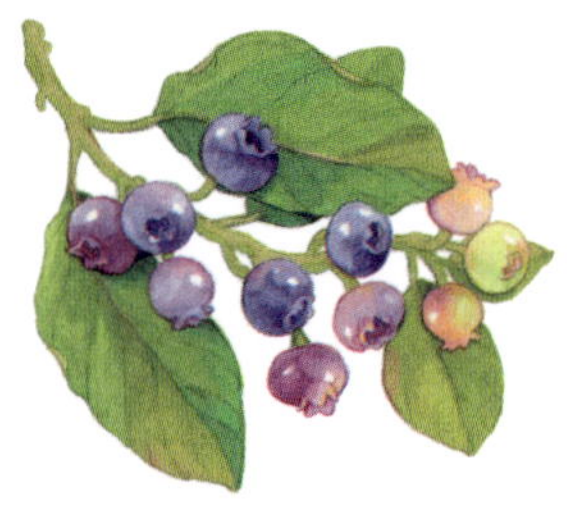

BLUEBERRY (*Vaccinium corymbosum*)

- Native to North America, cultivated blueberries were first domesticated in the early 1900s.
- They are one of very few foods that are naturally blue in colour; this is due to anthocyanin pigments in their skin.
- Blueberry bushes can produce fruit for more than fifty years.

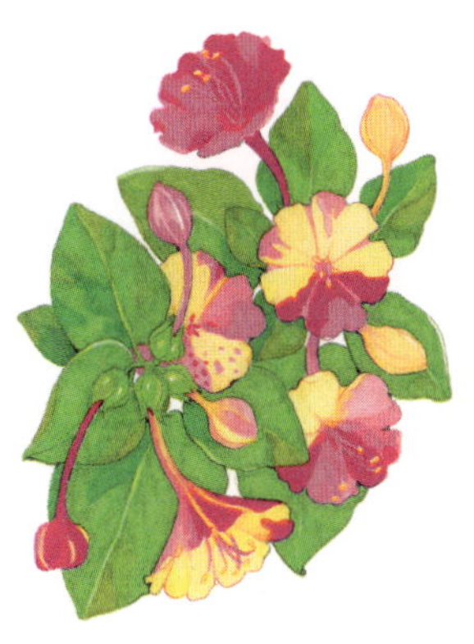

FOUR O'CLOCK FLOWER (*Mirabilis jalapa*)

- This plant gets its common name from the fact that its flowers open in late afternoon.
- A single plant can produce flowers of different colours from yellow through to pink.
- The flowers are most fragrant at night, intensifying in the evening to attract nocturnal pollinators.

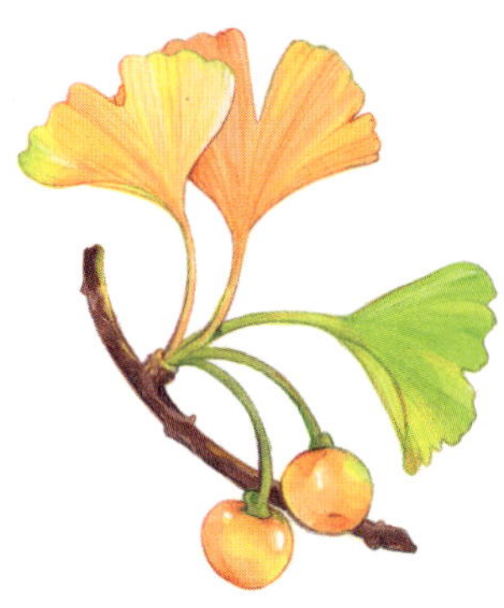

GINKGO (*Ginkgo biloba*)

- This is one of the most ancient and resilient species on this planet; it's the sole survivor of a group of trees that was on Earth before the dinosaurs.
- The tree's scientific name (biloba) literally means 'two lobes' because of the shape of the leaves.
- Ginkgo trees are either male or female, and it is the female tree that produces berries. Though it is rare, some branches of a male tree can become female over time.

PUMPKIN (*Cucurbita*)

- All parts of a pumpkin are edible; the flesh, seeds, leaves and even flowers can be eaten.
- Pumpkins were first domesticated in the Americas over 7,500 years ago.
- They can grow very quicky - up to 9 kilos a day - and reach massive sizes.

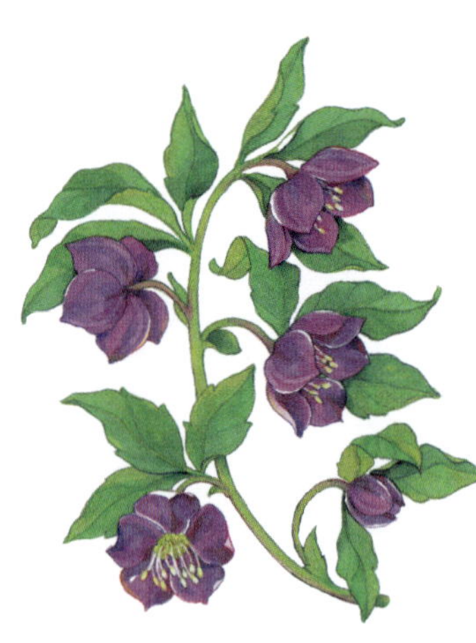

HELLEBORE (*Helleborus*)

- The common name of this flower is Christmas rose but it's not related to roses at all; it belongs to the buttercup family!
- In the past, hellebores have been used to forecast the weather for the following year.
- The flowers face downwards to protect their nectar from harsh weather conditions.

HOLLY (*Ilex aquifolium*)

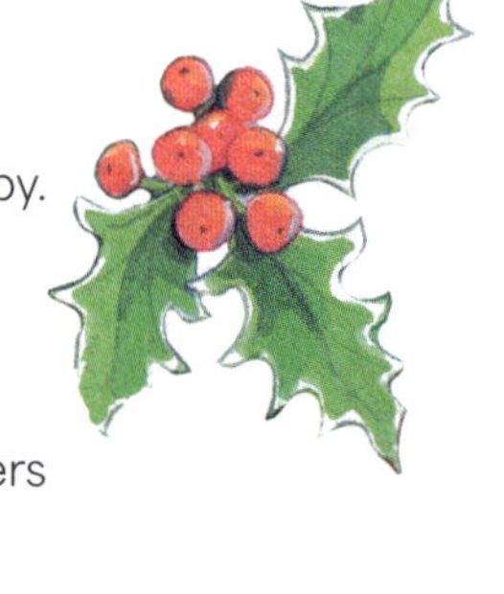

- Holly plants can be male or female; only the female plants produce berries, and only if a male plant is nearby.
- The prickly leaves are usually only found on the lower branches of a bush; higher branches often have smooth leaves.
- Ancient druids believed that holly had protective powers against evil spirits.

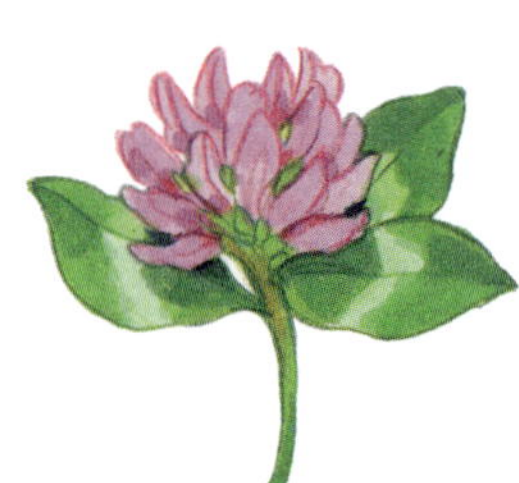

RED CLOVER (*Trifolium pratense*)

- Red clover was traditionally used for medicinal purposes. Today it is used to improve soil fertility and support the health of livestock and improve their diet.
- This flower symbolizes good luck, success, prosperity and industry.

FORGET-ME-NOT (*Myosotis arvensis*)

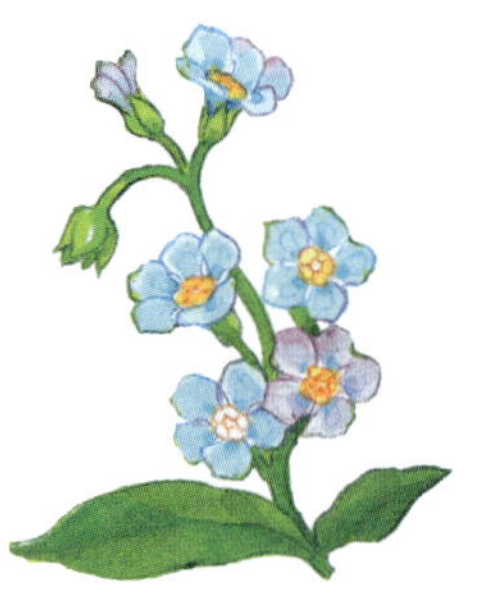

- The forget-me-not symbolizes love and remembrance
- In medieval times it was believed to have magical properties.

MARSH MARIGOLD (*Caltha palustris*)

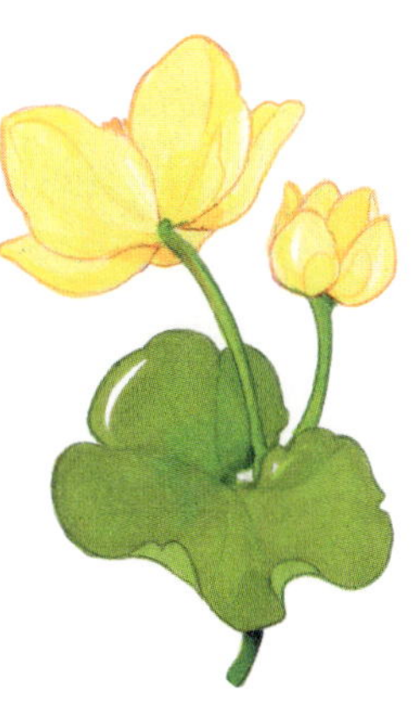

- Marsh marigolds play a significant role in the ecosystem, providing shelter for frogs.
- The plant can be in bloom from spring to late summer and is a good nectar source for bees and butterflies.

LAWN DAISY (*Bellis perennis*)

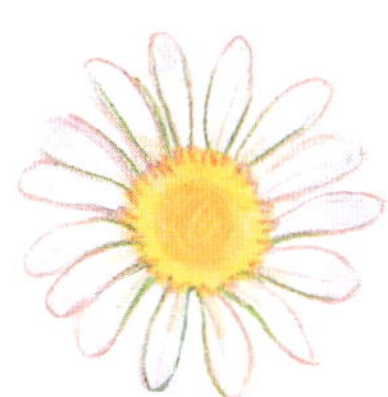

- The name 'daisy' refers to an Old English phrase 'day's eye', since the flower opens in the day and closes at dusk.
- Daisies symbolize hope, joy, purity and new beginnings.

CHICKWEED (*Stellaria media*)

- This plant got its name for being a favourite snack for birds, especially chickens, but it is also edible for humans.
- Chickweed was traditionally used for treating itchy skin and rashes.

CUCKOO FLOWER (*Cardamine pratensis*)

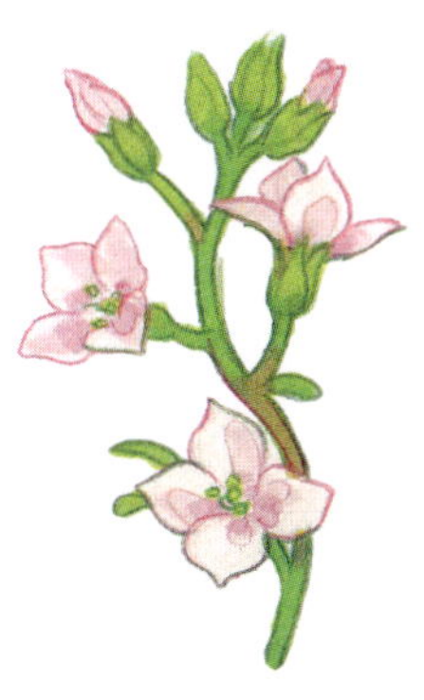

- Like the chickweed, the cuckoo flower also got its common name from a bird; its blooming time coincides with the arrival of the first cuckoo birds in spring.
- Also known as the May flower, milkmaid, lady's smock and fairy flower it is said to bring good luck.

Resources

Useful websites

For general information about plants: https://mgnv.org/plants/glossary/

For plant identification, especially in Europe, with very informative descriptions: https://luontoportti.com/en

To see plant pictures shared by others: https://identify.plantnet.org/

Inspirational books

Big Magic, Elizabeth Gilbert, Bloomsbury Publishing, 2016

The Cambridge Illustrated Glossary of Botanical Terms, Clive King and Michael Hickey, Cambridge University Press, 2000

Climbing Plants, Jan Tykač, illustrated by F. Severa, Littlehampton Book Services Ltd, 1985

Floral Folklore, Alison Davies, illustrated by Sarah Wildling, Leaping Hare Press, 2024

Florilegium. The Book of Plants, Basilius Besler, TASCHEN, 2016

The Intelligence of Flowers, Maurice Maeterlinck, Revelation Press, 2024

Ornamental Shrubs, J. Hofman, illustrated by J. Kaplická, Hamlyn, 1978

Roses. The Complete Plates 1817-1824, H. Walter Lack, illustrated by Pierre-Joseph Redouté, TASCHEN, 2024

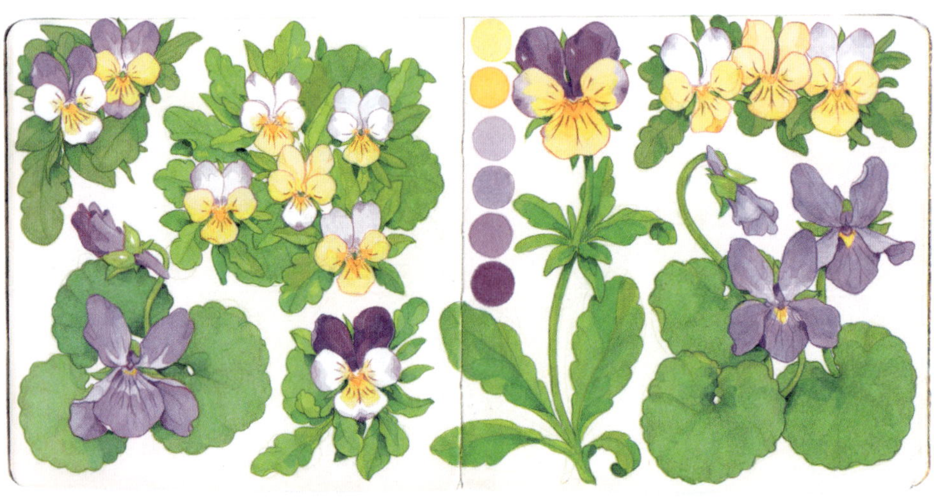

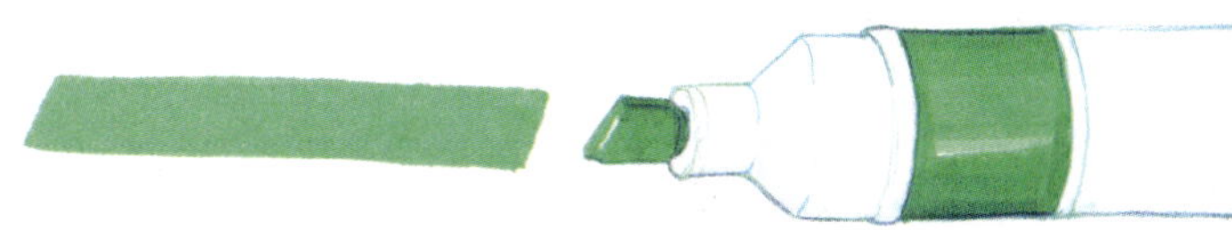

Art suppliers

ALCOHOL-BASED MARKERS

Winsor & Newton Promarkers: https://uk.winsornewton.com/
Arteza®: https://www.instagram.com/artezaofficial
Copic Ciao: https://copic-shop.co.uk

COLOURED PENCILS

Faber-Castell Polychromos: https://www.faber-castell.co.uk

GOUACHE

Winsor & Newton Designers Gouache: https://uk.winsornewton.com/

BRUSHES

Renesans: https://renesanspolska.pl

SKETCHBOOKS

Royal Talens Art Creation: https://www.royaltalens.com
SM.LT Art Bristol Sketch Pad: https://www.smltart.com

Index

Author acknowledgements

Thanks to Katie Moody for asking me to review her book, which led to making contact with Monica Perdoni at Leaping Hare Press. Huge thanks to Monica for reaching out with this book idea and believing in it. Thanks to Charlotte Frost and Anna Southgate for their support and valuable input. Thanks for the encouragement, the words of support and for giving me enough creative freedom but also structure to get the project done. This book wouldn't have happened without your guidance! Thank you to everyone else who worked on the book.

Thanks to my husband Paweł for always being by my side, for believing in me and for taking care of everyday life while I was busy working on this project. I love you.

Thanks to my parents for showing me how to love nature and letting me be the nerdy kid.

Thanks to my sister and friends, both online and in real life, for checking in and supporting my dreams.

Big thanks to my online community on Instagram and Patreon. Without you I wouldn't have the courage to follow a creative career path! It's an honour to be able to share my art with you.

Quarto

First published in 2026 by Leaping Hare Press,
an imprint of The Quarto Group.
One Triptych Place, London, SE1 9SH,
United Kingdom
T (0)20 7700 9000
www.Quarto.com

EEA Representation, WTS Tax d.o.o., Žanova ulica 3, 4000 Kranj, Slovenia
www.wts-tax.si

A catalogue record for this book is available from the British Library.

ISBN 978-1-80570-062-3
Ebook ISBN 978-1-80570-063-0

10 9 8 7 6 5 4 3 2 1

Design by Nicki Davis

Editorial Director: Monica Perdoni
Project Manager: Anna Southgate
Senior Designer: Renata Latipova
Senior Editor: Charlotte Frost
Senior Production Controller: Rohana Yusof

Printed in Guangdong, China TT032026

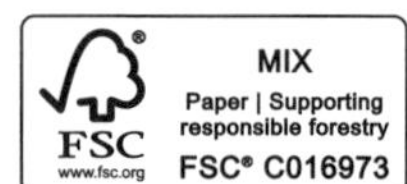